Missing Mila, Finding Family

Book Twenty-seven
Louann Atkins Temple Women & Culture Series

« MARGARET E. WARD »

Missing Mila, Finding Family

AN INTERNATIONAL ADOPTION
IN THE SHADOW OF THE
SALVADORAN CIVIL WAR

University of Texas Press ◆ AUSTIN

The Louann Atkins Temple Women & Culture Series is supported by Allison, Doug, Taylor, and Andy Bacon; Margaret, Lawrence, Will, John, and Annie Temple; Larry Temple; the Temple-Inland Foundation; and the National Endowment for the Humanities.

Requests for permission to reproduce material from this work should be sent to:
    Permissions
    University of Texas Press
    P.O. Box 7819
    Austin, TX 78713-7819
    www.utexas.edu/utpress/about/bpermission.html

⊗ The paper used in this book meets the minimum requirements of ANSI/ NISO Z39.48-1992 (R1997) (Permanence of Paper).

LIBRARY OF CONGRESS CATALOGING-IN-PUBLICATION DATA

Ward, Margaret E.
    Missing Mila, finding family : an international adoption in the shadow of the Salvadoran Civil War / by Margaret E. Ward. — 1st ed.
      p. cm. — (Louann Atkins Temple women & culture series)
    Includes bibliographical references and index.
    ISBN 978-0-292-72668-0 (cloth : alk. paper) — ISBN 978-0-292-72908-7 (pbk. : alk. paper)
    1. Intercountry adoption—United States.   2. Birthparents—El Salvador.
3. El Salvador—History—1979–1992.   I. Title.
    HV875.55.W367 2011
    362.734—dc22

                                         2011005492

ISBN 978-0-292-73553-8 (e-book)

*In loving memory of
Mamá Chila*

For all the children

Contents

Acknowledgments

For this twenty-eight-year journey, I cannot possibly name all the individuals who have accompanied me. I have tried in the text and notes to acknowledge the information derived from a conversation or interview, to name the person who gave me a photograph or an article, who translated a letter or wrote an entry in a family journal or on the weblog *Ana's Miracle* (www.anasmiracle.com). I regret any omissions and thank here every member of my extended family.

I am indebted to all of the searching organizations, including COFADEH and CODEFAM, but especially to Pro-búsqueda and Physicians for Human Rights and their staffs. And I am deeply appreciative for the way Nelson's birth family opened their homes and their hearts as they shared their stories, especially Lucila Angulo and her daughters, Vilma, Dalila, Haydée, and Tita Escobar, but also Luis and Miriam, Reinaldo and Ana-Doris, and Mariano and Reina Coto.

Wellesley College supported my sabbatical in 2004–2005, knowing that I would devote half my time to this personal project. Isabel Lecompte and Elena Legeros ably assisted with transcription of tapes and translations. Colleagues in the Spanish department supported me in various ways from 1983 on. Elena Gascón-Vera wrote a personal reference for our adoption. Joy Renjilian-Burgy recommended students who could help us and translated the first newspaper article one of them found. Marjorie Agosín and Lorraine Roses conducted videotaped interviews with visiting family members on two occasions. Finally, Nancy Hall and Veronica Darer allowed me to audit their classes.

So many family members, colleagues, and friends read and critiqued the manuscript at various stages or gave valuable advice about its publication. Thanks are due to each one, especially to my dear friends

Joan Arnow and Laila Maley Dawson, and to Rosanna Hertz, my colleague in Women and Gender Studies, who first gave me the opportunity to talk about this journey in her course on American families. The treasured members of my Women in German study group followed the project from its inception and commented on all parts, but most vigorously and helpfully on Chapters 5 and 6.

I have Sandy Thatcher to thank for believing in the importance of the book and for facilitating my search for a press, and Joanna Hitchcock for treating my submission so expeditiously. My outside reviewers gave thoughtful advice at an important juncture. Erik Ching reviewed the historical material carefully and suggested additional sources, and Helen Fehervary understood that Chapter 5, "Imagining Mila," was at the book's heart. I am most grateful to her for providing the key I needed to strengthen this pivotal chapter.

I am indebted to the staff of University of Texas Press for the care they took in editing and production, especially Leslie Doyle Tingle for managing the process, Jessie Hunnicutt for copyediting so meticulously, and Theresa May for providing understanding counsel throughout.

The children added their own distinctive voices and expertise to the mix. I am profoundly indebted to Nelson and Eva for their expansive willingness to express their feelings in conversation and in writing. In the final stages, Derek gave special attention to my translations from the Spanish, but any misunderstandings or mistakes should be attributed solely to me. Nelson lent his technical prowess whenever I needed it. For their writings, their suggestions, and their expressions of love, I am thankful to all the children; they were the catalyst for writing this book.

Tom has accompanied me each step on the journey, and he has always been my best friend and first reader. His editorial skill has been crucial, his love constant. My admiration for him and my gratitude to him know no limit. While I have formally dedicated the book to Mamá Chila and the children, he knows this one is also for him.

Missing Mila, Finding Family

Dalila's Hammock

SAN SALVADOR, EL SALVADOR, FEBRUARY 2005

L ying in the hammock in a shady corner of Dalila's patio, I can look up through colorful towels hanging on the line and a flowering poinsettia tree to the hulking gray-green presence of the volcano, seemingly serene in the rectangle of azure above. Three days ago I arrived from Costa Rica, after spending several weeks in an intensive course trying to hasten my acquisition of spoken Spanish. Dalila's niece, Eva, dropped me off at the airport in Alajuela, just outside San José, but I wasn't sure exactly who would meet me here in San Salvador.[1]

I should have anticipated the warm welcome. As I emerged from customs, a contingent of relatives from each side of the family converged, arms outstretched for *abrazos* (hugs). We created a caravan on the way to Dalila's house, where even more relatives gathered and a delicious meal was quickly prepared. The highway from the airport was as I remembered it, only it is the height of the dry season now, so the rose-colored blossoms of the Maquilishuat and Madrecacao trees, as well as the more distinctive brilliant yellow of the San Andrés, softened the visual effect of the hovels with thatched or corrugated tin roofs all along the way into the capital. Some men stood right by the edge of the highway, cutting coconuts with their machetes, hawking the pulp and milk to passersby. Women leaned over hot braziers filling freshly made tortillas with fried meat, beans, or cheese to create the traditional Salvadoran *pupusas*.

When I was here with Tom, Nelson, Derek, and Ernesto six years ago, I felt more like a tourist than family. Dalila, her sister Tita, and their five children were living in Soyapango then, a working-class district on the eastern outskirts of the city. Another sister, Inés, whom they hadn't seen in eighteen years, had come with her disabled daughter all the way from Mexico by bus in order to meet us. Dalila and Tita's tiny house was bursting at the seams. Tom and I stayed in a hotel downtown, and the boys stayed with their Uncle Reinaldo in an upper-middle-class neighborhood at the other end of the city.

I miss my husband and sons on this trip, but traveling alone has some advantages. This time I am sharing a room with Dalila, and I have a lot more time to converse with her. She has moved recently with her two grown sons to a neighborhood nearer to downtown. Next week I'll go to stay with Reinaldo and his family before I return to Costa Rica briefly, then fly home.

« »

My Salvadoran hosts represent each side of the family—maternal and paternal. Dalila and Reinaldo each play a minor role in this story, and they remember what things were like here in the late 1970s and early 80s. It's no secret that I am writing a book to celebrate the miracle of Nelson in our lives, and everyone has been so helpful. We know a lot more about his parents now, but we still have questions. Will Dalila and her sisters—will Reinaldo and his brothers—help me sort out the facts about Mila and Luis? Do I have the right to call forth their most painful memories? I wonder, too, whether I will have an opportunity to look for that photograph of Ana Milagro (Mila) that supposedly appeared in a local newspaper in the summer of 1981, just after her third child was born.

Earlier this morning Dalila showed me her new neighborhood. She wanted to take me up the hill toward the volcano before it got too hot. When we were nearly at the top of the steep incline, we stopped to catch our breath. "This is the place where I lived with my sister Mila for a while in the late 1970s when Eva was just a baby," she began without preamble, pointing to the pretty red and yellow, single-story stucco house in front of us. "No one knew where Luis was at the time, and Mila didn't explain. I didn't ask. In those days, you didn't. When she showed up again with a baby, I took her in without asking any questions."

While I was admiring the profusion of colorful plants in the tiny front yard and taking pictures of the house and garden, Dalila pointed out Mila's room, to the left of the front door. I plan to show these photos to Eva. She's never been back to El Salvador and has told me forthrightly she doesn't want to come here. She prefers to have her aunts and cousins visit her in Costa Rica. "Anyway," she emphasized just last week while I was staying with her, "I grew up here so I'm really a *tica* (Costa Rican woman) now." One of my assignments is to obtain a copy of Eva's birth certificate so that she can finalize her naturalization and apply for a passport.

« »

Resting in the hammock on Dalila's patio after our walk, my mind races down too many paths at once as I ponder all the curious circumstances—perhaps I should call them miraculous—that have combined to bring me here. I begin to read the morning edition of *La Prensa Gráfica*; one headline immediately catches my eye, for it reminds me that yesterday—February 1, 2005—marked the seventy-third anniversary of the death of Farabundo Martí, a charismatic leader of International Red Aid, an organization closely allied in the 1930s with the fledgling Salvadoran Communist Party. Martí was imprisoned, summarily tried, and executed in 1932 when an insurrection in the western part of the country broke out against the regime of General Hernández Martínez, which had overthrown the first democratically elected president in a coup.

Government troops were ordered not only to eliminate the so-called troublemakers—groups of students, artisans, and labor-union leaders that had been involved in the unsuccessful uprising along with farmworkers—but also to indiscriminately kill *campesinos* (peasants). The blood of campesinos literally ran in the streets of Nahuizalco, Tacubo, and other towns and villages in this largely coffee-growing region. It has been estimated that somewhere between ten thousand and thirty thousand lost their lives in just a few weeks, in what is simply referred to as the *Matanza* (slaughter).[2] Today it would probably be called an ethnic cleansing, for many of the peasants were indigenous. As Tommie Sue Montgomery puts it, "Anyone in Indian dress or anyone running from the security forces was fair game."[3]

Without exception, historians like Montgomery trace the Salvadoran conflict of the 1980s back at least as far as this coup and the uprising and reprisals that followed. In the late 1970s a new generation of revolutionaries drew inspiration from the telling of the story that had coalesced around the figure of Farabundo Martí, and they incorporated his name into the moniker of their group, the FMLN (Frente Farabundo Martí para la Liberación Nacional)—now a legitimate political party. The newspaper I am holding carries a picture of FMLNistas, or *farabundistas*, as they are also called, laying a wreath on Martí's grave in the general cemetery of San Salvador to commemorate his sacrifice and to remember the mass murder.[4]

Perhaps I should start my book with this unparalleled example of brutal repression in Central America, in a country ruled by an authoritarian regime supported by the oligarchy and the military. Or I could begin with the story of those like Luis and Mila who came of age in the late 1970s and were profoundly moved by the persistent economic disparities and political repression in their country, at a time when Martí had long been a legend.

I decide that I will have to start instead with the elements of the story that are most familiar to me—the way we experienced it. As I re-read this newspaper article I am reminded, however, that ours is not just a personal story; it reaches into the whole fabric of El Salvador's recent history, and I will have to include events that occurred long before 1983, when Nelson first entered our lives. I will need to find a way to place his little miracle firmly in the context of the prolonged tragedy that led to a twelve-year civil war (1980–1992), the death of at least seventy-five thousand Salvadorans, and the disappearance of countless others, the aftermath of which continues to the present day.

As I lie here trying to fix on a way to weave all the disparate threads together, I also find myself thinking of the varied, sometimes even contradictory voices of those who have lived some part of the story I want to tell. And I am touched by the loss of the voice that was silenced—the young mother who must have looked out the window of that little house into its luxuriant, sun-dappled garden. What was she thinking as she held Eva in her arms? Did she name the various flowers, using the sound of the words to soothe her baby? Or was she herself too distracted by the memory of their narrow escape, something she didn't dare share with her sister?

I find myself addressing her with all kinds of questions. Was "Iris," the name you chose for your nom de guerre, your favorite flower? It's mine. Even though I realize how difficult it will be to combine what we know with what I can only imagine, I take heart in this small connection I seem to have with the missing Mila.

«   »

Historians who have treated the Salvadoran conflict of the late 1970s and 80s in academic literature have suggested that one ought to try to grasp both the impersonal forces at work—the revolution itself—as well as the motivations of the individuals who carried it forward, sacrificing everything if necessary. I will have to do this. Inevitably, my take on the Salvadoran civil war is colored by my desire to make some sense of individuals I now care deeply about. What made them willing to risk so much? Can I grasp their convictions and their eventual doubts, their personal struggles and fears, their love for each other and their hope for a better future?

I will also have to interrogate myself as I try to convey the manner in which Tom and I came to our choices—less profound ones, no doubt, but just as crucial for the dénouement. While I have many documents to work with, I know they don't always convey the whole truth; the facts will continue to be open to interpretation. The narrative I can construct is not made of whole cloth, and I recognize that memories are malleable, subject to omissions and colorations over time by retellings in a variety of settings.

The Chilean American novelist Isabel Allende has suggested that memory is a mental process somewhat akin to imagination. It "is conditioned by emotion; we remember better and more fully things that move us." We thus tend to give our narratives more color, but we are thereby also liable to "create a private legend."[5]

Taking that risk, I believe these threads deserve to be joined in a variegated tapestry that will inevitably be as much familial legend as it is history. I have a strong sense that this multifaceted story that relies on the memories of others, as well as my own, can only be held together by my unfolding emotional truth. The book contains inconsistencies that remain unresolved and gaps that remain unfilled, as well as intentional generic dissonances. These features may jar some readers, but I need to let them be as they are, part and parcel of a whole journey of discovery and self-discovery.

Despite the contradictions and gaps, at its core the story I have to tell relies on a recognizable pattern, one that even resembles literary fiction. It is a tale of love and loss, yet one whose trajectory moves from disappearance to recovery, from anguish over death to solace in life. In a world where the conflicts of the day on every continent challenge the last bit of optimism we might muster, it seems worthwhile to recall a story that ultimately restores hope.

PART ONE

Our Story

ONE

Adoption

TEGUCIGALPA, HONDURAS, MAY–JUNE 1983

*M*emorial Day, a day to remember indeed! I wake up quite early—very excited, a little nervous. This will be the day we meet our little one—what will he look like? Thus begins my entry for Monday, May 30, 1983, in the little notebook that served as my journal for the month. I had brought it with me to Tegucigalpa—this city whose name we were just learning to get our tongues around—along with diapers, baby clothes, some toys, and a stroller we imagined we would need, even though we had no idea exactly how old the boy was.

For Tom and me, this date marks one of the emotional high points in the way this whole story has unfolded. For years we celebrated it as our son's adoption day—although it didn't mark its finalization, but rather the day when we held Nelson in our arms for the first time and were allowed to take him with us to the place where we would be staying until the court proceedings could be completed. Two years later, on the evening of May 30, 1985, I gave birth to his brother Derek—our biological surprise—in a Boston hospital. This reconfirmed May 30th as the date of our most important family celebration each year. On that Monday morning in 1983, though, I couldn't have imagined such a coincidence, nor dreamed of all the other unexpected ways that our adoption story would continue to develop much later on.

As we meandered through the streets of the Honduran capital the day before, Tom and I had been totally preoccupied with one question— what will he be like? We couldn't help but look at each little boy we saw in the plazas or on the streets, trying to guess his age, asking ourselves, will our son be like this toddler with the winning smile, or perhaps look a little like that one with the curly hair? We were desperately trying to make the time pass as we waited one more day for our appointment with the chief judge of the Honduran Court of Minors. I had a lot of time to write in my journal, getting in the habit of using the present tense to preserve the immediacy of my impressions.

We first walk down Avenida La Paz past the heavily guarded U.S. Embassy toward the central square. Men and women hawk lottery tickets spread out on the pavement and weighted down individually with a metal ring or a stone so that the buyers can look for a number they like. The zócalo (main square) is rather small for a city this size, not nearly as pleasant as the one in Merida, Mexico, we remember well from our trip to the Yucatan a few years ago. No water in the fountains here.

From the central plaza we wander across town to the Mercado Los Dolores, thinking we might find some indigenous crafts, but they appear to be building a road where the market formerly stood. We sit in a church to get out of the heat for a while, watching the people who enter—like us— to cool off and say a little prayer. Above the altar there is an ornate statue, perhaps of the Virgin of Suyapa, patron saint of Honduras. Her lighted neon halo stands in garish contrast to the plain, whitewashed walls. We head back in the opposite direction past the main post office and National Palace to a little plaza across from the Casa de la Cultura. Some people are trying to bathe in a small trickle of water that comes from a public faucet.

It's hard for us to sit still for as long as the people here seem to. We press on to the Park La Concordia with its miniature replicas of the Mayan pyramids of Copán and sit on a bench for much longer this time. Our pace is bound to change eventually. If nothing else, the oppressive humidity will force us to slow down. This is really a pleasant spot, well shaded by trees, but it's almost midday, and after more than three hours out on the street, we're thirsty. There is no place in sight to buy a soft drink.

We walk past the National Palace again and cross the Rio Choluteca into Comayagüela, Tegucigalpa's sister city—hardly any water in the river. Some people are trying to wash clothes in a few puddles. A soccer match on a makeshift field down in the riverbed attracts a crowd on the bridge. We go as far as the market area around Mercado San Isidro, then come back across on another bridge. By now, we're hungry too. And we think we might be lost, but we get our bearings as soon as we catch a glimpse of the pink-turreted Presidential Residence in the distance. We return to our airy upper room at the Maxwells' for a siesta, stopping one more time on the way to cool off in the lobby of the Hotel Maya.

We were looking at everything and everyone around us in something of a daze. Less than three weeks earlier, on Tuesday, May 10th, we had gotten a call around nine-thirty at night from our social worker, Mary Duggan. Everything we had learned about international adoption in the previous months was suddenly upended. Mary may have been smiling just a little on the other end of the line, as she could surely remember how disappointed we had been when we first met her in January and learned that the whole process would take much longer than we had expected. Even the initial application had dragged into late spring. After writing our personal statements that told about our family backgrounds and why we wanted to adopt, and after completing individual interviews, as well as gathering a number of necessary documents and testimonials, we had difficulty arranging dates for the joint interview and then a home visit. Mary threw up her hands: "How do you two imagine you are going to schedule things when you have a child to take care of?"

We acknowledged that as a two-career couple we would face some child-care challenges, but they didn't seem insurmountable. I pointed out that as a professor I had a more flexible schedule than most working mothers. We figured we would manage, even though Tom had left the professoriate and gone into college administration, meaning his day ran from nine to five—or even longer. Despite our initial scheduling difficulties, the home visit had gone well. Only the required group meetings with other prospective parents remained. After that, Mary would write up our "home study," the official statement that certified we had demonstrated physical and mental soundness, as well as financial stability, and that hopefully concluded we would be good parents.

With those first hurdles crossed, we had been concentrating on the question of a placement and had begun to face the fact that it might take a couple of years before we actually got a child. If we could identify an orphan through personal contacts, so much the better. The agency would help us with the rest. Otherwise, we would be asked to choose among its programs and be put on a waiting list. We understood that when we were eventually offered a specific child, we would be given a photograph and a medical report, as was routine practice. We would have about ten days to decide whether to go forward.

But here was Mary telling us that there was a child available if we were willing to assume more risks than usual, and if we could say yes by ten o'clock the following morning. She provided the bare outline of this startling development: "There is a little boy down in Honduras. I was notified about his availability through a contact we have. This social worker is based in Iowa, but he works freelance, helping embassy employees in Central America who want to adopt kids while they are stationed down there."

"A child for us? Right away?" Tom seemed doubtful. I hurried downstairs to get on the other phone. Mary was plunging on with her explanations: "Citizens who have adopted children abroad can't just bring them back to the States. They need to have a home study done by a licensed social worker, just like you." She continued without pausing, "Well, Michael Ster just came back from Honduras. He did a home study for the ambassador and his wife down there, the Negropontes. He doesn't know of any suitable family in Iowa that could just drop everything. So he's been calling around. I told him I thought we knew a couple that would jump at this chance. He has seen the child, but there is no photograph and no medical report, and he needs to know by tomorrow morning if you're interested. There seems to be some urgency at the other end."

"By tomorrow morning at ten," Tom repeated, as if to make it sink in. "I'll give you his number," Mary offered. "You can call him and find out more." Then she added, "I have to tell you, we've never handled an adoption from Honduras before, but we'll give you all the support we can. You'll have to concentrate on meeting the Honduran requirements as quickly as possible. Michael's contacts at the American Embassy in Tegucigalpa should help." "What about the home study?" I interrupted her. "We haven't done the three required group meetings yet." "Oh, don't worry about that. I'll write it up without them," Mary replied breezily. "You can complete those after you get back with the child—that is, if you two want to do this." Tom told her we would call the Iowan social worker right away and let her know in the morning.

«   »

Why us? We still wonder, twenty-five years later. It has occurred to me in retrospect that we might have had an edge simply because we were still in the midst of the home study process. Clients already committed to specific programs with documents all signed and sealed, possibly even the necessary visas in hand, would presumably not want to go through the hassle of switching to another country with different requirements, even if it would shorten their waiting period. Moreover, since Honduras did not allow for proxy adoptions, the prospective parents would have to be able to spend an extended period in the country, and that evidently meant right away. I imagine few would have been able to pursue this lead immediately.

I think Mary had sized us up pretty well. She knew a lot about our backgrounds, our hopes and dreams, even our vacation plans. She must have recognized that Tom, in particular, was a very decisive person, someone not given to second-guessing. She also knew that we were anxious to have a child as soon as possible, and we were poised to switch into high gear. My semester of teaching was nearly over, with only final exams still to grade. Fifteen whole months of sabbatical leave stretched out ahead of me, making it easier to meet the requirement that at least one adoptive parent be at home full time for the first six months. How often had I exclaimed, "If only we could get a child this year!" Mary also knew that Tom had arranged to take all four weeks of his vacation beginning in late May, as we were going to visit his family in Canada. She must have thought it was conceivable we would be willing to fly to Honduras instead of driving to Manitoba. We were, but we wanted to know more about the child first.

Tom put the phone down. I did too and ran back upstairs. We talked it over briefly, then called Iowa. Michael Ster expanded at first on the unusual circumstances, as if he also found the whole situation a little hard to grasp: "I've never dealt with a placement like this one! The judge of the Court of Minors and the head of the National Welfare Bureau both seem very anxious to have this orphan adopted out of country. Who knows why! The judge contacted the U.S. ambassador's wife, seeking a referral. You see, I just did a home study for the Negropontes. While I was in Tegucigalpa I got to see this little boy in the orphanage. He's beautiful. When I took out my camera, though, they wouldn't let me take his picture, so there's no photo and no formal medical report either. There wasn't time for that, but I can attest he's healthy. I wouldn't be surprised if this was the illegitimate son of the president or some other prominent person." I didn't say so right then, but I found his notion rather whimsical, although Tom always considered it within the realm of possibility and returned to it as a hypothesis from time to time when we reflected on the mystery surrounding our son's origins.

Ster continued: "If you agree to this placement by tomorrow morning, I'll call Diana—that's the ambassador's wife—and tell her to expect a call from you. She'll take care of everything." He judged the boy to be "over a year old" and described him as "small, but well-coordinated, with light brown hair, a round face, and a complexion somewhat lighter than most Hondurans." "And," he added, almost as an afterthought, "he has a wonderful smile." That was all we had to go on.

I don't remember what Tom and I said to each other before we went to sleep that night, but I am certain that we didn't have a long discussion about the pros and cons. I know that when we later attended the home study group sessions and were asked by the others to describe our decision-making process, I could truthfully say that we had not agonized over it. I told them what I still believe: "He just seemed to be meant for us." We knew that any adoption would involve risks, and I think we felt that this offer was providential in some way. It had come out of the blue at the very moment when we were ready for a child and had both the time and inclination to act quickly. Our answer just seemed obvious; the next morning we gave Mary our unequivocal "yes."

She might not have known anything about Honduran adoption laws, but Ster clearly did. Anticipating our positive response, he had already enumerated the various documents that would be required. I wrote them down on a piece of yellow tablet paper alongside the adjectives he used to describe the child. I still have it in our files, so I can readily reconstruct our first conversation.

I could tell that the Honduran regulations weren't so different from those of the Latin American countries with which our agency did have considerable experience—El Salvador, Colombia, and Brazil. And hadn't Mary promised she would help us get through the next stage by writing up the home study immediately? Moreover, it was obvious that some important people in Honduras had become involved in this orphan's placement. While we realized that personal intervention by a judge, the head of the welfare bureau, and the U.S. Embassy was not the norm in intercountry adoptions, rather than arousing any suspicion in our minds, their engagement initially reassured us.

«   »

Once we decided to embark on this path, Ster gave us the phone number of the embassy residence and explained that we could use his name to penetrate the layers of staff in order to get through personally to Diana Villers Negroponte, the wife of John D. Negroponte, U.S. ambassador to Honduras. Tom placed the call after dinner on May 11th, taking into consideration the time difference. It seemed like struggling through a labyrinth, he recalls, "but Michael Ster's name was our 'open sesame'! It did the trick." Finally, he got someone who spoke English, then Mrs. Negroponte herself. She sounded a little tentative at first, until Tom also gave my name.

We remember that she was gracious and solicitous—and above all, willing to take charge. Tom did the talking as I took notes. Based on those, her comments must have gone something like this: "Oh yes, Michael told me you would call, and he's also told me a bit about you two. I think you'll be the perfect parents. I'm very pleased that you want to adopt this child. Of course, you'll get a chance to see him before you make a final decision."

When we wanted to know if she'd seen the boy, she waxed as enthusiastically as Ster: "Oh yes. You'll love him. He is so cute and bright. And he's healthy too. You may have to treat him for intestinal parasites, but that's routine. I'll make sure to give you the name and address of our pediatrician. He's Honduran but did his training in Boston. Bring some clothes for an eighteen-month-old. You really needn't worry about a thing. If you encounter any problems, just call me."

Most important, she said that we could use the attorney who had just completed their adoption. "I'll make sure that our attorney, Lissette Sandoval, who handles most Honduran adoption cases, will oversee yours. I'll take care of the logistics here and find you a place to stay. The judge is very anxious to proceed, so you just need to focus on getting the paperwork taken care of as soon as possible. Once you have everything ready, you can call me. I'll see that the documents get down here by diplomatic courier. That is the fastest and safest way." She certainly did not offer any explanation for the haste, and fearing to jeopardize our selection as parents, we did not ask for one.

«   »

The story had really begun for Tom and me, of course, with our marriage in May 1975—or more precisely, several years later when we both held steady jobs in the Boston area and could imagine a future with children. After two years of a commuting marriage—he had been teaching Western European history at the University of Toronto while I was a professor of German at Wellesley College—Tom decided to abandon what had become an itinerant career as a professor for a position in college administration, retooling by means of an MBA in Public Management. By the time he finished his degree at Boston University, I had received tenure, but by then we were already thirty-five.

Having no success getting pregnant for almost another three years, we began routine infertility tests, which only showed that there was no obvious obstacle to our having biological offspring. Tom and I had always thought that we might adopt a child, although we did not act until after my gynecologist's admonition: "We can't explain why you two haven't gotten pregnant, but you know Margaret had that ovarian cyst removed as a teenager. That diminishes your chances, and the biological clock is certainly ticking. If you are willing to consider adoption, don't wait any longer."

As academics we naturally began by doing some research. In December 1982 we joined the Open Door Society of Massachusetts, which acted as a central source of information about domestic and intercountry adoptions in the state. In those days one could not just look things up on the Internet. We soon realized that we were likely to have a harder time with a domestic adoption, since both my age and full-time career were still looked on skeptically by many U.S. social workers. Tom and I actually knew several couples that had adopted children from other countries—namely, South Korea, India, Costa Rica, and El Salvador—although international adoption was not nearly as common in the late 1970s and early 80s as it is today.[1]

We talked with our acquaintances about their experiences and learned that requirements differed from one country to the next. There was not yet the multilateral Hague Convention that set internationally agreed-upon norms or procedures.[2] The issue of intercountry placements was especially fraught. There was no governmental clearinghouse as Tom had imagined, but only a patchwork of personal relationships maintained by various private agencies. Everything depended on ties an agency had developed with individual lawyers, orphanages, or child welfare agencies.

And other countries could suddenly change their laws without warning. An adoption agency might drop a program when it discovered irregularities in procurement or that standards of foster care were not being met. This hasn't changed, although the Hague Convention now provides a framework for regulation among its signatories.[3] We soon realized it would be especially important to make sure that we worked with a reputable agency, one that protected us from black market operators and helped us identify a child truly in need of a family, then provided guidance for the various legal hurdles we would face both here and abroad.[4]

By early 1983 we had decided to work with World Adoptions Services, a small local agency in Newton, Massachusetts, that handled not only international but also mixed-race and special-needs U.S. adoptions. Their modest offices were housed in a church basement located in the village of Auburndale, about five miles from our home in Wellesley. Friends of ours had adopted a one-year-old boy from El Salvador through this agency the previous summer, and we were thinking we might do the same. But the director had decided to cancel that program after a baby-selling scandal was exposed.

She said that she trusted the agency's contact but wanted to be especially careful. "Because of the ongoing civil war, the situation in El Salvador has really deteriorated. It is just too uncertain where the children are coming from," she told us. We were disappointed, but appreciated the care with which she and her staff seemed to approach every facet of the process, including the fact that fees for the home study were placed on a sliding scale depending on applicants' income. We would have to pay about $1,500 for their services from the application through post-placement. That did not include travel, lawyer's fees, or other in-country costs; these could differ widely.

As we started the application process, we read more about the kinds of adoptions we were now considering. I used a reading list prepared by Holt Adoption Program, a much larger private agency in Oregon that had originally specialized in adoptions from Asia. We began to ask ourselves whether we would be capable of taking care of a special-needs child, or whether we were willing to consider an older or nonwhite American child.

«   »

By late spring Mary had helped us focus even more intently on the range of issues that are liable to complicate any interracial, intercultural, or intercountry adoption.[5] We felt pretty sure about what we were capable of, and what we wanted. We told her we were open to adopting either a boy or girl up to two years old. We still had a strong preference for a child from Latin America, but we had decided that we would not rule out an Asian child or an African American or mixed-race U.S. child of roughly the same age. Our willingness to accept a boy and to forego having an infant was no guarantee of getting a placement quickly, but we discovered that it enhanced our chances since the greater number of prospective parents wanted infant girls.[6]

We had found out that even in the international arena our options were more limited because of our age. In most instances it was the mother's advanced age that was considered prohibitive, and in February I had turned thirty-nine. Colombia—one of the countries with which our agency had an ongoing program—would not even consider a mother over the age of thirty-five for an infant or toddler. Many other countries would not place a child with a mother who was more than forty years older than the child, a provision that made us nervous. What if we languished on some waiting list for so long that we were unable to adopt a child two or under?

Because we were encouraged to be proactive in finding an appropriate placement, we explored various sources, not just ones the agency told us about, including suggestions from friends and family. Someone who knew someone was enough of a lead. I am surprised now, as I look through our entire adoption file, to find that we were still writing such letters in early May, only days before Mary's transformative phone call. I had forgotten the details, but I see that we sent letters or made calls of inquiry to organizations in Minnesota and Texas, and to orphanages or personal contacts we had in Costa Rica, Indonesia, and Taiwan.

From this ultimately unsuccessful effort to identify an adoptable child on our own, as well as from the materials the agency provided and the books we were reading on the subject, it really began to sink in just how complex the whole process was going to be. We had all but decided that our agency's contact in Natal, Brazil, was probably our best chance. If we didn't hear something positive from any other source before we left for Canada at the end of May, we would join that waiting list. Then, everything changed overnight.

«   »

During the few weeks between that surprising phone call and our departure for Honduras, we had our hands full trying to get all the paperwork completed. We studied the list Ster had dictated over the phone. Fortunately, we had already obtained the local police clearances from all the places we had stayed for six months or more—complicated by the fact that both Tom and I had lived more than once for such periods in Germany. We also had the certified copies of our marriage and birth certificates in hand. We had started early on those, because we knew every country would require them, and Tom's had to be authenticated in Drangstedt, Germany, where he had been born in a field hospital in July 1944, after the family's apartment in Bremerhaven was bombed out.

For the home study we had already provided letters from our primary care physician attesting to our good physical and mental health, as well as bank records and tax forms showing our income and savings. However, we still needed a slew of personal letters of recommendation, and statements from our employers concerning our financial security. All these affidavits had to be presented in multiple copies, the authenticity of each copy verified by a notary public, then each notarization certified in turn by the State of Massachusetts. It all seemed like a bureaucratic nightmare.

Our families and friends were apprised of the unexpected development, and our vacation trip to Canada was canceled. Instead, Tom's parents would come to see us once we were back with their new grandson. Looking over the original set of documents that were returned to us by the Honduran court after the in-country adoption, I am reminded of the tremendous support we received, not only from our families but also from all the people who provided us with letters of recommendation right away. Mary had our home study written up within only a few days. Everyone rallied around our cause, helping us get ready and providing us with clothes and basic equipment for the child and enough toys for him and the orphanage.

When we found that our local Wellesley police could not take our fingerprints on May 14th—a Saturday—we leaned on the fact that Tom was then director of finance at Regis College to get the neighboring Weston police to do it. Then we ran into our first roadblock. After taking our prints, the sergeant said it could take weeks—perhaps even months—for us to get the needed clearance back from Washington, D.C. Tom threaded the labyrinth again and reached Mrs. Negroponte on the phone. "Is there anything you can suggest?" he asked.

She told us to contact Senator Ted Kennedy's office and ask to have our criminal background check expedited. She had no doubt that the senior senator from Massachusetts would have the necessary clout. Exactly who pulled the strings we do not know, but the bureaucratic obstacles were indeed swiftly overcome, and only a few days later we received the expected clearance from the FBI stating that we had no criminal record.

«   »

As soon as the word was out that we were on the verge of adopting a child in Honduras, Sister Thérèse Higgins, president of Regis College, introduced us to a nun who had recently come to Boston after teaching for fourteen years at a Catholic school in La Ceiba. Sister Christina spoke of her appreciation for the beauty of the Honduran countryside and her love of its people. She promised to loan us a book with photographs, and she gave us some helpful hints about handling the mañana culture we would find there. I told my hard-charging husband that he should probably commit those to memory, for he was sure to need them.

Sister Christina also wanted to alert us to the current political climate. While nominally ruled by the first civilian government since 1963 (when a coup had installed a military junta in place of a democratically elected president), Honduras not only was the original "banana republic" but also had remained under strong U.S. influence and was run de facto by a military strongman. The man in charge was not President Roberto Suazo Córdova, but General Gustavo Álvarez Martínez. In 1983 Álvarez was the head of both the Armed Forces and the National Police; he had also created a secret army intelligence unit called Battalion 3-16, a special force trained by the Argentine Army and the CIA that was later held responsible for a range of human rights abuses including surveillance, disappearances, torture, and murder of regime opponents during the 1980s.[7]

Sister Christina had promised to give us the names and telephone numbers of people who could assist us if we ran into any trouble. The coffee-table book and a list of suggested contacts arrived by mail. In addition to members of her religious order and lay educators in the north, we were surprised to find the private number of none other than General Álvarez, to be used, she wrote, "only in a true emergency." In addition, she provided another "last-resort" contact: the head of United Fruit Company! I was reminded of a comment in an article I had just read in *Ms. Magazine* on international adoption: "Ironically, women seeking to adopt who consider themselves feminists and political liberals may suddenly find they are working quietly in tandem with right-wing, nondemocratic governments."[8] What were we getting into?

«   »

On May 16th I took the train into Boston and walked from Park Street Station uphill to the golden-domed State House in search of the office of the secretary of state. There I needed to get confirmation that the notaries who had certified our various documents as copies of originals were licensed by the state. For a fee, each piece of paper got a certificate attached to it testifying thereto and carrying the appropriate signatures and the great seal of the Commonwealth of Massachusetts.

The following day I placed this impressive sheaf of papers with those green raised seals and our passports on the desk of the Honduran Consulate in a miniscule office on East 41st Street in Manhattan. The woman behind it eyed me suspiciously. She looked first at the passports. "Where is he?" she asked brusquely, holding up the photo page of Tom's passport. "At work," I replied. "No one told us he needed to present himself in person. As you can see, my husband's passport is here along with all the necessary affidavits, including the required Honduran consular document that declares that we are not members of the Communist Party, nor do we 'harbor any sympathy for that exotic doctrine.'"

In case she didn't like the fact that we had different last names, I added, "The documents for the adoption include our marriage certificate, of course." She went to consult with another staff person. When she came back she named the price for the certifying Honduran stamp and the signature of Herman Allan Padgett, consul general. Again, we needed one for every copy of every document.

She was more reluctant to issue me entry visas, insisting that we needed residence visas if we expected to stay in Honduras for a month or more to complete the adoption. I asked myself why Mrs. Negroponte had failed to mention this possibility to us, as I registered my surprise: "We were under the impression that tourist visas would be sufficient." The clerk intimated that she was not inclined to issue me any kind of visa for Tom. As I was wondering whether it would help to mention our connections to the U.S. Embassy, she made it clear that if I could pay for everything in cash she would overlook the irregularity. I knew this was probably a bribe, but we would lose more time and incur even more expense if Tom had to show up in person. I paid her in cash and headed back to Boston.

By May 18th we were able to notify Mrs. Negroponte that we had all the documents signed and sealed more than once. She gave us an address in Miami where we were to send them by express mail. From there they would get to Honduras by embassy courier, she explained. Then they only needed to be translated into Spanish and reviewed by the judge at the Court of Minors. She would call us as soon as everything was prepared. Today, as I peruse online the ambassador's secret diplomatic correspondence from those very same days—posted at the time of the hearings for Negroponte's confirmation as intelligence chief in April 2005—

I can't help wondering what messages from the State Department might have been traveling in the same pouch as our adoption papers.[9]

Around the same time, I filed an application for advance processing of orphan petition form 1-600A with the U.S. Immigration and Naturalization Service at the JFK Federal Building in Boston. On May 25, 1983, our eighth wedding anniversary, we received a "favorable determination [. . .] concerning our ability as prospective adoptive parents to furnish proper care to a beneficiary orphan under Section 101(b)(1)(F)."[10] The document granted us a year to complete the adoption process. After bringing a child into the United States, I would have to submit more paperwork and documentation concerning my adoption in the source country. (Tom was not yet a citizen.) But the first steps had been taken.

Within a week Mrs. Negroponte called to let us know that our documents had been translated and received the required court approval. She urged us to make our plane reservations and come right away. "Don't worry," she said again. "I'll take care of everything." But, of course, we did worry.

It hardly seems feasible to me now, but I can see that on Friday, May 27, 1983—less than three weeks after Mary's phone call—we actually departed Boston. At the last minute, one of my colleagues in the German department, a mother of two young boys, gave me a book on the subject of toddlers. For almost half a year, we'd been entirely focused on researching the international adoption process, gathering materials for the home study, and hunting for a child. We thought there would be plenty of time to read books on child rearing once we were playing the waiting game. But now we were on our way to meet our child. I was too excited to read the book on the plane.

«   »

Takeoff felt like a leap of faith. Despite Mrs. Negroponte's assurances, it was disconcerting to have no idea where we would live. All we had was the name of the attorney who would meet us at the airport; we had no idea what she looked like. It wasn't our usual style of travel to just leave for some foreign country without a clear itinerary and a place to stay. Our anxiety mounted as the Tan-Sasha plane out of Miami stopped off first in Belize and then in San Pedro Sula, near Honduras's Caribbean coast. We could make out banana plantations crisscrossing the plateau, but there was no sign of the city. It was getting dark already at five o'clock as we approached our final destination, Tegucigalpa's Toncontín International Airport—one of the most dangerous in the world we'd been told, because of its proximity to mountains and its single, short runway. Heavy storm clouds hung over the high peaks that ring the capital, but it was not raining yet. There was hardly time to register the twinkling lights of the city below as we descended through the clouds rapidly and banked sharply to land. Tom vowed never to fly into this place again. His stomach—always a little sensitive to motion—was in knots.

As we waited in line to go through immigration and customs in the airport, still fretting about whether our visas were in order, one of the flight attendants came back to tell us that her aunt, Lissette Sandoval, was waiting in the arrivals lobby. Her aunt was the lawyer who would be taking care of us. This coincidence brought us a little relief. Then the border patrol agents told us we did not need residence visas after all. When Lissette later heard about the clerk's insistence on a cash transaction in New York, she asked me whether I had been given a receipt. "No," I responded, a little sheepishly. I recorded my first impressions of our attorney and the city in my journal.

We pile into Lissette Sandoval's large pickup. She is friendly but somewhat reserved, a diminutive woman, slender, with an aquiline nose and fine, short black hair. I judge her to be about our age, in her late thirties. We learn that she actually does the adoption work on the side, after hours, usually from her home. That's where we should call her most of the time rather than the office. Tom makes a note of both numbers.

Although there are storm clouds all around, Lissette tells us the rainy season is a month overdue, and there is already a severe water shortage. Even some of the tourist hotels have to ration water because of the extreme drought. "But you won't be staying in a hotel," she adds. "Mrs. Negroponte has arranged for a host family. That will be less expensive and more comfortable. Their house is in Colonia San Carlos, near a nice little shopping plaza on Boulevard Morazán, only a few blocks from the U.S. Embassy." I can almost hear Tom breathe more easily in the front seat. When we tell Lissette we've brought a lot of donated toys, she suggests they should be given to the state institution that needs them much more than the private orphanage where our child has been staying.

She takes us to meet the Smiths. We learn that Anita and Bill, who have been here for only ten months, have already adopted three children— two little boys, ages two and three, and a baby girl, eight months old. Michael Ster conducted their home study too. I'm a little sorry to find out that this is not where we'll be staying; Anita is so eager to help. Lissette can't linger, because she has to pick up her three-year-old, an adopted daughter.

There seems to be a whole network of adoptive parents here who have already been through what we're facing. Before leaving, Lissette promises to check whether we might see our son tomorrow. She's doubtful, though, because we're unlikely to get permission without first seeing the judge, and that will have to wait until early Monday morning.

Our host family lives in this same neighborhood; they aren't home since the eldest daughter took a fall while at riding school and they wanted to have her checked out. We're really tired from the long flight and all the anxiety of not knowing what to expect once we landed. Now we're just anxious to get to our final destination and fall into bed, but all we can do is wait. We are sitting outside listening to the night sounds—ripe mangoes drop from the trees while fruit bats fly overhead as we drink freshly squeezed grapefruit juice and eat homemade peanut butter cookies. It seems a little unreal.

Finally Magda Maxwell comes to pick us up, apologizing for the delay. She is a vivacious woman, born in Peru, who works in the housing office at the embassy. When Mrs. Negroponte inquired about a place for us to stay, she volunteered her house. We'll pay the Maxwells nominal room and board and can stay as long as we have to.

The drive is literally around the corner, and they welcome us like family. We're a little taken aback at the luxurious surroundings. We have use of all the downstairs rooms and the walled garden, a private bathroom— all onyx—and servants to cook and clean.

Anita has given us some bedding for the crib that we find already standing in the roomy bedroom the younger daughter has ceded to us. The three Maxwell children, Nicole, Christopher, and Gretchen, range in age from ten to fifteen. They seem excited at the prospect of having a toddler in the house. Built-in babysitters. We have some trouble placing Carl. He's not from Peru, like Madga. Where then? The Philippines? "No," he explains, laughing. "I'm an Inuit."

Like Bill Smith, Carl works as an engineer for USAID (U.S. Agency for International Development). He tells us he's involved in road-building projects in some rural areas of Honduras. I can't help but think of my late father. He too was a structural engineer who built roads and bridges, albeit in Pennsylvania, New Jersey, and New York. We'd long ago decided to call our son by his full name followed by Tom's surname. It's sort of strange to have this wonderful name—Nelson Ward de Witt—and no child yet to call by it. I fall asleep to the rhythmic thought: soon—soon.

As Lissette had correctly surmised, we had to spend two more days in this state of suspended animation, longing to see him. While waiting even more anxiously for her to pick us up on Monday morning, May 30th, I found that writing calmed my nerves: *We don't even know when our lawyer will pick us up. She said "early," but what does that mean in mañana land? By 7:45 we were at breakfast, the last ones. The kids have already left for school.*

We're dressed up; we want to make a good impression on the judge, but we've noticed everyone else seems to be quite casual—the men in cotton jerseys or loose-fitting guayabera shirts. Tom didn't need to bring two suits! It is extremely hot and very dry. Every night clouds gather ominously, but so far offer only a drop or two. As a precaution, Carl has posted water conservation regulations, but luckily their cistern is nearly full. At nine o'clock Tom can't stand this waiting any longer. He calls Lissette's home number to find out when "early" is, but she's not home.

Like so much of what was happening to us, even small details seemed to be out of our control, an uncomfortable position for two people used to being "in charge." We didn't know what to expect or what would be expected of us, yet we were slowly learning to accept that things would take their own course and work out somehow.

No sooner does Tom come back out on the patio after making the call than Lissette rings the doorbell. We set out immediately in her blue truck, first downtown to the Instituto Hondureño de la Niñez y la Familia, the juvenile and family court, a nondescript building with many people milling around in the hallways. We are clearly privileged since we're ushered in right away to see a red-haired judge, Teodolinda Pineda de Aguilar. She speaks with us in Spanish, and Lissette translates: "This is a little boy who has been through a shock and needs a lot of love. From reading your home study, I feel sure that you can give him that." She doesn't say anything very specific about what the "shock" was, but we gather a violent separation from his parents. She does make it clear that he has been officially declared an orphan and is adoptable under Honduran law.

We meet two social workers, one associated with the orphanage where our child has been living—we gather for about nine or ten months—the other court-appointed. The latter will have to inspect our arrangements for keeping Nelson in our care before he can be released to our custody. No problem. The judge smiles; she can tell we are anxious to meet him. Even though it is only twenty days since we first heard about this child, we feel as if we've been waiting a lifetime. The judge gives permission; we can go out to the Aldeas SOS orphanage in another part of town to see if we like him and really want to proceed with the adoption. Then we'll have to appear before her again.

Of course, I was wondering what the place where Nelson had spent such developmentally important months would be like. Lissette had impressed on us how much better this orphanage was than the one run by the state.[11]

I'm clearly not prepared for this place. Tom has to hop out of the truck and open a broken gate. A chain-link fence studded with diapers drying in the sun encloses a red clay yard where a few older children are playing. They don't appear to have many toys though, not even balls to kick around in the dust. They wave to us.

We enter the cement-block compound with square openings for windows. We are led from the main office upstairs past a well-stocked pharmacy. The nurse indicates that contributions from their international donors are used for essentials—food and medicine. Lissette steps on a huge cockroach. We go from one large room full of infants and toddlers to another. Each has cribs lining the walls.

Some children are lying listlessly in their beds; others are standing and watch us pass, silently. Tom looks at one wide-eyed child after another and wonders aloud whether we might not adopt more than one child while we're here—now that we have all the paperwork done. I look at him sideways and, while I share his underlying emotions, reply in a whisper, "Get a grip." I can't imagine our coping immediately with three under the age of three like Anita and Bill. That's when we find out most of them can't be adopted anyway. Many will simply grow up here until they are picked up again when they're old enough to help their families scratch out a subsistence living. We're reminded of the fact that Honduras is the poorest country in Central America and, after Haiti, the poorest in the hemisphere.

Finally we reach the last room on the upper floor. The nurse walks to the crib in the far corner by a window and lifts out a little boy with sturdy legs and big feet, much too big for the running shoes I've brought. I can see that right away. He's wearing only a cloth diaper and faded T-shirt. The staff nurse and Lissette both point to us and say in chorus, "Mamá, Papá." We hardly feel prepared for this moment, but suddenly I am thinking more about how they have prepared him for it. Have they?

Then I hand Nelson the little bear Sister Thérèse had given us for him—a Paddington Bear with a blue felt coat and red hat—odd to be giving him a bear in a raincoat in a place so desperate for rain. He clutches it—perhaps it's the first stuffed animal he has ever had. Tom and I are each allowed to hold him awhile; we kiss him and soothe him, although he doesn't seem upset, just sad and a little uncertain. He doesn't cry at all or reject our caresses.

Now comes the hardest thing we've had to do so far—put him back in the crib and say good-bye. We can wave to him again from the truck, since he is standing up near that corner window watching us drive away, not smiling, not crying, but holding on to that teddy for dear life. It brings tears to my eyes. Let's get back quickly please, so we can take him home and hold him forever.

Next it's back to the Court of Minors. We tell Judge Pineda how beautiful we think he is, with his round face, wavy chestnut hair, and expressive, coffee-colored eyes. How could we refuse him? She smiles broadly. Our interview is shorter this time, our "yes" irrevocable. Next the court-appointed social worker comes with us to see where we will be keeping him.

How could she not be impressed with Carl and Magda's house? We are. Given all the poverty we've seen here, cheek by jowl with wealth, we feel almost embarrassed. On the vacant lot at the corner of this street, squatters are living in a one-room shack. We find ourselves explaining that we're not used to living in a three-story villa with marble floors and maids to cook and clean. At home we share the housework, and by North American standards, our house is small—we've had to submit a picture of it— but, "yes, our son will have a room of his own."

The social worker asks us some questions about what we expect of our child. "What are your wishes for his future? Do you want him to be a doctor or lawyer, perhaps?" she coaches us. "No, not necessarily." She looks a little disappointed. Luckily, Anita has forewarned us that they fear we will want to make their children into our servants. We try to answer truthfully: "We want him to have the benefit of higher education like ourselves so that he can become whatever he wants to be."

Back to the court a third time, we hardly speak with the judge for more than a minute or two. Having heard the report of the social worker concerning our housing arrangement, Pineda agrees to release Nelson to our custody while the adoption proceeds under Lissette's able guidance. She orders the proper document prepared and takes her leave.

That day, in our excitement to meet our son, to hold him, and to have him with us permanently, we didn't press the judge who had control of his destiny for more concrete information about his past. In the ensuing years, we have asked ourselves many times, why not? Were we afraid it could cause problems? In any case, we thought there would be additional court appearances as the adoption proceeded, but much to our surprise, the three on May 30th were the only ones.

After a while we headed back the same route we had taken earlier in the morning. In the midday heat the place seemed even dustier, the children even more forlorn. Again, our hearts were in our throats as we passed by all these other children in cribs. I left some lollipops and crayons with the social worker from the orphanage. Sister Christina had suggested this, but it seemed like so little. I tried briefly to imagine what conditions were like at the state orphanage that would get the toys, but soon all our concern was directed to our little boy.

Nelson seems to recognize us but remains passive. He won't let go of his teddy, so I undress him while he holds on to the bear. We fold the few items he has on and leave them on the mattress. When I pull out a clean diaper and his new clothes, a little blue and white striped T-shirt and jogging shorts of soft blue jersey with white trim, he smiles for the first time. Will he someday be a clotheshorse?

When we are ready to leave, we are told to stop downstairs to talk with a doctor who wants to say a personal good-bye. Lissette explains later that the young man has grown up in this same orphanage. He smiles and tells us, "Ronny is a special little boy. I care a lot about him, and I'll want to know how he's doing." It was the first inkling we had that we would be asked to file regular reports on our child's progress. "He's healthy but needs a lot of attention. He's been considered a rather difficult child; he always wanted to be the first to eat. He's had a skin rash, nothing serious. Later we'll give you his vaccination certificate." He provides us with a short list of the foods that Nelson has been eating, then adds, "He likes to drink Coke." I frown.

We quickly concluded, however, that it was probably better to have a feisty, purportedly "difficult" child who liked Coke than one of the listless ones we had seen upstairs.

«   »

With hindsight—after much more information about his origins came to light—we realized just how little Judge Pineda had been willing to reveal of what the Honduran authorities must have known at the time. She did mention during one of these interviews that she had refused a prospective adoptive family back in December 1982. Why tell us that? We still have no answer to this particular question. It was such a curious bit of specificity when everything else seemed so vague that I could vividly recall it when his actual background was first revealed to us.

Our first evening in Honduras, the Smiths had passed on the outlines of what they believed to be Nelson's story. Maybe Michael Ster had told them how mysterious the case seemed, and Anita, putting two and two together on meager information, remembered reading in the paper about a kidnapping that had ended in a shoot-out. It had taken place in the northern industrial town of San Pedro Sula about ten months before, and a little boy had been orphaned. She thought this might be our child. That would fit with the bit about the "shock" he had experienced and his having been in the orphanage for ten months. Would they have brought a child all the way to Tegucigalpa, we wondered? We filed Anita's speculation in the back of our minds.

For the moment, our attention was entirely centered on our new role as Nelson's parents. This much was clear—the Honduran authorities didn't know who he was. There was no birth record, and we learned that a birth certificate would have to be created as part of the adoption process. After that, a Honduran passport could be issued, and later we could apply at the U.S. Consulate for the immigration visa to bring him back home.

We had only a few minutes to select an artificial date of birth for him. We chose August 25, 1981. The 25th seemed an easy day to remember because of Christmas Day and our May wedding anniversary, and by choosing August we gave ourselves plenty of leeway to make sure we got him back home on the free "child under two" one-way air ticket we had. As someone born in mid-winter, it even occurred to me during those few minutes that late August might be a perfect time to have birthday parties.

Because there was no birth certificate, no one knew his real name. In the orphanage they were calling him Ronny, and later we saw that "Rony [sic] Funez" was used in all the official Honduran adoption papers. We had already decided to give him a new name, one that signified how much he now belonged to our family, but when I heard them call him Ronny, I was certain we were making the right choice. I didn't want anyone to think we had named him for then-president Ronald Reagan.

We did not support either Reaganomics or the president's foreign policy in Latin America, which tried to cloak every conflict in cold-war rhetoric, ignoring the individual histories of those countries. It was a little bonus to discover that Nelson was actually a rather familiar first name in Honduras, a questionable legacy of the English buccaneers who had influenced the Caribbean coast. As I write now, I am also struck by the coincidence that the first identifiable victim of the notorious Battalion 3-16, cited in a series of exposés that appeared in the *Baltimore Sun* in 1995, was a Honduran named Nelson Mackay Chavarría.[12]

Our Nelson had been through a lot—we had been told as much—but he clearly had survivor skills; he was resilient. We knew that young children suffer from separation anxiety. He'd lost his birth parents at such a young age—we didn't know how or when exactly, but surely the sudden separation had left residual feelings of fear and anger. Would he now resent being plucked from the surroundings he had gotten used to since then? Would he be missing the young doctor at the orphanage who was so fond of him?

Although we understood that many months had passed since he had been orphaned, we figured our child would probably carry deep emotional scars. We could only hope that he had not been subjected to the trauma of witnessing some terrible violence. We had already opened our hearts for him, but would he be able to return our love and affection unreservedly? These were the questions that were foremost in our minds as we took him "home" to the Maxwells'. Our first few hours together were entirely reassuring, as I noted in my journal.

Nelson seems a little afraid when we leave in the truck and holds on to me tightly. We have to drive to another section of town first to pick up our attorney's daughter, who spends a half-day in a Montessori preschool. As we all get out of the truck, the children come right over to inspect "the baby," who is somewhat unsettled by all this attention. In the orphanage he evidently couldn't get enough; now maybe it will feel as if it is too much all at once. After this stop, I'm wedged in the back seat with Nelson, Lissette's daughter, and another little girl; no one worries about booster seats or seat belts, but at least we're not riding in its bed like so many people we see on the roads here, sometimes holding a sheet over their heads to protect themselves from the sun.

Lissette promises to come by with the first set of adoption papers for our signature sometime tomorrow. "I'll handle everything," she assures us. "When the second social worker that needs to interview you gets back from San Pedro Sula, I'll arrange to have her come to the house; no need for you to go back to court." We're a little surprised at this.

What excitement when we arrive! Gretchen, Chris, and Nicole alone are going to give Nelson all the attention he wants, but our little boy is still pretty shy, preferring to sit in my lap. Magda is speaking to him in Spanish, but while he appears to understand her, he has only one functional word of his own that we can discern—"agua" (water)—an appropriate demand in such a time of drought.

The business about wanting to be the first one to eat certainly rings true. Nelson has a good appetite and tries anything we offer him for lunch. And he wants it right away! Food is almost as important to him as water. Even a Cheerio dropped on the floor has to be retrieved. Out on the patio we take our first photos.

The only immediate problem is that Nelson is afraid of Butch, a friendly beagle the Maxwells are also boarding. Maybe he has had a bad experience with a dog; whenever he hears barking, he whimpers a little. After lunch we're all pretty tired, so we go upstairs to try to take a nap. He's not sure of his surroundings yet, so we let him fall asleep between us on the big bed. As soon as we think he's sound asleep and put him in his crib, he's wide-eyed. But he plays quietly with the toys we've placed there. From time to time he looks over just to make sure we're still here. I doze, then wake and look back at him looking at me. We smile at each other. Bonding begins.

We could see from the conditions in the orphanage that Nelson had had little opportunity to develop either fine or gross motor skills. With so few staff to care for so many children, they just kept the toddlers in cribs most of the time. We figured he probably lagged behind in language acquisition too. Would he be able to catch up on all these fronts? Again my journal records that our first hours together were reassuring.

He is so curious and eager to savor each new experience. He watches me blow bubbles in amazement and tries to touch them. He manipulates nesting cups and opens and closes the bureau drawers. Everything is a source of wonder and delight. Around three o'clock we head out to Boulevard Morazán for his first stroller ride. Nelson gives out a loud laugh every time Tom has to lean him backward to go up or down a curb. We swing around the house again and then go over to see the Smiths. Nelson is terrified of their two large dogs so they tie them up out back.

I compare the kids' statures. If their David is two, then Nelson probably is only about eighteen to twenty months old. The clothes I have brought fit perfectly. Anita has just the right thing for his big feet—a used pair of sneakers and some red leather sandals for now, and another slightly larger pair of running shoes to grow into. I will trade them for the smaller ones I brought and some other things she can use, like bottles, because Nelson is already drinking from a two-handled cup.

A big black cloud around dinnertime seems like a sure harbinger of rain. We feed Nelson first in the breakfast nook. He's no slouch, taking two helpings of meat and mashed potatoes, zucchini, and even cucumber salad. Then, while we eat, he sits in his little yellow director's chair and plays. Our dinner hour gets chaotic when the winds suddenly come up. We all jump up to close windows and doors and tie up flying hammocks, but it turns out to be another false alarm. The three Maxwell kids leave the table to play with Nelson, tossing a ball to knock over a tower made of boxes— his first real silliness with lots of laughs. The rain finally comes in a deluge much later when we're all in bed. Paddington Bear was prepared for this tropical downpour after all. It seems like a good omen at the end of an emotionally exhausting but wonderful day, our first as a family.

We actually had little time to worry about how Nelson would react, for after those first anxious days of waiting, he was put rather suddenly in our care, something we had not really expected. We just tried to embrace him and show him all the love that we could. After some initial hesitancy, he turned out to be cheerful and responsive beyond our wildest dreams. Michael Ster had been right—he had a wonderful smile, and he knew how to laugh. He clearly loved life. He accepted our hugs and began to cuddle in return. We thought—quite simply—that he was adorable.

We took Nelson to the nearby Clinicas Medicas the next day for a thorough physical exam by the Honduran pediatrician Mrs. Negroponte had recommended. The only thing that frightened him on this occasion was the measuring tape. He was thirty-two inches tall and weighed twenty-three pounds. He already had sixteen teeth. Dr. Tomé judged him to be a little older than we had thought—around twenty-one or twenty-two months. Although he prescribed two kinds of vitamins and a ten-day treatment for parasites, he found our toddler quite healthy. "I think your little boy has good prospects because he is such a curious fellow," he added.

Indeed he was! Released from his crib-bound existence, Nelson appeared to go through entire developmental stages in short order, as we introduced new activities: stacking toys, putting things in a mesh net and taking them out again, playing tug-of-war with his red rings, wrapping things up in a cloth book, blowing bubbles himself, and especially throwing and kicking a ball around the enclosed yard.

However, within only a few days Nelson evidently felt confident enough of our new bond to begin to test its limits. Tom and I soon found we badly needed that book on toddlers' behavior that my colleague had given me as a going-away present. Anita added to our parental library with another book, appropriately titled, as I recall, *The Difficult Child*. At times, he was still all sunshine and smiles; at others, he could be an absolute tyrant, especially in the afternoon if we had to interrupt his nap because we had an appointment.

He reserved his best theatrics for those times when we began to issue the simple prohibition, "No." He would look at us, screw up his sweet little face, and flash us a defiant look as he threw himself on the ground and screamed as loudly as he could. He could carry on a tantrum for forty-five minutes, if he thought the cause sufficient. Even in our distress, we had to admire his strength of will and voice. Magda and Carl laughed knowingly, "Don't worry about it, ignore him, it doesn't bother us a bit." It bothered us terribly, nevertheless, and we wondered more than once how we would have dealt with such displays of temper in a hotel room. In the direst instances, we even asked ourselves why we had not held out for a babe in arms. What had made us think we could handle a child in the midst of the so-called terrible twos? Our initial parental confidence was sorely tested.

The following excerpts give some sense of both the highs and lows of these first weeks, as together we overcame our fears and learned to negotiate: *Nelson is still afraid of Butch. He laughs and waves him away and then cries out "Wow-Wow" when the dog is already running in the other direction. If he weren't so obviously frightened, it would be very funny. [. . .] Nicole reads a book to him. He's more interested in turning the pages, an activity that absorbs him for a long time. We're impressed with his attention span. Only when he gets really tired and cranky does he move aimlessly from one thing to the next; otherwise he is absorbed with each new task or learning situation. [. . .]*

Nelson begins to explore the house again as we sit down to dinner. I check out where he has gone and find him standing on a kitchen chair playing with rose petals the maid has given to him—what fun to see them flutter down all around like confetti. All three of us laugh at the beautiful sight. Then the electricity goes out—a common occurrence. We're given a kerosene lantern to take up to the bedroom. [. . .]

He will only take a bath standing up. I don't imagine he's ever seen a big tub like this one or this much water. He loves to sit in his crib afterward with some stuffed animals or a cloth book to pass the time until he just conks out. When I think he's asleep I remove as many toys as I can. Sometimes he sits bolt upright in bed as if to say, "How dare you take them away," and throws his blue musical rabbit at me. Sometimes we hear him crying or whimpering, or he scratches himself in his sleep. His skin shows a lot of little scars. What is he remembering; what is he dreaming?

After only a week with us, Nelson was much more confident on his feet. He could climb the stairs and kick a ball with gusto. He liked to push the stroller around the block rather than sit in it all the time when we went out for walks. We had signed various adoption papers that our lawyer brought by the house and were just waiting for the interview with the still-absent social worker. After that, we planned to take a trip while the adoption was finalized, since Lissette was fairly certain that our presence in court would not be required.

Originally, we had hoped to go to Copán, but Nelson still didn't have a passport. Without one we would not be allowed onto the archaeological site because of its proximity to the Guatemalan border. Instead, we found we could catch a ride to San Pedro Sula with Carl, who had business up north. After that we thought we might visit the school where Sister Christina had taught in La Ceiba.

Tom and I were getting much better at anticipating Nelson's moods. I found we could avoid the first likely outburst of the day by giving him a banana before even starting to fix breakfast, and by peeling it very quickly! We knew not to interrupt a nap if at all possible. Of course, there were some times when we had to do just that, and others when we just had to say no. We thought it would be wise to see how he fared on shorter outings before we committed to a longer journey. I recorded our first.

Routine seems very important, but we can't always control the timing of naps and meals. In preparation for this afternoon's outing with the Maxwells to a "members-only" club about thirty miles outside of Tegucigalpa, I put Nelson to bed in mid-morning after checking his diaper. He howls in rage, but I ignore it and close the door, and eventually he settles down. Honduran friends of the Maxwells' that are members of this club have invited us to join them and their seven (!) children for the day. It will be our first time out in the countryside, so we look forward to it.

We drive through Comayagüela, then stop in Comayagua to see the famous cathedral there. After that the road winds through hilly countryside up to a pine-forested ridge where this glorified park is located. In the city and immediate outskirts the main roads are paved, but full of potholes, and the side streets are all dirt. By comparison this main highway out in the campo is not too bad despite treacherous curves and crazy drivers.

Cattle of all descriptions roam around freely. At one point I think we are going to hit a cow that is just trotting along in the middle of the road.

The pine trees on many of the hillsides are dry as tinder. There is rural poverty everywhere. As in town, the juxtaposition between rich and poor is often quite stark. Here the hovels are interspersed with small, well-kept farms. We see women walking along the road carrying heavy loads on their heads.

From this elite club you get a beautiful view of the surrounding mountains. There is a huge swimming pool area, covered to protect people from the hot sun, and great facilities for kids of all ages: a kiddy pool, a fort, swings and slides, a little lake for boating, a train ride, and, of course, a soccer field. I think of the poor boys in Tegucigalpa who only have the dusty riverbed. I see one woman with twin girls—probably about three—all gussied up in frilly dresses with petticoats, and ribbons and curls. How will they be able to enjoy it all?

The day is full of new and exciting sensations for Nelson—uneven terrain to walk over and the rough bark on the tall pine trees to touch. The pool is even more daunting than a bathtub, so he sits on the side and throws his orange ball to me, laughing whenever I miss and it splashes into the water. He falls asleep in my arms on the way home, his ball in one hand, a precious pinecone in the other.

«   »

After this promising start, general lethargy began to set in because of the heat and humidity, Nelson's uneven temperament, and the occasional headache or slight fever from which both Tom and I suffered. Having grown up in Winnipeg, Tom had a lot of trouble adjusting to the tropical climate. We were spending more time in the house and garden and the nearby shopping center than we had anticipated, as we waited for that all-important interview with the court-appointed social worker. I remarked in my journal on the comforts we enjoyed.

At least here at the Maxwells' there is always a bit of a breeze and a full cistern; others have hardly any water despite the recent heavy rains. I don't know how we'd manage Nelson's messes without water. We're still treating him for intestinal parasites. [. . .]

Lissette doesn't arrive with the social worker until around four p.m. By then I have a splitting headache, but the interview only lasts half an hour. After all the days of waiting for her it feels like an anticlimax. She asks us why I have kept my maiden name, why we chose Honduras, whether we will adopt another child, if we share our home with anyone else, and, again, what kind of future we plan for him. For most of these questions

there really is no good answer, but we try to sound confident. Afterward we
walk over to the clinic to get a cold Coke out of their machine—a little cel-
ebration for Nelson.

He's awake before six a.m. today, and since the interview is now be-
hind us and the sun shining, we decide this is a good morning for a trip by
bus out to a quiet rural town known for its pottery and wood crafts, about
fifteen miles away. We make it down hill just in time to flag down the
eight a.m. bus as it is pulling out of the terminal. Having a child in your
arms helps in such situations.

I'm surprised, but people here seem to readily accept that we are a
family. If they inquire, it is always in a friendly way. I sit next to a man
who introduces himself to me as a Baptist minister. He's traveling with his
youth group, who sing hymns for the whole hour it takes to chug up the
steep grades to Valle de Ángeles. He's Honduran, but he tells us his mother
came here from Jamaica; he also shows us pictures of his wife and kids.
He volunteers that she has gone off to serve as a missionary in Nicaragua.
With the children, I wonder?

By the time we get to the village there is an unexpected downpour.
Usually they come in the late afternoon or evening. We get off at the end of
the line and stand under a roof until the rain lets up, then walk to the cen-
tral square, where young people are decorating for some festival. We find a
nice craft shop on the main street where we pick up a few things—mostly
carved woodenware—to take home to remind Nelson when he's older of the
country he comes from. He eats a banana while we shop, warily watching
every stray dog that wanders by the door; there are a lot of them. We decide
to walk down the road until we can find a bit of shade under a tree, then
wait to hail the first bus returning to town. We're back in time for lunch.

The next Sunday morning after church, I was invited over to the
home of another friend of the Maxwells', a helicopter pilot. Tom stayed
home with Nelson. I jotted the following down in my journal later on:
I'm not even surprised when Dick casually admits that he regularly flies
into El Salvador. His comment confirms what we have read before com-
ing here, that the United States is using Honduras as a base for counterin-
surgency operations in other Central American countries. By having pilots
like Dick based here, our government can circumvent the restriction on the
number of military "advisors" allowed in El Salvador.[13]

Tom had come down with a fever and was in bed by the time I got
back from lunch. I gave him some aspirin, thinking it was much like our
other fevers up to now, and I accepted an invitation to join the Maxwells
for dinner in the home of one of Chris's school friends. To give Tom a

real rest, I took Nelson with me. The mother had prepared some spicy Thai specialties from her homeland, but we finished off the meal with apple pie—Nelson's first. He was on his best behavior, playing with the other children, watching their parakeets and parrot, even warming up a little to the family dog.

By the time we got home Nelson was dead tired, but Tom was nearly dead. While we were gone his fever had suddenly shot up to over 105. Alone in the house, weakened from diarrhea and delirious, he had nevertheless managed to drag himself into the bathroom, fill the tub with cool water, and get into it. All night I applied cold compresses, just to keep his raging fever down a few degrees. The next morning I called the embassy nurse. "He's already lost so much body fluid," I said. "Bring a stool sample to be analyzed," she replied. I was used to this because we'd been doing it regularly to test Nelson for remaining parasites.

First I drop off Nelson's sample at the Clínicas Médicas and then Tom's at the embassy infirmary. The nurse gives me something to have Tom drink with juice or soda to restore electrolytes. She also gives me some more specimen containers. By three p.m. I'm able to go back for the results of both tests. Nelson is finally parasite free. But despite all the precautions we've tried to take, Tom has gotten a serious bacterial infection from contaminated food or water. I'm able to get him some penicillin at the pharmacy, but suddenly I get the chills too and start running a low-grade fever in the late afternoon. I'm just exhausted. Tom is very weak and will have to stay in bed for several more days, so our trip north is off; Carl left this afternoon without us.

«   »

We had been in Honduras for nearly three weeks. While we were preoccupied with Tom's health crisis, we still toyed with the idea that we might rent a car and take a two-day trip as far north as Lake Yojoa once he recovered. We wanted to see more of the country if we could, but we didn't want to go too far. We had no idea how much longer the adoption might take, and there was no guarantee we wouldn't suddenly be summoned to court. We dreamed of leaving for Boston by the end of June with everyone intact, if only we could get the adoption papers, obtain a Honduran passport for Nelson, begin the U.S. visa process, and reserve flights. For the moment, everything remained up in the air.

In the first days after our arrival we had been disappointed not to be able to reach Mrs. Negroponte at all; then we learned they were changing the telephone exchanges at the embassy residence. Finally, we made contact and were invited to have afternoon tea with her on Thursday, June 16th. Tom was weak but feeling better, and looking forward to an outing after being in bed for three days. I wrote about our visit. Oddly, it is one of the few passages in my journal where I used the past tense.

The embassy residence is perched way up on one of the hills that surround the city, the house set in a beautiful park—walls with razor wire for security all around. Stately palms line the driveway. Mrs. Negroponte told us she has plans to add coffee bushes and vanilla trees. According to Magda, who went with us, the tennis courts and swimming pool are available to all families connected with the embassy. Since it was raining when we arrived, white-coated servants came out with umbrellas to usher us in.

Mrs. Negroponte greeted us cordially at the front door, explaining that most of the rooms on the first floor are unusable right now because of a leaky roof. She showed us to a small living room in the back. Tea was served in bone china cups with delicious apricot pie and banana bread. We met the Negropontes' thirteen-month-old daughter. She's just starting to walk but is not that much shorter than Nelson. We're beginning to think he's short for his age, whatever that is exactly. He wasn't much interested in playing with her, but he loved her chatter telephone pull toy and alarm clock. Both create lots of noise! For a change he was so intent on these playthings that he showed no interest in eating.

Mrs. Negroponte asked us about our experiences here so far, and we had a chance to thank her for everything she had done to smooth the way. She apologized for her initial hesitancy on the phone when Tom called from the States. Michael Ster had given her my last name, and she didn't recognize Tom's. I was surprised that she would remember this detail. She also told us the story of how they had come to adopt.

More important, Diana Negroponte also said something in passing about Nelson's origins that sticks with me: "Nelson's biological parents must have been very exceptional people of strong will and firm conviction. Who knows out of what socioeconomic situation they came that made them do what they did."

I wrote that down exactly in my journal, wanting to hang on to it. She didn't say exactly what they did or why she concluded they were "exceptional people," although we thought she might be referring to the kidnapping and shoot-out, first suggested to us by Anita and later seemingly confirmed by Lissette. It certainly was an unusual comment that stood out amid all the small talk. Did she know more? She had phrased it only as a rhetorical question, but wasn't she suggesting that his parents had been involved in some action based on socioeconomic, even political motivations?

« »

One of my problems in writing now is that I can no longer sort out how much we understood then of the whole backdrop against which our adoption was taking place, since I dwelt almost exclusively on personal matters in my journal. I recently discovered an undated article in our adoption file that appears to offer some proof that we were not totally naïve. I must have clipped it at the time from the *Christian Science Monitor*, which I liked to read for its excellent international coverage. The title of this review article by James Nelson Goodsell is "What to Read on Central America," and it lists four books, one on the role of the CIA in Guatemala, two on El Salvador, and one on the Nicaraguan Sandinista Revolution, translated from the French edition. I'm certain that I didn't have time to read these before we left for Honduras, but I grasp at what it appears to illustrate—our desire to deepen our understanding of what was going on in Central America even before our adoption.

I can even prove that just four days before our visit to the embassy residence, we saw an article under the byline Diana Villers Negroponte published in the *Miami Herald*, in which she countered accusations that had been made about her volunteer work for World Relief, a nongovernmental organization connected to the National Council of Evangelicals. I cut out this article, and it found its way into Nelson's first photo album. On April 3rd the *Herald* had reprinted an article from *Mother Jones* magazine, in which the author accused Mrs. Negroponte of working for a "group that ran supplies to anti-Sandinista Indians on the frontier." In her rebuttal she reminds the reader that the relief organizations were all functioning under the umbrella of the U.N. High Commissioner for Refugees, and that their humanitarian mission could not be carried out without the help of volunteers: doctors, nurses, teachers, engineers, and even college students. The accusations of CIA collaboration, she concludes, are "absurd, untrue," and, moreover, "harmful," because they may discourage both donors and prospective volunteers:

> The accusation has been made that I and, by implication, the other
> volunteers involved in La Mosquitia have been running guns to the
> anti-Sandinista forces. [. . .] Some have concluded—presumably based
> upon the news that the Miskito, Rama and Sumo tribes are fighting to

regain their land from the Sandinista government—that the relief supplies sent to the refugees in Honduras contain military wherewithal. The only ammunition is food, medicines, seed, basic agricultural tools and building material for simple construction. The distribution of these supplies is undertaken by volunteers and a strict census of the camp population ensures that only family members present receive their food rations. One pound of nails, allocated to each family for building their home, is hardly enough to puncture Sandinista trucks on non-existent roads!

It seems we were aware that both Ambassador and Mrs. Negroponte were controversial figures in the larger political context of the time, but I commented only briefly in my journal on this dispute and expressed only admiration for her: *One has to admire her willingness to work out in the field with refugees in such a remote area under tough conditions, running the risk of contracting malaria or dengue fever.* There is no sign of critique on my part; I was preoccupied with thoughts about illnesses that could be contracted. Did we discuss the article before we went to see her? I can't recall.

The article cites the overall refugee population in Honduras at the time as thirty-seven thousand, a figure that includes not just the native Miskito tribes, mentioned above, who had fled Nicaragua to the south and were now being resettled in the far northeastern part of the country, but also thousands who had been displaced by the civil war in El Salvador, warehoused in huge camps like La Virtud, not far from the border. Many of these refugees were being moved at the time to Mesa Grande, a camp in the interior. I regret that we did not broach this subject at all in our conversation with Mrs. Negroponte, or ask for some clarification of her passing remark about Nelson's birth parents. We did not meet the ambassador, and we don't know whether either of them knew more about our son's story, a question that really only became compelling much later.

«   »

It is almost impossible to reconstruct twenty-five years later how much we understood of the interconnections in the political landscape of Central America. We considered ourselves fairly well informed, as we read both the U.S. and German press, but coverage of that part of the world was spotty. High profile killings—the assassination of Salvadoran archbishop Oscar Arnulfo Romero on March 24, 1980, and the murder of four American churchwomen the following December come to mind— had whipped up small waves of outrage in the United States that quickly subsided. Our awareness of the conflict in El Salvador, wracked since the mid-1970s by fraudulent elections, government repression, death squad violence, and civil war, was the reason we had wanted to adopt a Salvadoran child. Yet these same factors led to the uncertainties that had made our agency cancel its program there.

In all this time, we knew that U.S. military aid continued its upward trajectory. But did we know that both Honduran and Salvadoran forces, some trained in the States, had been involved in the killings at the Sumpul River along the border in May 1980, where peasants—women, children, the elderly—were massacred as they tried to cross into Honduras? Did we realize that there had been another similar massacre of civilians trying to flee across the Lempa River into Honduras in March 1981, and that both Salvadoran and Honduran troops were involved, using helicopters supplied by the United States? I don't believe so.[14]

Because we were in rural New Hampshire during the previous summer, we evidently did not see the article by Robert E. White, former ambassador to El Salvador, titled "Central America: The Problem That Won't Go Away," which appeared as a front-cover story in the *New York Times Magazine*. White stated, "It is not Russia, Cuba or Nicaragua that make the revolutions of Central America—it is injustice, brutality and hunger," and he argued that Americans needed to better understand "the history, culture and motivations of those who fight and die in this neglected center of the hemisphere."[15] I think we would have agreed.

I do recall reading excerpts of Joan Didion's book *Salvador*, with its vivid account of death squad violence and the fate of the disappeared, in the *New York Review of Books* the following October. We didn't subscribe to *Newsweek*, though, so we missed the incriminating story it ran in November 1982 that specifically accused Ambassador Negroponte of being the "spearhead" of clandestine operations in support of the Nicaraguan "contras." But how could we have missed the reports of this in other newspapers?[16] Was it because we were not focused at all on Honduras at that point, I now wonder?

The ties between the U.S. Embassy in Tegucigalpa and Nicaraguan as well as Salvadoran counterinsurgencies may not have been as obvious then as they were to become in the 1990s, especially after the Iran-contra scandal broke, but I realize only as I write this book how much more we could and should have known.[17] In the fall of 1982 the Honduran government had asked for additional helicopter support after a high-profile hostage-taking incident in San Pedro Sula involving a large number of government officials. While we were away, General Álvarez had come to Washington, D.C., and by the time we got home in late June 1983, the U.S. plan to set up a training camp for the Salvadoran troops on Honduran soil was being questioned in the press. At this point I began to regularly clip articles about Central America for my files.

As we considered the little we had been told about our adopted son and how he had been orphaned, it did occur to us that the background might be highly political. The authorities were obviously unwilling in the summer of 1983 to let us in on their theories. Had we not been so focused on our growing relationship with Nelson, had we not been so intent on just getting home with him after the fright over Tom's bacterial infection, we might have acted more aggressively and asked the judge, our lawyer, or even Mrs. Negroponte for more information. I know we sensed from the beginning that there was some mystery at the heart of his story and that all these figures were unwilling to state specifics. As I look at the written record in my journal, I can see that we simply hesitated to ask too many questions. Would it have endangered the adoption? I may have thought so, as I pondered why the judge had made such a point of the fact that an unnamed French family had been refused six months earlier. Had they asked too many questions?

«   »

While still waiting for our adoption to be finalized, we went on an outing to the National Museum a few days later. On the way back, we stopped in Concordia Park. In my journal, I had returned to the present tense: *We sit on a bench under the trees, thinking about how we lingered in the same spot less than a month ago wondering about Nelson— what would he look like, how would he relate to us? In these three weeks we've been together he already acts as if he knows we are his parents. He likes to go off and explore but always keep us in view. He is keeping up an animated "conversation" with one old man who luckily seems to find him amusing. We try to feed the pigeons some Cheerios, but the birds don't go for them the way Nelson does.*

There wouldn't be much more time for leisurely walks in the parks and plazas or for writing in my journal. Less than a week after our tea at the embassy residence, events began to overtake us. Tom remained weak, and we had given up any idea of touring the country. He had been calling Lissette on a daily basis to monitor as best he could any progress on the legal front. She was not loquacious, offering only one bit of information at a time, but suddenly she held out hope that we would be able to depart before the end of the month. Then, on June 22nd, she gave us the good news that the adoption had been finalized in court the day before. We could move into high gear again.

We had only a few days left to wrap things up and became preoccupied with all the bureaucratic details related to the visa to bring Nelson into the country as a landed immigrant. We were satisfied just to take a morning walk around the neighborhood. By this time, Nelson always preferred to push his stroller instead of riding in it, so we decided to leave it with Anita and Bill, who were planning to move into a much larger house in another neighborhood, where they would have more room for their burgeoning family and could regularly rent one room to prospective adoptive parents. They might need an extra stroller, we thought, although it was doubtful that there would be enough adoptable children to support their plan, as I noted in my journal.

We sense Lissette's frustration when she arrives late for our appointment this afternoon with a couple from Chicago in tow. They have just come down unannounced to hunt for a little girl one to three years old. They are going to try an orphanage in Valle de Ángeles after failing to find a child to their liking in Tegucigalpa! We're amazed at this. Carl offered that he had heard while he was in San Pedro Sula that there were one hundred infants abandoned in that city each year. But it doesn't necessarily mean they are available for adoption. Lissette reiterates for the benefit of this couple that most of the children one sees in Honduran orphanages are not adoptable. One either can't locate the mothers to sign off, or the families intend to return someday to reclaim their children.[18]

For us, only one more hurdle remained—getting Nelson into the United States. He still needed his Honduran passport. The various offices we visited over the next forty-eight hours became a blur. We first found a place to get his photo taken. Nelson looked rather sheepishly at the camera; there would be no smile for the authorities. I remember that I had to make an appointment for a medical exam from an approved list of pediatricians. For some reason Dr. Tomé was not listed. Magda was out, and it was the first time I had to speak Spanish on the phone. I had my little speech all written down and hoped the person at the other end would be able to see us at the time I specified. If someone started asking me questions, I would be sunk. Luckily, I succeeded in making the appointment.

The medical exam was perfunctory. We were just glad to have the required piece of paper. I recall an interminable wait the same afternoon at the U.S. Consulate. "When you get to Miami you'll submit this whole packet," the clerk said as he finally handed me a large envelope; it contained copies of all the documents concerning our adoption with translations into English. "They'll place a stamp in his passport and give him an alien registration number. Then when you get back to Boston you have to submit the form sent to you earlier." Now we just needed a flight out.

Thursday, June 23rd. Everything seems to be falling almost miraculously into place. In the morning we first stop by the travel agency, but they can't say whether we can get on the Tan-Sasha flight on Saturday morning. We need to be on that early flight because we have to allow extra time in Miami to take Nelson through immigration. After going with Magda to get a tire for her van (she needs three, but the inventory is so low they aren't allowed to sell her more than one), we go back to the travel agency around 1:30 p.m. They have been able to confirm us. It hardly seems possible; we'll be leaving exactly a month after our arrival! Thanks to Tom's persistence—calling Lissette nearly every day—our adoption may have set some records for speed.

We were out doing some shopping the next day, our last in Tegucigalpa, when a phone call came for us from Lissette—something about wanting to see Nelson before we left. I wondered why, since she had just seen him the day before. *When Magda got home, the maid was able to explain the full gist of the message—it was the judge who wanted to see him one more time. Our hearts sank for a moment. Was there some last-minute snag? We called Lissette right away, but she said it was already too late; Judge Pineda had left her chambers for the day. "She is requiring that you send me a letter every six months with a progress report and pictures of Nelson that I can pass on to her."* We promised to do so.

Carl and Magda took us to the airport the next morning. *We are so anxious to go. Nelson seems to sense that something important is happening when he sees us load up all the suitcases. I packed most of his things last night while he was asleep. Our tearful good-byes to this family we have come to think of as our own is tempered by the fact that we know we'll see them again. Magda is bringing Gretchen to Boston in the fall. We've recommended a boarding school right down the street from where we live. While Gretchen gets settled, Magda can stay with us.*

As we walk out on the tarmac to climb the stairs to our plane, Nelson looks in pure amazement at this huge version of a toy he has played with so avidly for days. His first words in English that summer were "car," "truck," "bus," and "plane," and to his first phrases, "my ball" and "more please," he soon added another: "Up we go!" His first flight was clearly a formative experience.

The plane was a real puddle jumper, stopping at La Ceiba and San Pedro Sula, as well as Belize, before heading for Miami. *We have a last chance to glimpse the Honduran landscape. We're sorry we didn't get to see more of it from ground level. The mountains rise suddenly from the plain with its plantations along the coast at La Ceiba, and there is a dramatic landing as you descend steeply over the aquamarine waters of the Caribbean. Lots of scuba divers get on here. Nelson needs some room to wiggle around, and we are lucky to have an extra seat for most of the trip. He is gregarious, making friends with the lady behind him and the man in front with his ready smiles.*

We breeze through customs, but have an excruciatingly long wait at immigration—an inefficient operation with just two officials on duty in a far-off, hot corner of the terminal. Most of the people in line have not been told they need photographs, so these have to be taken on the spot, slowing things down even more. Since Nelson already has his pictures, the official only needs to stamp a temporary visa in his Honduran passport after he looks at our packet of papers. It's official; he's got alien registration number A38-259-689. We have to walk nearly the length of the terminal back to our gate. I carry Nelson, who has gained several pounds in these four weeks, while Tom struggles with our two rather heavy carry-on bags.

«   »

We had called from Miami and were grateful to have a colleague of mine waiting for us at Logan Airport in Boston. Nelson was asleep in my arms by the time we got to the harbor tunnel. Our friend took a picture when we got to our little red house in Wellesley.[19] It is one of my favorites from these days, one of the few with all three of us, and it captures the moment so well.

Tom, with his full dark beard, is wearing his Panama hat at a rakish angle. We're standing on the narrow front stoop. It must be early evening, because the porch light is on, casting a glow on the family grouping. The light in the entryway is also visible, as Tom has already opened the front door. His hand is still on the knob as he holds it open for me, but he has hesitated just a moment, grinning broadly as he turns to glance back at us. I'm standing a little to one side, holding Nelson tightly, supporting

him with my left arm under his strong thighs, and my right around his back. His stubby, muscular legs in the gray sneakers with blue stripes— the ones Anita had given us—hang down like dead weights out of his blue and white shorts. He has on a light blue short-sleeved polo shirt, and his left arm is tucked securely under my right. His wavy chestnut brown hair looks a little disheveled, and he is obviously very tired, but he's not asleep. He manages to take in our arrival to what will be his new home, but his head is planted firmly on my right shoulder, just hiding my smile that must match Tom's. You can see it in my eyes.

We had arrived home with Nelson safely in our arms, but with many of our questions unanswered. Others we had not yet formulated or even imagined. In March 1984 we re-adopted him before the Probate and Family Court in Dedham, Massachusetts, an extra step recommended by our agency. When we anticipated some family travel to Europe and knew that Nelson's Honduran passport would soon run out, I filed an application in February 1986 to petition for his naturalization. (Tom was still a Canadian then.)

More than a year later, we got notice of the final hearing. He was to come—along with hundreds of other immigrants—to historic Fanueil Hall in Boston for a swearing-in ceremony. By some coincidence, the date—June 25, 1987—was exactly four years to the day after we had brought him into the country. At six, Nelson was old enough to appreciate some of what was happening. His brother, Derek, age two, looked on as Nelson held up his right hand to take the oath of citizenship and had his picture taken with the certificate.

Our curious fellow grew up uncertain of his birth name or date, yet confident that we cherished him. We tried to answer his questions about his birth parents whenever they came up, but there was not much to tell of which we could be sure. We emphasized that as far as we knew his parents had been killed, we thought perhaps violently, perhaps in a political incident. Nelson learned to live with the uncertainty about his past and never really plagued us with questions. He naturally wondered who he was and what his biological family was like. And, as he became an adolescent, that longing to know quietly deepened.

In fact, Tom and I underestimated how much he suffered from the anxiety of being different from the rest of his family, and of not knowing who he really was. Issues of identity loom large during the teen years, but if Nelson was conflicted because of the question of his origins, it was a subterranean struggle. We didn't talk much about it, as I recall, because the little we had to say had already been said. There were other, more immediate issues to deal with. Adolescence is always a challenge for parents and children, and we were no exception. Then, everything changed just as unexpectedly as the way he had come into our lives in the first place.

TWO

Rediscovery

MASSACHUSETTS, AUGUST–DECEMBER 1997

When the next part of this story unfolded for us in the summer of 1997, fourteen years had passed since our adoption, and Nelson was a teenager, looking forward to learning to drive like most near-sixteen-year-olds. Tom and I have experienced most of the highs and lows in our lives with Nelson together, but the next turning point happened on a Sunday night when Tom was home alone in Auburndale, Massachusetts. I was in New Hampshire with my mother, and the kids were away at overnight camp.

This part of the story also has a prologue, although I can no longer say precisely when that took place. Nevertheless, I remember it well. After we returned from Honduras with Nelson in June 1983, one of my first outings was to the Spanish department at Wellesley College. I didn't hesitate to tell my colleagues about the mystery surrounding his origins. I even shared Anita Smith's theories about the shoot-out in San Pedro Sula.

Some years later, one of these colleagues told me of a student she had who was going to visit an aunt in San Pedro Sula that summer. Tom and I thought this was the perfect chance to investigate our one slim lead. We hired the student to hunt in local newspaper archives, hoping she could unearth some information about what might have orphaned our son in 1982. We had come away from Honduras pretty sure that it had involved a kidnapping and a shoot-out. We recalled that our lawyer had confirmed these aspects, but Anita had been the only one to suggest a specific incident.

I went back to my journal for the details and was reminded that the judge told us Nelson had been in the orphanage about "nine or ten months." And then there was the quote I had written down by Mrs. Negroponte, who had said his parents were "exceptional" and "strong willed." We gave the student all these stray bits of information.

She returned from Honduras in the fall with a front-page article from *La Prensa*, a San Pedro Sula daily, dated October 11, 1982. It featured graphic photographs of the bodies of three "kidnappers," two men and a woman, who had been killed by special police during the "daring rescue" of a fourteen-year-old girl—granddaughter of a local businessman and daughter of a physician. According to this account, the "audacious operation" had lasted a mere "eight seconds"![1]

The group had kidnapped Ruth Marie Canahuati Larach as she was being driven home from school by her chauffeur and held her in a tiny closet for forty-five days, hooding her when she was brought out to sleep on a mattress at night. The small house of concrete blocks had been built rather quickly five months earlier, expressly for this purpose, and then occupied—according to neighbors—by two men, a woman, a young child, and a maid, who came to the home regularly. The group appeared to be a normal family and aroused no suspicion. In reality, the group was a Honduran "gang," whose ringleader, identified as Efraín Javier Pérez López, was already wanted by the police for murder. Presumably they were negotiating with the wealthy Canahuati Larach family for ransom when the police ferreted out their hiding place.[2]

The woman, identified as Gloria Devina Osorto Bardales, is pictured lying on her back in a narrow hallway, her legs stretched out into a bathroom whose door was left open behind her, as if she had just exited. Her facial features are totally obscured by her blood-tangled hair, probably the result of a fatal head wound. Pérez lies nearby, just in front of the closet where the girl was held, his face turned to the side in a pool of blood, but he is also shown in a police mug shot. The second man, identified as Rosendo Cruz Bonilla, is shown lying flat on his back, stretched out on the bed where he had been shot, blood dripping down his face.

Curiously, while all three individuals are identified by their given names, the article says little about their motivations. They are portrayed as criminals without any particular political or social agenda, although one caption refers to unspecified "subversive material" hidden in the ceiling. Photos show their arsenal of typewriters, boots, wigs, and weapons, including a dozen handguns of various calibers with ammunition. Dynamite, intended to destroy their abandoned getaway truck, was purportedly "deactivated by special agents" at the time of the kidnapping. It was not a pretty picture.

Moreover, the specifics that mattered most to us remained obscure.

At one point, the infant referred to in the article is presumed to be the child of Pérez and the dead woman. Elsewhere in the same article, however, the "colonel" in charge of the raid states "that the baby, whose whereabouts are not known, was only used as a 'cover,'" and the theory is put forward that the couple "pretended to be the parents of a baby who was taken for walks around the neighborhood as a way of ascertaining whether they were being watched or if they were in any danger of being discovered."

Not just the location of the child is unknown. Even its gender remains undeterminable, for within the space of a few sentences it is first referred to as their "hijo" (son) and then as a "niña" (girl). At least the child was out of the house with the maid at the time the killings occurred, we thought with some relief, even as we hesitated to believe that this was Nelson's background. Still, we had to at least consider that the missing infant in this story might be our son.

We read and re-read the article carefully. We speculated that the child could have been found and taken to Tegucigalpa until the sensational aspects of the case died down, so that he could be declared an orphan and placed for adoption. Was this the reason for all the secrecy? I thought of the clientele at the exclusive club we had visited. Presumably no Honduran family wealthy enough to adopt would want a child thought to be the offspring of known criminals. Was this the reason he had been offered internationally?

Then again, the newspaper article also suggested the child had been merely a cover. Had it also been kidnapped by the gang? Was the reason for periodic reports to the judge due to her fear that family members might yet come forward and inquire about the child? Or did the child belong to the "maid," perhaps? Was she a part of the gang? Had she or the child ever been found? Each question only led to others, and all of them to a dead end. The student said there had been no follow-up articles on subsequent days. The teenage girl had been "miraculously" restored to her prominent family; as far as the public was concerned, the case was closed.

Some aspects of this incident certainly seemed to fit with what we had been told. Other parts—especially the timing in early October—did not entirely jibe with the few facts we knew. That would place our adoption only about eight months later, not nine or ten. And the image of this gang did not exactly confirm Mrs. Negroponte's assertion that Nelson's biological parents must have been "very exceptional people of strong will and firm conviction." Why, we also wondered, would the U.S. ambassa-

dor's wife be enlisted to locate a family for the child of common criminals? Or was it all just due to happenstance?

We asked ourselves these and many other questions. How reliable
had our sources been? Did Anita really know what she was talking about?
Had she been correct to link our child to this kidnapping and shoot-
out up north? Had the officials purposely lied about the time that had
elapsed since the presumed death of Nelson's parents and our adoption,
or were they just careless with their estimates? Both seemed possible.

Why had we not demanded more concrete information about his
background from the judge? We looked closely at the photos of the three
people. Could we detect any family resemblance between Nelson and
these individuals? And, even if we could, did we want our child to grow
up thinking that his parents might have been kidnappers, his father a
murder suspect? The more we thought about it all, the less certain we
became.

While I no longer know precisely when this article surfaced, I do
recall that Nelson was quite young. I remembered clearly that we had
been cautioned by our agency to listen carefully to the questions posed
by our child about his adoption and to answer as honestly as we could,
but in Nelson's case there had always been so little to say.

The story always began with our visit to the orphanage, and we emphasized that we did not know anything for sure about his first year of
life. I remember how startled I was after Derek was born in 1985, when
four-year-old Nelson asked me one day while I was nursing the baby,
"Did you nurse me too?" "No," I answered, "but I'm sure you were loved
and taken care of this way." Before I could even add "by your birth
mother," he himself chimed in: "Oh yes, it must have been the nice
nurse in the orphanage!"

At that age, he wasn't questioning what might have come before that.
I recall another similar episode when he was five or six. He learned that
a newborn calf at a farm we often visited in New Hampshire was also
named Nelson. He promptly struck up a conversation with the farmer,
who then asked where our son came from, to which he replied cheerily,
"Oh, my parents just picked me up in an orphanage in Honduras."

As he got older, we talked openly about the fact that his birthday was
one we had chosen, and both our boys understood that we didn't know
Nelson's birth name either. Eventually, we also talked about the fact that
we assumed, but did not know for sure, that his parents had both been
killed in a shoot-out, always emphasizing that we eschewed violence.

I am almost certain that this Honduran newspaper article came to us even before we moved to Auburndale from Wellesley in 1988 when Tom assumed the presidency of Lasell College. At that time, Nelson was seven and about to enter first grade, and Derek only three. There seemed to be no way to introduce this story as a way to think happily about Nelson's origins. The graphic portrayal favored by the Central American press might prove very disturbing. We knew there was too little information here to tie him conclusively to this particular incident, and we ourselves were not convinced. We had the article translated by one of my colleagues in the Spanish department and placed it in our safe-deposit box for future reference. When he was older and better able to cope with the violent details, we could show it to Nelson and explain our reservations. We never did.

Tom had the habit of looking at the front-page photos of the two men whenever he opened the safe-deposit box. Nothing in the eyes, nose, or mouth of Pérez, the man in the mug shot, reminded him of our son. And the photograph of Cruz, bare chested, spread eagle on a rumpled bed, reveals a man with a lanky build. His rib cage is clearly visible and his arms are long and slender. Nothing about his physique suggested that of our growing boy, with his short, sturdy stature and his muscular neck, arms, and calves. The woman's features were indistinguishable. We let it be.

« »

Our elder son proved to be both creative and inquisitive; he liked to problem solve. As a child I'd find him looking at some fairly simple mechanism like a doorjamb and knob, and he would tell me how he was imagining what it all looked like on the inside as he tried to figure out how it functioned. He had a special love for visual arts and used them as a way to get out of an argument or a tantrum, withdrawing to his room to paint a peace offering.

He also enjoyed going to museums in Boston: the Museum of Science, the Children's Museum, and the Aquarium, of course, but also the Museum of Fine Arts and the Isabella Stewart Gardner Art Museum, where one of his babysitters was an intern. I see one of his preschool teachers from time to time, and over twenty years later, she still talks about the "art museum" he constructed in her classroom and the fantastic exhibition he mounted.

Nelson was somewhat shy but nevertheless socially adept. He had this wonderful smile and love of silliness. He was inventive and playful, and other children naturally liked to spend time with him. To this day he wins new friends easily and keeps up with untold numbers of old ones. What seemed unusual to me, though, was the way at a young age he was able to be in the middle of things socially, yet be an observer of the action at the same time. I can remember how he would come home from kindergarten and analyze for me all the social interactions that were going on between various groups of children on the playground. We also noticed how compassionate he was. He rejected cliques and would readily embrace the odd person out—the new boy in his second-grade class from Portugal, for instance, who could barely speak English.

When we moved from Wellesley to Auburndale, Nelson transferred to an elementary school that was much more diverse, as it had inner-city kids bused there as part of Boston's Metco (Metropolitan Council for Educational Opportunity) program. Williams Elementary also served as a magnet school for Japanese children living in the city of Newton, of which Auburndale is just one village.

As far as I know, he only once had a negative experience around the issue of race or ethnicity, when a kid thought he was "dirty" because of his skin color. That happened at a summer day care in New Hampshire, where he was with a group of youngsters who evidently had never seen a nonwhite child before. Perhaps the contrast with his very pale little brother made the other children take particular note of his skin color.

We comforted him and explained the ignorance of the other children about his place of origin, then talked with the teachers and asked them to make this a learning experience for all of them. They could talk about international adoption and have a geography lesson at the same time. Nelson seemed to feel comfortable about the place from then on. The slur was not repeated.

As he was growing up, Nelson always excelled in athletics, although for him the most important thing was just playing the game and being part of a team. He preferred to play three or four sports each year, rather than devoting himself to one. Despite his short stature he liked to play basketball, as well as soccer, but lacrosse turned out to be his best sport. He was willing to use his body strength, and with his low center of gravity and ability to suddenly accelerate, he could maneuver around opponents and escape quickly down the field as he cradled the ball.

Reading and writing were another matter. He had begun to struggle in elementary school. The discrepancy between Nelson's high intelligence, his creativity, and his curiosity—which were obvious—and what he was able to achieve academically was becoming apparent. In first grade his teacher had exclaimed, "His stories are often better than the ones in the book," but the point, after all, was to decipher "the words on the page." But she also insisted that lots of kids reversed their letters. "It's nothing to worry about."

When written assignments became more complex in second grade, however, and Nelson—full of great ideas—could not complete them in the way he imagined, he sometimes broke down crying or exploded in a tantrum. When he had finally calmed down and we tried to find out what was the matter, he was as baffled as we were. One thing was clear: learning in school was often a frustrating experience for him.

By third grade we were quite concerned about his reading level, which lagged far behind his peers. I was planning to take him out of school for six months as I had a semester sabbatical leave and had been granted a Fulbright research fellowship. After much discussion about what to do, we had decided to temporarily split up the family.

Nelson would go with me to Berlin, where I hoped to place him in a school setting that would give him an opportunity to experience a new language and culture and allow me to pursue my project. Derek, only five and in kindergarten, would stay home with Tom, and the two would visit us in April for a few weeks' holiday and again at the end of our stay, in June. I insisted that Nelson be tested before we left in February, and we learned that he had a serious language-based learning disability.

It took Tom and me years to fully grasp how profound a problem our son's dyslexia was. As he got older, he needed a series of ever more sophisticated tests to analyze the problem. These allowed him to qualify for extra time on quizzes and tests or to be exempted from a fourth year of foreign language study. We always had the results explained to us in a conference, with Nelson and his teachers present. I'll never forget when one specialist, who had just administered a whole battery of tests, said to a dumbfounded math teacher, "If he gets the right answer, don't take points off because he didn't show his work; he is not getting to the answer the same way you are. He has a synthetic mind with special strengths in visual-spatial learning, and he's mathematically probably a lot smarter than you are."

We were well aware, of course, that Nelson could learn some things—like how to build or program a computer—very quickly, although not by the book. Because Tom and I are verbally oriented, it was difficult for us to really grasp how Nelson's brain was "wired differently." His characteristic profile brought me to tears each time I looked at the latest results, for they showed that—despite the many different kinds of intervention we had tried—the gap was only widening between his high intelligence quotient, his growing knowledge base and creativity, and his ability to process written language.

In elementary school the "whole language" approach had not helped. We hired a specialist to teach him the Orton-Gillingham method of breaking down words into syllables. He picked up the technique in record time, but it didn't make that much difference. His reading was still labored, his grasp of spelling and punctuation weak, making every school assignment that involved both reading and writing a marathon. If he didn't pace himself, it could lead to disaster, and what child doesn't procrastinate when faced with big projects and long papers?

As a result of the extra time it took him to process what he read, Nelson often suffered from cognitive overload. Taking him out of school mid-year in third grade turned out to be a positive move. He learned in all kinds of other ways during our time in Berlin. Every Saturday after we had eaten our brunch of potato pancakes with applesauce, we would choose another museum or special place in the city to visit.

Tom and I were not entirely sympathetic, though, when year after year Nelson would get off to a strong start and then fall apart, announcing in February that as far as he was concerned the school year was over. It took time for us to appreciate that he was just mentally worn out. The issue of cognitive overload raised its head sometimes, too, when the whole family was on vacation. Over-stimulation could lead to an unanticipated angry outburst when he was young, or stubborn silence as a teenager.

In retrospect I think we underestimated how much Nelson suffered, not only from the dyslexia itself but also from the fact that in this way, too, he was different from the rest of us, who liked nothing better for relaxation than to curl up with a book or to play word games.

In addition to relying on books on tape, I continued to read to him aloud; story time had always been sacrosanct in our family. He retained information extremely well by ear. That's how he learned German during those few months abroad. On the very first day in his Berlin school, where—on the strength of his math skills—he was placed in a fourth-grade class, I was told that he also exhibited his superior social skills by stopping a fight from breaking out on the playground. How he managed to do this with his rudimentary German, I'll never know.

Given his learning issues, we had decided that it would be better for Nelson to be in a small private school environment where he would get special attention during middle and high school. Fortunately there were minority students and adoptees among his many friends at Beaver Country Day School. He was so bright that he wanted to be in all honors courses. This was not realistic given his learning style, and one fall we faced near disaster when he got put in an honors English section because that was the only one that fit his schedule. Ultimately Nelson proved resourceful, and he was privileged to have many wonderful teachers and tutors who cared about him and whose help he accepted more readily than he did ours. He continued to do well enough to be on track to go to college.

He still had a keen, artistic eye and was studying photography in high school along with more traditional subjects. His senior year, he decided to take developmental psychology as an elective. For this course, as for others, we had to order the textbook through Princeton Center Books for the Blind and Dyslexic. Otherwise he never would have gotten through it. But in the nursery school practicum that accompanied the course he was a natural. The kids loved him. Younger children have always gravitated to Nelson, and he enjoys caring for them. For years he was a beloved camp counselor at a YMCA camp.

« »

On May 30, 1997—at the end of his freshman year in high school—we celebrated Nelson's fourteenth adoption day. It was also Derek's twelfth birthday. After school was out, the boys spent most of June and July at our house on the lake. My mother—their ninety-year-old Granny Ward—who had grown up in this area of southern New Hampshire, joined us after a trip to Europe. At the end of July we packed the boys' trunks, and Tom delivered them to Camp Frank A. Day in central Massachusetts for its second four-week session before he headed back to the Boston area. Nelson was looking forward to participating in "leader corps" that summer, a program for senior campers that would prepare them to become counselors-in-training the following year. Derek was now a "junior." We anticipated having an end-of-the-summer birthday party for Nelson when they returned. And we looked forward to our time with them on the traditional visiting day two weeks hence.

I think it is safe to say that August had become their favorite month of the year. Camp Day was the place where they had really bonded, and because of it they also shared friendship circles. Once he fell in love with this camp, Nelson wanted nothing more than for his little brother to join him. He begged and pleaded when Derek was only six, showing "D" all the great things about the place on visiting day. We took a chance the following summer that Derek would like it as much as Nelson, who should have been in the "juniors" unit, but stayed with the "midgets" to look after his little brother whenever he was homesick. Their bond became stronger with each successive shared year at camp.

In addition, by 1997 both boys had been going to Beaver since the previous year; Derek was in the lower school, Nelson in the upper. I had heard from one teacher that when Nelson had a free period he would take time to go over to the other part of the building to pick Derek up from class and walk him to his next. That didn't surprise me at all. Although Nelson could tease and tickle his little brother mercilessly, I knew he was tenderly devoted to him.

« »

I have asked Tom to describe in his own words what happened on July 27, 1997:

It was a normal mid-summer evening. I was alone at home reading, after having delivered our boys to camp earlier in the day. The phone rang relatively late—after nine p.m., not the usual hour for solicitations, but that was what I thought it was. I did not even try to catch the name of the caller, nor the organization he rattled off, and I was about to end the call quickly with the usual, "No thank you, we're not interested," when the caller stopped me in mid-sentence and asked: "Are you Thomas de Witt, and did you adopt a little boy, Nelson Ward de Witt, in Tegucigalpa on May 30, 1983?"

Totally taken aback, all I could utter was, "Not exactly," for the legal record would show the adoption had been finalized on the 21st of June, and we had re-adopted Nelson in Probate Court the following spring. But I was just stalling for time to recover from the immediate shock. I knew very well that Nelson had been released to our custody on May 30th, and we ourselves had always called it his adoption day.

How could some perfect stranger know this? I was apprehensive. Was someone finally checking up on us after all these years since we had stopped sending those "required" updates the judge wanted every six months? (We had gotten to know a couple that had adopted two boys in Honduras. When I asked them what they wrote in those semiannual reports, they looked at me surprised: "Reports? We don't have to send any reports." After we heard that, we just decided to go cold turkey. We stopped sending reports, and nothing had happened.)

My gut reaction was tempered by a sense of curiosity, however. Who wanted to know this and why? I worried about our privacy being compromised and wondered what else the caller already knew about us. His simple, direct question and my knee-jerk response, as well as all these thoughts, had taken no more than a few seconds—a little like having your whole life pass before you as you're drowning, I suspect. As I waited with bated breath for the second shoe to drop, he must have sensed my wariness, for he hastened to assure me, "I'm not here to take your son away."

He reintroduced himself as Dr. Robert H. Kirschner. "I'm on the staff of Physicians for Human Rights, an organization of health professionals, scientists, and concerned citizens, with its offices in Boston. I'm a pathologist in the International Forensic Program at DePaul University College of Law in Chicago. My job is to facilitate DNA testing that enables PHR to identify the remains of those massacred in places like Guatemala, Rwanda, and the former Yugoslavia, so human rights abuses can be exposed, and families can lay their loved ones to rest."

He also explained that his current project, in El Salvador, was potentially more joyful, because it held out the hope that families could reconnect with their disappeared children, some known to have been adopted both within the country and abroad.[3] He then proceeded to tell me a remarkable story—it seemed Nelson was not a Honduran. Relatives had been looking for him ever since the Salvadoran civil war had ended with the signing of a peace agreement in January 1992 and the publication of the U.N. Truth Commission report the following year.[4]

Dr. Kirschner explained that beginning in 1994, a Honduran human rights organization had cooperated with several organizations in El Salvador. They had finally ascertained that "Rony [*sic*] Funez, adopted by Thomas de Witt and Margaret E. Ward in 1983" was probably the missing boy for whom a Salvadoran family was looking. He was reading from the final investigative report over the phone. It was hard to absorb. He mentioned an older sister and brother, aunts who were members of the grassroots organization that had written the report, and a grandmother who had propelled the investigation. I remained silent for what seemed like a long while, just stunned. Then I responded, "I don't believe that is our son."

Dr. Kirschner must have heard my reluctance and sensed my fear. He must have made many similar calls. He knew how to convince me to stay on the line by quickly insisting that—in cases like this one—the role of the organization he worked for was to protect the legal rights of the adoptive families, while also offering hope to the birth families that they might eventually get to know their children, who had disappeared in the 1980s. He emphasized that the legality of our adoption was not being questioned, that our rights would be protected.

Furthermore, while the Salvadoran and Honduran organizations that had collaborated in the search knew our names and address, the family did not. Unless we agreed to have them released, they would remain in the dark about the child's whereabouts. It was entirely up to us. He reinforced this point by telling me of two European families that had refused all efforts toward a reunion. The Salvadoran birth families knew their children were alive and well but nothing more.

Clearly he hoped that we would be more receptive. He outlined the next stage that could lead to DNA testing and—if that proved the biological link conclusively—a family reunion, if we so desired. He promised to send a packet of supporting documents along with the investigative report the next day. He said that it contained photographs of the missing boy's siblings and letters from some relatives that had been translated into English. I agreed to be in touch with him after my wife and I had studied these. I hung up, feeling suddenly drained of emotion.

I called Margaret at once and tried to convey everything that he had just told me. She could hardly fathom what I was saying. For her, too, it all came like a bolt out of the blue. We recalled how the article about the shoot-out in San Pedro Sula had left us confused and skeptical. "Perhaps this will be similar," I said, hoping it was all a mistake. Even with Dr. Kirschner's considerable powers of persuasion, I was not convinced, but Margaret was more willing to concede that this just might be Nelson's true story. She said, "I'll come as soon as I can make arrangements for someone to look in on Granny while I'm gone." We wanted to be able to look at the materials together. Dr. Kirschner had promised that the dossier would be sent by overnight delivery.

The packet with the investigative report arrived at my office at Lasell College on Tuesday morning, July 29th. I couldn't work. I pored over the supporting documents and shared the photographs and poignant letters with members of my senior staff who knew my family very well. Every one of them was convinced that this was Nelson's birth family.

Dr. Kirschner had enclosed a cover letter addressed to me, in which he thanked me for my initial cooperation: "I realize what a shock my call must have been so many years after your adoption of Nelson." He went on to explain that the organization that had prepared the final investigative report was an association of families of disappeared children in El Salvador. He also drew attention to something I had asked about on the phone—there was a copy of a birth certificate included in the dossier. Even more stunning was his added revelation that Nelson's supposed biological father was still alive and living in Panama.

By evening Margaret had arrived. I met her at a local restaurant where we planned to celebrate my fifty-third birthday, which was the following day. We began to spread the documents out on the table when the waiter clumsily splattered red wine all over me as he opened the bottle. A new tablecloth was brought, and the manager offered to pay for my dry cleaning, but all we cared about were the papers. Margaret had luckily managed to snatch them up in time.

«   »

The dossier consisted of a three-and-a-half-page investigative report in English, prepared by Ralph Sprenkels, a young Dutchman who worked for the Salvadoran searching organization Pro-búsqueda (Asociación Pro-búsqueda de Niñas y Niños Desaparecidos), and some supporting evidence. A photocopy of a birth certificate showed that the child for whom they were hunting was born Roberto Alfredo Coto Escobar on May 22, 1981, in San Salvador. My first thought was, If this boy is Nelson, he's already sixteen! There were copies of relevant articles from 1982 Honduran newspapers on which the investigative résumé relied heavily, and a few passages from these journalistic accounts were cited verbatim.

A photocopy of a portrait of Roberto's birth mother was also included, as well as one of her identity card. There was another whole page of small family photos, including several more of his mother and one of his grandmother, but mostly photos of the boy's sister, Eva Nátaly, and his brother, Ernesto Arnoldo, at different ages. Because his maternal grandmother had initiated the process, all the photos and three letters addressed to "Roberto" came exclusively from that side of the family. There was no sign of the father referred to in Dr. Kirschner's letter. Tom's account continues:

> As soon as she got her first look at the materials, Margaret began to dispel my lingering doubts. First she looked at the photos of the boy's brother and sister. She noticed the resemblance right away. Ernesto Arnoldo, while thinner, looked so much like Nelson as a youngster. If you covered the lower part of his face—as Margaret illustrated—the eyes and eyebrows could be mistaken for our son.
>
> Then she read the report. She pointed out that many details in this account appeared to dovetail with those of our adoption: the name "Ronny," the same private orphanage, and, she thought, the identity of the judge, who was even pictured and quoted in one of the newspaper articles. One other unusual thing struck her almost immediately. The investigative résumé referred to two other children who had been orphaned by the same incident. Two French families had adopted these girls on December 1, 1982. She recalled at once the strange remark by our judge about having refused a French family for Nelson six months before we came to Tegucigalpa. That would have been the beginning of December! Margaret planned to check the adoption documents in the safe-deposit box the next day to make sure the judge's name was the same. But she was absolutely certain about the other point, and she would later find the notation in her journal to prove it.

Oddly enough, the seemingly extraneous information we had been given in 1983 about a rejected French family resonated with me right away. That date in early December—about which the judge had been so uncommonly specific—and the fact that a French family had been involved must be more than a coincidence, I thought. It was like finding a little key that fit into the lock of an old diary.

I had always wondered how the Honduran authorities could have had a couple come all the way from Europe and then told them they could not adopt a child who had been previously offered to them. Now I could imagine a scenario that made some sense with what we had been told. It occurred to me that a French couple that had come to adopt one of the two little girls probably reacted as Tom had, and sought to adopt two children at once. The judge had evidently turned down their offer to adopt the boy caught up in the same affair and continued to search for another family.

These details tipped the balance for me, perhaps because it was something that I was able to deduce myself, and it fit perfectly into the rest of the compelling narrative. I checked our adoption files the next day. I hadn't remembered her name exactly, but the judge mentioned in the article was indeed the same red-haired Teodolinda Pineda de Aguilar whom we had seen, and whose signature and stamp are on the first document that authorized the release of "Rony [sic] Funez" to us. It didn't matter whether my imagined story line was exact. I needed little more confirmation than this—and the photos of his siblings.

«   »

In the cover letter, dated June 10, 1997, Ralph Sprenkels argued that the evidence—gathered by a human rights organization in Honduras, COFADEH (Comité de Familiares de Detenidos Desaparecidos en Honduras), and passed on to another in El Salvador, CODEFAM (Comité de Familiares de Víctimas de las Violaciones de los Derechos Humanos de El Salvador), and subsequently to Pro-búsqueda—strongly suggested that Roberto Alfredo Coto Escobar, Ronny Funez, and Nelson Ward de Witt were one and the same. "The only way to prove this link beyond reasonable doubt is through DNA testing," Sprenkels wrote. He confirmed what Dr. Kirschner had told Tom, that Physicians for Human Rights (PHR) was assisting Pro-búsqueda in the area of genetic testing and contacting families.

The letter also offered the following overall assessment: "Given the circumstances of involuntary separation, both the child's and the family's fundamental rights were severely violated by the Honduran Government. This responsibility does not apply to the adoptive family, but does question adoptions as a practice within the context of an armed internal conflict." This statement put us on our guard because of the way it questioned the adoption. Despite Dr. Kirschner's assurances, we feared someone might be trying to undermine our legal status as Nelson's parents. We doubted that anyone could undo the double knot we had tied when we re-adopted him in Probate Court in Massachusetts, but we were wary.

Sprenkels continued in a more reassuring vein. Should the results of DNA testing confirm the conclusion they had drawn concerning Nelson's origins, we could choose to communicate in writing or by phone with members of his biological family, and Pro-búsqueda could help us arrange a "re-encounter," with the support of trained psychologists on their staff. "We hope that you are willing to facilitate your adoptive child's recovery of an important part of his identity. [. . .] Both our organization and Roberto Alfredo's family want this process to be as harmonious as possible, based on common understanding between the adoptive family and the biological family, and respecting the child's special situation and opinions."

This last remark reinforced our own sense that what happened next would depend on Nelson. He was sixteen, luckily, not three, six, or ten. He was not in his majority yet, but certainly mature enough to form his own opinion about what he wanted to do. Tom and I felt very fortunate, however, that the kids were away at camp for the next few weeks. This gave us time to recover from our initial shock. We wanted to fully digest the material we had been sent, to ask our friends and family for advice, and to think carefully about how to present it all to our sons.

As we read and re-read what had been sent to us, we realized that the grandmother, Lucila Angulo, had begun the seemingly futile search for the boy in 1992. The formal rediscovery process initiated by her testimony in August 1994 to CODEFAM had taken the four organizations involved almost three years.[5] We could surely wait a few more weeks to break the news to our children. We agreed that a conversation on the camp's visiting day was out of the question. In the meantime, Tom contacted the deputy director of PHR, who sent us some of its newsletters and copies of a series on the disappeared children of El Salvador that had been published the previous summer in the *Boston Globe*.[6]

«   »

As I read the investigative report again in order to write this chapter, I can vividly recall the powerful emotions with which I perused it the first time, always asking myself, Can this boy be my Nelson? The organizations that had been entrusted with the search did not know then as much as we know now, and in the interest of providing a coherent narrative, they relied heavily on the journalistic record and even glossed over its apparent contradictions. But they provided us with the basic outline of a riveting plot.

The child, Roberto Alfredo, had been born to Ana Milagro Escobar and Luis Noé Coto in El Salvador but had been orphaned in Honduras, where Mila was on a secret mission. His parents had been members of a guerrilla group later subsumed under the umbrella of the insurgent co-alition called the FMLN (Frente Farabundo Martí para la Liberación Nacional). "Members of this organization were being persecuted and murdered by Salvadoran government troops on a daily basis," and their revolutionary activities "were dangerous and highly secretive," the report offered by way of explanation.

On May 19, 1982, just three days before the boy's first birthday, the "Cobra" battalion of the Honduran police force, FUSEP (Fuerza de Seguridad Pública de Honduras), carried out a surprise attack on a safe house in Tegucigalpa, freeing a wood industry executive, Jacques Casanova Wolffsheim, who had been kidnapped on March 10th and held for ransom.[7] The investigators draw the conclusion that the woman gunned down that morning along with two *guerrilleros* was the boy's mother. She is pictured in the paper lying on the floor in a pool of blood, but her face is turned to the side and her features obscured almost entirely by her hair—not unlike the woman in the San Pedro Sula incident—making a positive identification difficult. She is described in the newspaper accounts as "quite young, almost juvenile in appearance, short, fair-skinned, with long, straight brown hair."[8]

In addition to Casanova, who was unharmed, two children were evidently recovered from this house, and a third child—an infant—was found in a second safe house in a different part of the city sometime later. At this second address the revolutionaries kept an arms cache, and several other members of the group were either killed or captured there. The journalistic record that accompanied the report remains sketchy about this second attack, however. COFADEH nevertheless assumes that all the Salvadoran guerrillas were eliminated and buried "anonymously in the Tegucigalpa area."

This FMLN cell had been living like an ordinary extended family in several upper-middle-class neighborhoods of the Honduran capital. How could the authorities know with such certainty that they were members of the FMLN and not Honduran revolutionaries? More important, how had the squad of special police managed to spare not only the life of the hostage but those of two small children, plus a "58-year-old domestic," during a shoot-out lasting "five minutes" in close quarters, according to one newspaper? And what had happened at the second address? Had the others been killed, or captured and then tortured? What had happened to the older woman, who is mentioned only once?

As shocking as it was, and as many questions as it raised in our minds, the story somehow rang true, in contrast to the San Pedro Sula incident we had considered earlier. Because of the unusual intervention of the U.S. Embassy in our adoption, we had always thought that the case might have some political import. We understood by 1997 that kidnappings of politicians and businesspeople for ransom had been one of the key techniques used by Salvadoran guerrillas to fund their struggle in the 1980s.[9] But still we wondered, how had the Honduran police found this group out?

As in the report of the kidnapping and shoot-out that we had filed away in the safe-deposit box roughly a decade before, pictures of the dead are featured in the journalistic record, and there is a certain fascination with the "spectacular" aspects of the event, heralded as "unparalleled in the history of our country." A great deal of attention is paid to the type of weapons found, the number of shots fired to kill the three adults, and the appearance of the basement "prison" where Casanova was held. Even the contents of the well-equipped kitchen are inventoried. We find out, for example, that the first guerrillero held an Uzi and the second a Galil machine gun, and that hand grenades and tear gas formed part of their arsenal. Moreover, the "cárcel del pueblo" (prison in the house) contained everything from a book on practical electronics to "a can of Lysol" and "a bottle of Phillips milk of magnesia," as well as "a pink towel" and "a pink blanket." The kitchen had "chicken, beans, rice, vegetables, cereals, canned food and other goods, a stove, a refrigerator, an electric mixer, and other utensils for food preparation."

By comparison, the details we cared most about remained murky. The newspaper reports actually give disparate accounts concerning the conduct of the first raid. Either the group was so taken by surprise that they were unable to return fire or the police were fired upon both before and while entering the house; the police entered either through the garage or the front door. One caption says the woman opened the front door and was shot dead immediately; in another she is said to have been shot in the hall, a few yards behind the first man, who was killed before he could even fire his gun. Even the number of guerrillas in the cell is reported as five and six members.

Unlike the October 1982 incident, the victims in this case could not be individually identified. No given names are used. Furthermore, the

ATIENDE LA POLICIA A NIÑOS QUE VIVIAN CON PLAGIARIOS

second house and third child do not surface in the reports until months later—without any details or photographs. The journalists and the investigators also give wildly differing estimates of the ages of the two girls and one boy left behind, from the very specific "40 days old," used to describe the infant discovered in the second house, to anywhere from six months to two years for the other children.

The boy—most consistently estimated to be a year old—is the only child pictured in the newspaper articles provided. A member of the women's police auxiliary is seen holding him as the general commander of FUSEP, Colonel Daniel Balí Castillo, looks on.[10] The baby is turned not toward Balí, who holds his outstretched hand, but directly toward the camera. An enlargement of his round face, provided in the dossier, despite its fuzziness, reveals a striking resemblance to the wistful way

Nelson looked at us when we saw him for the first time exactly a year later.[11] While they had not seen him since he was five months old, several aunts in El Salvador evidently identified the boy in this newspaper photo as Roberto Alfredo.

The article (for which Pro-búsqueda provided a translation), published twelve days after the shoot-out, appears under a headline printed entirely in capital letters:

POLICE ATTEND TO CHILDREN THAT WERE LIVING WITH KIDNAPPERS

The police have said that the kidnappers, militants of the Farabundo Martí National Liberation Front (FMLN) of El Salvador, that occupied the house number 2707 of La Campaña, supposedly had abducted two children in the neighboring country for the house to appear to be lived in by an integrated family. Balí Castillo visited the infants to find out personally about the health of the children—a girl and a boy—who fortunately survived the police operation in which three of the kidnappers were killed. The children receive attention from the Women's Police, but it is still not clear what will happen to them.

The investigative summary explains that the children were given names by the women's police auxiliary who were taking care of them. The boy they called Ronny.

Another article dated over three months later, September 4, 1982, features a personal appeal by the judge of minors, "Teodolinda Pineda A.," who is pictured, to the parents of the "three children" to make themselves known to the authorities. This reinforces the theory that they were kidnapped, rather than being the offspring of those who had been killed. I was reminded of a similar thesis put forward in the other incident, in which it was also supposed that the child might not be the biological offspring of the kidnappers but a mere cover for their clandestine activities.

Interestingly, the judge also reveals in the article that the three children orphaned by the incident involving the two safe houses were still in state custody. She asserts that if their true identity could not soon be determined, some "generous persons" might adopt them.[12] The investigative report adds that the children were subsequently placed in the care of the Aldeas SOS orphanage. If that transfer did not occur until September, I concluded, then the nine or ten months we were told Nelson had been at the orphanage was indeed accurate.

While the Honduran government evidently dragged its heels in the rediscovery process, the investigative résumé explains that eventually the information about the adoption "was provided verbally to representatives of COFADEH" by the Court of Minors, although the court "did not agree to have photocopies made of the adoption files." It hardly mattered. Once they had been given our full names, an Internet search by Pro-búsqueda was sufficient to find our contact information.

Most of the remaining information in the résumé is based on the testimony of the boy's maternal grandmother, Lucila Angulo. She told the investigators that about a year before Roberto was born, she had left El Salvador with his siblings, Eva and Ernesto, raising them first in Nicaragua and then in Costa Rica, where she still resided. An unidentified messenger who sometimes brought letters from her daughter told her that Mila had been killed in Honduras; he could not provide her with any information "about what had happened to Roberto Alfredo, or any other details about the circumstances of Mila's death."

Little was offered in the investigative report on the subject of Roberto's biological father, other than his name and the fact that he was based in Nicaragua at the time of the shoot-out but now lived in Panama. Nevertheless, it states that he was "willing to donate a blood sample in order to perform the DNA testing." In conclusion, Sprenkels places the whole narrative in the larger framework of Central American insurgencies during the 1980s:

> It is important to see the events described in this investigative résumé within their context. During the 80s in Central America, there were insurgency movements in almost all the countries of the region, and most strongly in El Salvador, Guatemala, and Nicaragua. The FMLN was a very large organization in El Salvador, but only very select and very secret small groups operated outside of El Salvador. Everybody that participated in these groups had to change their identity and the other members of the group would not know the true name of any of the members, because of security reasons. Persecution against these groups was systematic in the entire region, and to be associated with any of these groups in El Salvador, Guatemala or Honduras almost certainly meant death or forced disappearance. It is not until the end of the Cold War and the Peace Accords in El Salvador (1992) that sufficient guarantees existed to set up serious investigations about Human Rights violations during the 80s.

We were able to get a sense of the family that was searching for their Roberto from the three letters that were included in the packet—one from his grandmother, the others from her two eldest daughters. I give them here in the translations provided by Pro-búsqueda at the time:

Dear Grandson,

I send you my best wishes, hoping you are doing well and are enjoying the company of your mother and father. You can't imagine how long I have been looking for you. Every night I prayed and asked God to help me find you. You can't imagine what great joy I felt in my heart when they told me that you had been located, and you can't imagine how much I would like to see you and hold you in my arms. [. . .] I hope you will answer this letter very soon and send us a photograph of yourself to see how much you have grown. I want to know you in person. Until soon, my little boy, please say hello to your mother and father. We would very much like to meet them also. Your grandmother says goodbye, with all the love in my heart, and many hugs from all of your family.

Lucila Angulo

Vilma Escobar's letter, addressed "Dear Nephew," shows a great deal of sensitivity for our situation, as she expresses concern that the new knowledge about our child's origins might "be a reason for worries in your home." She continues:

We don't know what your [Roberto's] reaction will be when you find out about the history of your (biological) mother and father. We don't know how much you know about your own history. During the first years we had no idea what happened to you and where to go to find out about you. [. . .] You can't imagine the anguish we have lived with during all these years of your disappearance. Your localization has been the greatest gift that God could have sent us. My mother has not been able to live in peace these last 15 years asking God that one-day you would be found.

She concludes with a remark that made Tom and me more confident as we tried to imagine the reunion they were clearly hoping for: "Sincere greetings for your parents, because the truth is that they are your real parents. See you soon. Lots of kisses from your aunt who hopes to meet you soon."

The third letter from Dalila Escobar surprised us because it was written in English rather than being translated from the Spanish. It gives the names and ages of all six sisters on this side of the family and tells briefly how the seventh and youngest daughter, Mila, met Luis in school, fell in love, got married, and became a member of "the guerrilla (a group of persons that fight for what they think is just)." Dalila says that they knew nothing about Mila's clandestine activities that sometimes took her to other countries in the region:

> She died and then you were lost for a long time. There are many things I would like to tell you but maybe when you come here [El Salvador]. I hope your parents accept you come here to know you personally. [. . .] We don't want to disturb your life and your feelings. We only want you to know your biological family. We are very grateful with your parents. They took care of you, without their help you probably would be died [*sic*].

These letters warmed our hearts, for they were full of true affection and genuine concern, not only for the boy they wanted to meet but also for us—his parents. And they seemed to appreciate that after fourteen years this news would be a shock to our family. There was a great deal in the dossier for us to mull over, even worry about. Our chief concern, though, was how Nelson might respond.

How would he view the pictures of his siblings, his mother? We had tried to raise our children to eschew all violence, never allowing them to have toy weapons of any kind, not even water pistols. How would he react to the fact that his parents may have been guerrillas? Could we explain adequately what they had been fighting for in El Salvador that would make their resort to violence understandable to him? Would he be prepared to have the DNA test? Would he be overwhelmed by this family's need to see him and embrace him? The prospect that he might suddenly shut down and not want to know more about his origins seemed to me to be as worrisome as the possibility that he would eventually forsake us for them, emotionally if not literally. And how would Derek react to the idea that there was another family out there, who—at the very least—wanted to get to know the brother he doted on? Would he feel even more threatened than we did?

We tried to concentrate on the immediate question of when and how to tell the boys the story when they got home. We knew that they would be dead tired after a long awards-night celebration and the end-of-summer good-byes to friends and counselors, but we wanted to initiate the conversation as soon as possible. Tom brought the kids and their trunks to our place in New Hampshire, where we planned to celebrate Nelson's sixteenth birthday, spend a few days doing the camp laundry, and then transition back to Massachusetts and the start of the school year.

Although we had shared everything with my mother by then, Granny suggested it would be best if she went over to my cousin's nearby cottage for dinner that evening, so we could give the kids our full attention. When the boys walked in the door, I realized all they wanted to do was crash. I let them sleep off their exhaustion all afternoon, but when I woke them for dinner, I cautioned, "Don't just eat and run from the table tonight. We have something very important to discuss with you two!"

They looked at me from their bunks, still groggy and probably a little puzzled by my demeanor. I laughed, "Oh no, nothing terrible, we're not getting divorced or anything remotely like that. But it is something very important." Their curiosity piqued, and no doubt hungry, they got up and staggered downstairs.

As soon as we had eaten, we brought out the dossier and placed it on the table. Tom began with a copy of the PHR newsletter that featured a front-page picture of Dr. Kirschner drawing blood "for genetic testing from a putative parent in El Salvador." I wondered whether Nelson could make out the bold headline, "DNA Testing Links Missing Salvadoran Children with Parents."[13]

As I anticipated drafting this chapter a few weeks ago, while both boys were home, I asked them to remember the way they had experienced this particular evening. Nelson unhesitatingly recalled, "The minute Dad showed me the picture of Dr. Kirschner and explained that this man had called about me, I just knew that my birth family had been found." Derek, who had turned pale as soon as we began to tell the story, recalled the incapacitating sense of fear that had gripped him as the import of what we were explaining began to dawn on him: "I was only twelve, and twelve-year-olds are not entirely rational. All I could think of was that Nelson was going to be taken away from me. But of course it hasn't turned out that way." Later he expanded in writing as follows:

> I don't remember any other time, before or since, that my parents sounded so serious when they mentioned that they needed to talk with us after dinner. Right now I'm sitting no more than thirty feet from where I was that night, and I can still remember the look on their faces and on my brother's. As they explained the situation, I probably must have turned as white as a sheet, which is impressive for me considering my normal pallor. My first thought was that now that Nelson's "real" family had found him, they would want him to live with them and I would never see him again. Looking back, it sounds silly, but I really felt scared for a bit that I would lose my brother forever.

Nelson has also written at length about that day, using the present tense, which makes his recollection even more vivid:

> It's the last day of camp, Saturday, August 23rd. I think it's six or seven in the morning. I've been up all night. Most of it was spent in cabin 7A. [. . .] The bugle goes off, and now more people are up. Everyone's up and hanging out in front of 7B. There is a crowd, so I climb up into Lizzy's bed on the top bunk because there is nowhere else to sit. I'm so tired that within minutes I'm asleep. But then the second bugle goes off and it's time to gather at the flagpole.
>
> Now my Dad is here and it's time to say good-bye. What an amazing summer! I can't believe it's over. As I am saying good-bye I notice Yoli is crying, which I think is weird. She doesn't strike me as the type to cry. I'm so tired; all I can think about is going home and sleeping. I hand Josh the envelope with a tip from my parents and thank him for the best summer I ever had at camp. Derek and I pile into the car, and Dad drives off.
>
> We get home and I go right to bed. Mom starts doing the laundry. Five hours later I wake to my mother telling me it's time for dinner. Then she adds that she and Dad need to have a serious talk with us right after dinner. The thought of them getting a divorce flashes through my mind for a second, but that doesn't make any sense, and I quickly push it away. It seems weird. They have never done this before, but honestly I'm too tired to think about it. Half asleep I stumble down the stairs of our house in New Hampshire. We eat dinner. I'm still half asleep and don't say much.

As we are clearing our plates my Mom says again rather seriously, "Now, don't go anywhere; we need to talk." I'm thinking to myself, "Yeah. I know. I'm not going anywhere." My brother and I sit down again. Now my parents are sitting next to me, one on either side. I'm really stumped; what's going on?

My father has a FedEx package on the table. From it he pulls out a magazine or a newsletter. On the cover is a man. He points to the picture and says to me, "This is Dr. So-and-so and he works with children in El Salvador." It was at that point that I knew I found my family. I don't know how I knew, but I did. Dad went on to explain that this man works for an organization in El Salvador that helps find lost children. I was hardly listening, I just knew what was coming next, and it took everything I had not to completely break down. I had been waiting for this for so long. Then he finally says it: "They believe they have found your birth family."

He goes on to say that I have a father in Panama and a stepmother, an older sister and brother. No mention of my mother yet. It turns out that I was born in El Salvador, not Honduras. Both my parents fought in the civil war in El Salvador as guerrillas. . . . I feel numb. I'm not sure what to make of this. In all honesty, I had never even imagined having a brother and sister and so many family members. As for my father . . . well, I guess I never really thought about him. The only person I really wanted to see was my mother.

There are pictures too. My parents say they have been looking at the photos and think that my brother and I look a lot alike. I glance at the picture, and I don't see the resemblance. There are also letters written to the lost baby "Roberto." That's me. Robert—I don't know if I like that, but my mother's name is Escobar and I think that's a cool name. It turns out my birthday is May 22nd. My August birthday is in a few days, but this kind of changes things. I'm really sixteen already.

Dad says they want to do a blood test to see if we are actually related. He asks me if I would be willing to do it. The question surprises me. Of course I am, but truthfully I don't need a blood test. I already know it's them.

We went over the entire dossier with the boys that evening. As I recall, we read them the whole three-and-a-half page report aloud and discussed what conclusions we would have drawn based on the evidence before us, had genetic testing not been available. We looked at all the pictures very closely. When Nelson saw the portrait of his young mother with her round face and her serious eyes, he started to cry. He had just found out she was dead. After so many years of uncertainty about his origins, though, getting all this information about his family was like an epiphany. For him, it was a no-brainer. He wanted to have the DNA test done as soon as possible, but he was already sure. He looked at the photos again and again in the next days and took them to school to show his friends.

By now, Tom and I were also entirely convinced—it was his family. But so were *we*. I could empathize with Derek, who had grown increasingly withdrawn as we considered our next moves—the genetic testing, drafting a letter to the family in anticipation of the results being positive, even beginning to plan a reunion in December when we would all have vacation time.

First, we phoned Dr. Kirschner about Nelson's decision, and within days a letter arrived enclosing a lab card for his blood sample and a detailed explanation of the method to be used so as to prevent contamination. The sample was taken at a clinic and returned to him by mail on the Friday of Labor Day weekend, August 29th. Before long Dr. Kirschner notified us that he had also received blood samples from two maternal aunts in El Salvador, so the DNA testing could proceed without further delay. Evidently a sample from his biological father was not considered necessary.[14]

More important for Nelson, a letter written on July 1st by Luis Coto and forwarded to Dr. Kirschner by Pro-búsqueda was also enclosed. Nelson had certainly noticed how little had been said about his biological father in the initial report. There had been no picture of him either, and he was understandably anxious to hear from him in person and to learn what he looked like. Now he was ecstatic. "A letter came from my dad!" he exclaimed excitedly. For the second time, Tom's heart sank, as the weight of what it might mean to share his son with another father came to him in an instant. Nelson remembers it this way:

> It's 6:15 p.m. and it's already dark out. I just got back from school, and I'm the first one home. I dash up to my room and drop my bag. I fire up the computer and head back downstairs to get something to drink. As I go to turn on the outside lights I bend over and pick up the mail. On my way back to the kitchen I start to go through it. Bill, bill, junk mail . . . but what's this? A note from Dr. Kirschner containing another letter.

Tossing the rest of the mail on the counter I'm staring down at a letter addressed to Roberto Coto from a Luis Coto. It's a letter from my father. When we got the original package from Pro-búsqueda there were only letters from two aunts and my grandmother. I take a second to look at it before opening it. It's three pages typewritten. I frown for a second. It's all in Spanish, and I can't read any of it.

I head back up to my room, letter in hand. Half an hour later my dad yells from downstairs, "I'm home"

"Hi," I reply, making my way out into the hall.

"How was your day?" he questions.

"I got a letter from my dad," I say excitedly.

My adoptive father would tell me later these words and the tone of my voice made his heart sink because for fifteen years he was the only one I had called "Dad."

I don't think it's the letter that I'm excited about. I realize I can't wait to meet these people and see what they are like. For that I will have to wait, it will be another couple of months before I get to meet them.

Tom had said nothing to cloud Nelson's joy, and the letter from Luis—once we had gotten it translated—moved all of us:

ROBERTO: I am writing to you on this occasion because I want to know how you are, where you are. It doesn't matter what your name is now. I just want to tell you that when I found out that you were alive my heart stopped suffering. My son, this situation isn't easy for you or for me. The family you have here is very anxious to know you. We want to tell you that we love you and that we need you, but we don't want to cause you any confusion, my son. If you are happy where you are at, don't worry. I just want to tell you that we love you and that we want to get to know you. I want you to know in one way or another that we carry you in our daily prayers. ROBERTO, my name is LUIS NOÉ COTO, I am your father.

At the time you were born in El Salvador, I was in Nicaragua, and because of the circumstances of the moment, I had no control over or knowledge about what was going on. Your mother could only inform me that you were born, and it was impossible in those days for your mother and me to see each other. We tried to be together once more. In order to make this possible, your mother and you left El Salvador and traveled to Honduras. Your mother was put to work, and I was also in Honduras, but because of negligence of the people we were working with, I wasn't allowed to be with you and your mother, even though I tried to locate you.

ROBERTO, maybe one day I can explain to you personally what happened. ROBERTO, my fear of writing you has been that you would get confused, but let me tell you that, in spite of all that happened, and the circumstances in which I lost you, I always had the hope that GOD would protect you. And this actually happened, according to the information I have about your adoptive parents.

I want you and your adoptive parents to know that it is not my intention to change the life you are currently living. This is not what moves me to seek you. Only you will be able to decide what to do after you have seen our letters. I only ask for you—for the love of the memory of your disappeared mother—to give us a small opportunity for you to get to know your brother and sister, your father, your aunts and uncles, in short, our entire family, which is anxious to know you.

ROBERTO, I want to emphasize two things that are very important to me: first of all that I LOVE YOU, independently from whether I'll be able to have you with me or to get to know you in the same manner I know your brother and sister, who pray for you every single day. Second, while we didn't know anything about you, we suffered your absence in silence and with much pain. Now that we know that you are well, our suffering is so much less. But we can't feel completely happy because we haven't seen you yet. Nevertheless, we don't want to make you suffer, telling you the true story about what happened to your family and about your roots. Considering and reflecting upon all this, I send you these words, which I hope you will be able to interpret correctly and with your heart, so that you can forgive me and give us the opportunity to know you, embrace you, and give you this love that has been guarded with pain for so many years. MY SON, I ASK YOUR FORGIVENESS FOR ALL THE THINGS THAT I COULD NOT DO FOR YOU . . . SEE YOU SOON AND MAY GOD CONTINUE TO PROTECT YOU AND BLESS YOU ALWAYS.

YOUR FATHER AND YOUR BROTHER AND SISTER.

Clearly, we were careening toward an emotional encounter with all these people who were so anxious to meet our son in person. Would there be a collision? Would he be able to return the love they professed so openly for him? Receiving the positive results of the DNA testing from Dr. Kirschner over the phone about ten days later seemed almost like an anticlimax. We hadn't really expected anything else. The full written report prepared by the scientists at Professor Mary-Claire King's laboratory in Seattle concerning the "nucleotide sequence analysis of mitochondrial DNA" was not sent until the end of October; by then we had already made arrangements to fly to Costa Rica in December.

« »

We no longer needed to rely on Pro-búsqueda's translation services, as we could turn to the Spanish department at Wellesley and hire bilingual college students as needed. That speeded up the pace of communication. We wrote a two-page, single-spaced letter to all the members of the family from whom we had heard so far.

In it we tried to express how we felt about what had happened so suddenly after fourteen years, explaining briefly how we had come to adopt Nelson and that we had thought both his parents had been killed. We told them about our professions, his many interests and activities, and—most important—about the fact that he had a younger brother, Derek. We also wanted to demonstrate that we understood something about the Salvadoran civil war and the "sorry role" the U.S. government had played in that twelve-year conflict.

We then outlined our plan to come to see them in Costa Rica, not El Salvador. It seemed to us to be the more logical place for a reunion, and frankly, we thought it would be safer. We had already made hotel reservations in the town of Heredia, not far from where we understood that his grandmother, his Aunt Vilma, and his sister, Eva, lived together. We told them that we would stay for a week, and we expressed the hope that some of the relatives in Panama and El Salvador could join us during that time. I raided our photo albums so that I could send each of the addressees some photos of Nelson at various ages. We didn't know at the time how unreliable the Costa Rican postal service was; his grandmother never received hers.

We also told them in our letter that we had been "worried about the impact this would have on all of our lives," and that their letters had reassured us, filling us with great joy. We concluded, "Nelson took the news very well and has become very eager to see all of you. In his Spanish class at school, he has told everyone about this exciting development and taken the name Roberto, which is his birthright." Nelson drafted his own short but heartfelt letter and signed with his new full name:

> Dear Family,
>
> I never thought that the day would come when I would be writing to my biological family. I have always wondered who I was and where I came from. Hearing that I had a family that was looking for me was one of the best things that ever happened to me. I have grown up to believe that I had no more family left, and if I did I would never see them. Even after accepting this, I never gave up hope that one day I might meet my family. Nothing I have ever imagined comes close to this. I am so happy to have found out all this information. I cannot wait to come to visit you. I have waited so long for this to happen and finally my wish came true.
>
> Love,
> Roberto Alfredo Coto Escobar

« »

The weeks passed incredibly swiftly, and our anticipation was heightened by more and more letters that arrived during the course of the fall in response to ours. Luis wrote a second time, telling us more about his family in Panama. He said that he ran his own silk-screening business from his home in David and introduced his Panamanian wife, Miriam, a pediatric nurse, and their daughter, Jennifer Éstefany (age six), Roberto's half-sister. "Each line we read [in your letter] filled us with hope and love toward you both," he wrote to Tom and me. "I give thanks to God for this impending encounter with you and to you for having done all that I could not do for Roberto. I want you to know that I have in my heart a great respect and profound gratitude toward you both. There are no words nor ways in which I can repay you your kindness."

Nelson he addressed in a separate letter as "Beloved son," as he once again begged his forgiveness for both omissions and commissions in his youth:

> I have read your letter carefully and could not contain my tears of joy that each one of your words made me sense you close to me, despite

the time and distance that have separated us. Only God knows the intensity of my joy at the prospect of getting to know you personally and to think that you already feel like a part of our family. [. . .] Some years ago I had a dream about a very tender meeting with you, but you can't imagine the emotion I have knowing that you are really alive. [. . .] I love you with all my heart, and I give thanks to God for the grace that you have received adoptive parents who are so kind to permit this grand reunion. It reflects on their hearts and the human compassion that they possess, and their love, which has in turn formed you.

Ernesto also wrote a short, somewhat formal letter, addressed to his "Esteemed brother," in which he explains that he has always been called Toto and that he would soon graduate from high school. He reveals that he had always tried to imagine how it would be to have a younger brother, as he thought about "the things we could do together. Now I know that I have one, and that I am going to share many things with him. [. . .] We will see each other soon. I don't know what this day will be like, but I know I will remember it forever. Very affectionately, your brother, Ernesto Arnoldo Coto Escobar."

A whole raft of Salvadoran aunts and cousins chimed in, with letters and pictures, and it began to dawn on us that there might be quite a reception in Costa Rica, as three of these maternal aunts expressed the hope that they could come from El Salvador with some of their children for the occasion. Aunt Tita's daughters, Mireya, Claudia, and Diana, had written to introduce themselves, and Nelson chose the one of similar age, Mireya, to be his Spanish-speaking pen pal for a school assignment. He wondered whether they might not be able to communicate via e-mail, since he had learned that she, too, liked computers. Mireya promptly gave him her e-mail address at work. She also asked whether the game of lacrosse that we had mentioned in our letter was played in the snow!

Finally, Nelson received the first direct communication from his sister, Eva. It was forwarded to us by Pro-búsqueda. This time, with the help of a dictionary, I was able to translate it into English myself, as my passive knowledge of Spanish was rapidly improving. In it she describes herself as someone who "likes music, works hard, and is trying to manage to become someone." She talks of having dreams and illusions that she and Roberto might have similar emotions and will be able to understand each other in some special way:

Dear brother:

Hello! I hope that all is well with you when you receive this letter and that your emotions are like mine. I believe that writing a letter is like having a conversation, so I will begin without much ado, but really not knowing what to say, what to tell you, not knowing if I should begin by asking you things or by telling about myself. I guess that I'm going to recount something about myself so that you can get to know me a little, since it's not possible to answer my questions.

I am 19 years old, I am short, fair in complexion, and I have green eyes and chestnut-colored hair. That's a little about what I am like on the outside, and as for the inside . . . well, for the inside, I'm not sure about who I am inside, I don't know myself, but I think that everyone experiences this to some extent.

Do you know what I mean? It's really always the feeling of a "hole in my soul" (like Aerosmith puts it), always the sense that something is missing, which isn't material. Nothing fills up the inside entirely, and I don't know what causes this. I think that it is the lack of our mother, which I always felt very deeply, but apart from that, also the uncertainty of not knowing anything about you. Always thinking that one would never discover you, and just now thinking about writing this letter with the uncertainty whether you will understand me or not. But for me to know that someone has found you has been a great joy. My heart did a 360-degree turn, and all this revived these old feelings in me.

I (like you) am a child who left El Salvador, and I don't remember anything about that country. Of our mother I have only a vague memory that has stayed with me always, and of you—well then—to be sincere, I never met you and I have no memory of you, but always I have a little piece of my heart that you have always occupied. It seems incredible that you have always been a stranger. To know that soon we can overcome that, that we can get to know you at last, after all this time, has made me very emotional, and I have no words to express what I am thinking and feeling. [. . .]

There remain many questions in the air, which soon—God willing—we will be able to clear up. I don't know what reactions will pour out when I meet you, but although I can express little, I want by means of this letter for you to know that you have been in my thoughts and that I love you and that I am grateful to God for reuniting you with me. Forgive me if I cry. I don't know what you will think, but I am quite sure that I will burst out in tears because of the enormous joy of seeing you for the first time.

I give thanks to your parents for having taken care of you and for permitting that we get acquainted. Surely, it must be boring to read this, so I will stop for now, but not without mentioning that we will be waiting for you here.

Eva

THREE

Reunion

HEREDIA, COSTA RICA, DECEMBER 1997

D espite the outpouring of goodwill expressed in the letters that had flooded our mailbox through the fall, I was anticipating that we would face a considerable language barrier when we actually met in December. We gathered that several members of Nelson's biological family knew some English, and both our boys were taking Spanish in school, but they were far from fluent. I planned to go armed with dictionaries and phrasebooks, but I expected it might be helpful for everyone to be able to express their deepest feelings in writing, so I brought along a journal we could share.

I had found a notebook I thought was particularly appropriate for the occasion, as its cover seemed to me to symbolize our best hope for understanding. A heart appears superimposed on a map of North and part of South America in such a way that the right lobe covers both the east coast of the United States and the Central American countries; a luminescent door key stands at its center. For me that stood for the fact that a grandmother's anguished heart had provided the key that had finally unlocked our son's mystery. While anxious about the coming encounter, in my best moments I truly believed we were on the cusp of something miraculous. Lucila Angulo's loving persistence had brought us to this point and infused me with hope. The letters we had exchanged suggested that an outpouring of love on all sides could overcome years of separation and help Nelson to integrate his identities without our having to lose ours as a family.

During the course of the week we spent in Costa Rica, almost everyone who participated in this wonderful reunion wrote a personal reflection in our journal. Entries in English and Spanish alternated at first, until Nelson's biological family wrested the book away entirely. I had to take notes on separate pieces of paper, and Tom spoke on tape since we had taken along a micro tape recorder. I thought the journal would be something Nelson could read later on, to bring to mind what each of these people dear to him had experienced during this week when we took our first steps toward each other. In his entry, Luis rightly called it one of those unforgettable "grand or sad moments that have transformed what we do and our desire to live for something worthwhile. These special moments form part of our reason for living."

Ralph Sprenkels of Pro-búsqueda, with whom we had been exchanging e-mails, had promised to join us in Costa Rica to make sure the reunion went smoothly, but let us know shortly before our departure that he had taken ill and could not come. Tom and I were not anticipating any major difficulties and had told him it was not necessary for the organization to send one of their psychologists. We did, however, seek some contacts on our own, just in case something went dreadfully wrong or we needed more support than we could give each other.

My former college roommate, who had grown up in Mexico and traveled with her family extensively in Central America, gave me the name of a professor in San José, Costa Rica, whom she knew well. Another trusted friend, who had recently taken his sabbatical at a seminary there, gave us the names of an American couple on the faculty whom we could contact if need be. It was reassuring.

Fortunately, I was again on sabbatical leave during calendar year 1997, which gave me more time to process everything that was happening to us during these few months, but as a result I had also promised to accompany Tom on a business trip to Japan and Hawaii in November. We were involved in a considerable amount of entertaining for the college as the semester ended and the holidays approached, and there were many trip-related preparations. The run-up to December 20th proved unusually hectic.

When asked what he wanted for Christmas, Toto had replied, "Thanks for the kind gesture of asking us what we would like as a present, but I want you to know that I can't ask you for anything. The best gift is that you are coming to meet us." The sentiment was heartwarming, but it didn't help me much. I couldn't imagine going empty handed, and I had no idea how many members of the family to expect. I decided on generic gifts—music tapes for the teenagers, stuffed animals for the children, picture books of Boston for the adults, and candy, the latest school photos, and small craft items made in the United States for everyone.

I also raided our family photo albums a second time and prepared three small ones to take along. They featured Nelson's growth from age two to sixteen and showcased the places we had lived and traveled together: Newton, New Hampshire, Florida, New York, Pennsylvania, Manitoba, Germany, and Spain. Of course, many photos featured both our boys. I thought his family would be able to guess how close Nelson and Derek were. Understandably, both of them were having some difficulty concentrating on schoolwork as they anticipated what was in store for us during their vacation.

Then, only two nights before our departure, we had another surprise—a dry run for the week to come. One of Lucila Angulo's many grandchildren, Betty, a loquacious young woman, phoned us from nearby Chelsea, Massachusetts: "Me and my family would like to come to see you. Is tonight OK?" Her parents—Nelson's Aunt Tina and Uncle Efraín—had just come from San Vicente, El Salvador, to visit, and they wanted to meet their newly discovered nephew. The group, including Betty's eleven-year-old stepson, didn't arrive at our house until nearly ten o'clock on that school night.

Genuinely pleased to meet them, Nelson was able to overcome the first awkward moments—probably exacerbated by the fact that we were living in a rather formal setting, a three-story Victorian college president's house. He promptly took them upstairs to his room, so that he could send an e-mail message to his "pen pal" Mireya in El Salvador, explaining who was at our house that very minute and extend our combined greetings to everyone. It was the first indication that the Internet would quickly bind the teenagers in a way that would undercut our traditional perception of the distances between people and places.

Mireya—who was working after school and at night in order to earn money so she could eventually go to college—replied immediately that Aunt Dalila and Aunt Haydée were already on the way from San Salvador to Costa Rica by bus with their youngest sons, Fernando, a year older than Derek, and César, a year older than Nelson. Because of the nighttime dangers on the highway, the trip necessitated an overnight stay in Managua, Nicaragua. "As soon as my mother [Aunt Tita] gets off work in a few days, I'll leave with her and my two younger sisters, Claudia and Diana, by the same route," she wrote.

In my mind's eye I could imagine all these people setting out single-mindedly on their various travel routes converging on Costa Rica, the point of contact with the child that had gone missing fifteen years before. It would be the first time that most of them had laid eyes on him.

We wondered whether Luis, Miriam, Toto, and Éstefany would be able to come from Panama as well. Their letters suggested it was their fondest desire, but we had not heard anything definite about their travel plans.

« »

My journal entries began the next day on a mundane note; as usual writing helped to calm my nerves: *Nelson came home from school out of sorts yesterday because he forgot his good headphones, as well as his carrying case with his favorite CDs, and he won't be able to retrieve them until the building reopens in January. It's a struggle to get him to choose which clothes he wants to take along and to get him to pack his other personal belongings in his backpack. [. . .] He finally agrees to take a jacket after I tell him that even in Costa Rica it will be cool in the mornings and evenings this time of year. [. . .]*

Saturday, December 20, 1997. We wake the boys at 4:10 a.m., and I'm amazed; everyone is ready to go when the taxi arrives twenty minutes later. Usually, we have to wait for Nelson, but not this morning. Intense anticipation is the key emotion carrying us through this whole long day. Logan Airport is already very crowded. Although we booked in September, our choices were limited, and we have to fly into Fort Lauderdale, pick up a rental car, and drive to Miami in time to catch our flight to Costa Rica. We are sitting in two different rows on both flights—Tom with Nelson and Derek with me. As far as I can tell, Nelson seems to be taking everything in stride; he's spending his time sleeping and photographing cloud formations. Outwardly, at least, he appears serene.

Nelson remembered it ten years later this way:

I met my birth family for the first time when I was sixteen during my Christmas vacation in 1997. It was an incredible experience, one that I will never forget. Looking back on it now, it's all a blur of memories. Filled with excitement, confusion, love, and happiness. When I found them, I found myself.

The first thing I remember is sitting on the plane listening to music. I'm always listening to music, especially on long trips. I don't remember what I was listening to, but I think I had really crappy headphones. It always bugs me when I don't have a decent pair of headphones, and for some reason this sticks out in my mind. Even though I had been to a few different countries before, I had never been to Central America, and I really had no idea what to expect.

In my journal I tried to capture our first view of the landscape: *There is a beautiful descent, with forested volcanic peaks poking up through the clouds, then the mountains that fringe San José appear, and we land at the airport in Alajuela on the elevated central plateau of Costa Rica, a little ahead of schedule. Passport control is routine, but we have to wait what seems like an eternity for our checked luggage.*

Nelson recalls how embarrassing it was to be immediately mistaken for a native:

> We arrived in the late afternoon, and as we walked through the airport I remember going down a long flight of steps on our way to customs. I was still listening to music as we waited to pick up our bags. It was a long wait. As we stood there a woman approached me and started to ask me questions in Spanish. She had a piece of paper in her hand, and I believe she wanted me to take a survey. I just stood there and ignored her. I felt bad because I'm sure I came off as being rude, but I had no idea what was going on and all I could think about were the people waiting outside.

My journal records other details: *After a perfunctory customs check, our four bags are sent upstairs on a conveyor belt where we can retrieve them a second time. As we carry them down a short, dimly lit interior corridor, I have to insist to several porters that we can manage, bravely stating that we are being "met by family." Then I glimpse a crowd at the exit, including a short man with a round face, slightly protruding ears, and a shock of dark hair with a distinctive white patch. We recognize Luis Coto from photos. He catches sight of Nelson and starts waving vigorously.*

Suddenly the whole crowd by the exit has surged forward, propelled by an emotional tide. A wave of hugs and tears breaks over us as we reach the sidewalk just outside the terminal. I can see Nelson, almost a head taller than his father, crying on Luis's shoulder. Then he and his grandmother are doing the same. His half-sister is clutching him around the knees.

Tom, Derek, and I are standing a little to the side with the luggage at first, as the immediate focus of attention is on "their Roberto." A few moments later, overwhelmed by the whole scene, we also begin to weep, embracing each other first, and then members of Nelson's biological family. Many of us are taking pictures. The flashes create colored spots before my eyes, adding to the blur caused by my tears, but I can make out that Éstefany is still clutching Nelson and won't let go, even as others take their

turns to embrace him—his sister, his brother, his maternal aunts, I pre-
sume, and what seems like innumerable unidentifiable cousins.

In his account, Nelson also recalled this moment:

> We finally cleared customs and headed out of the airport. There were
> people everywhere and most of them were cab drivers asking if we
> wanted a taxi. We just kept saying no and moving forward. Then there
> was a clearing and that's when I saw them for the first time. In front of
> me stood an older version of myself and by his side was a little girl of
> seven years. Immediately they hugged me, my little half-sister getting
> stuck in between my father and me. For a moment I tried to let her
> out, but it was no use; she wouldn't let go. My father had been waiting
> sixteen years to see me, and it felt like he would never let me go ever
> again.
>
> After that, it's all a blur of meeting my older brother, my sister,
> grandmother, stepmother, cousins, aunts, and uncles. There must have
> been over thirty people at the airport waiting to meet us. I have no
> idea how long we were outside the terminal with everyone just hug-
> ging, crying, and trying to communicate with each other. We have a
> picture from that night. It's blurry and you can't really see anything.
> All you can make out are lights streaking across the photo. My mother
> has said from time to time that this picture describes the emotion of
> that night, and I think she is right. It was just one big blur.

My initial journal entry continues: *For a long time, as additional*
"abrazos" are exchanged, our knot of humanity disrupts the orderly exit of
other passengers, who urge us to move on. We're finally trundled off into
two large red taxi vans for the short drive to the Bougainvillea, a hotel that
had been recommended to us. Nelson is holding his half-sister Éstefany in
his arms and playing clapping games with her.

Nelson has written of his feelings at this moment of being both lost
and found at the same time:

> The next thing I remember is piling into a car with my little sister
> close behind. She sat next to me, never letting go. My mother snapped
> a picture of the two of us. Later we would make a mouse pad from this
> picture and to this day that mouse pad sits on my desk. As we drove off,
> I remember feeling completely lost; everything looked so different, and
> I had no idea where I was. Even so, I felt at home and safe. I looked

down at my sister. Here was this little girl who I had never met before, but I meant the world to her. It was a strange feeling and one that I would feel again and again as I got to know my biological family.

In the van, I noted how Luis radiated his happiness, as he sat beside this son he had never seen before. But I could also tell that he was simultaneously able to register Derek's vulnerability, as he tried to make him feel included in their warm welcome. A few cousins peeled off in their own cars and went home, but about twenty members of the family accompanied us to our hotel.

The hotel is set in a beautiful landscaped park on a hillside in St. Tomás de Heredia. Far below in the distance, we can see the lights of San José coming on gradually in the dusk. After we check in, the whole group stays to eat. What better way than a shared meal to begin to connect. The Muñoz family joins us; Luis, Miriam, Toto, and Éstefany are staying with them for the week, as they were neighbors and became close friends while Geraldo Muñoz served as Costa Rican consul in David. Luis asks him to offer a prayer of thanksgiving before we break bread together.

Aunt Haydée also uses this occasion to say a formal word of thanks for our willingness to arrange this reunion and to share our son with them. Eva's boyfriend, Roy, a medical student who has studied for a semester in St. Louis, offers simultaneous translation as needed, but gratitude really requires no translation.

I find myself seated next to Lucila Angulo, whom the family affectionately calls Mamá Chila. We, too, have begun to call her that. Everyone does. It is Nelson who helps me overcome my shyness by insisting I fetch the three little photo albums so that his grandmother can see all the pictures of his childhood right away.

Mamá Chila was also the first to contribute to "our" journal the following day:

> To my beloved Nelson/Roberto:
> God granted me this miracle to be able to know you. I prayed to him night after night, not wanting to die without knowing where you were, and God granted me my prayer. I can't explain to you how I felt when I saw you in the airport. I wanted to shout; I don't know, I can't say how I felt, only that I cried, and it seemed like a dream.
>
> From your grandmother, who never forgot you (your Mamá Chila)

« »

As soon as she returned the journal to me, I continued my entries: *December 21st. Roosters crowing in a nearby farm wake me up before five o'clock. As I revisit all the worry of the previous days and the excitement of last night, my mind is racing. No point trying to go back to sleep. By six Tom and I get up and have a walk, first through the beautiful gardens behind the hotel, where we catch sight of a toucan, and then uphill to the small village of St. Tomás with its church, school, public soccer field, and small coffee farms. It seems fitting that it is St. Thomas day. There are some villas up here, but primarily middle-class houses, many decorated with Christmas lights. The hillside provides a beautiful vista of San José, and we're happy to be above the exhaust fumes and noise, but still only a fifteen-minute ride away in the hotel's courtesy van.*

After waking the boys and having breakfast, we enjoy looking at the pre-Columbian treasures on display in the lobby and the work of contemporary Costa Rican artists that adorn the walls of the dining room and corridors. We are waiting to be picked up. Tom understood that Geraldo, who lives even farther up in the mountains, would come by with the Coto family by ten o'clock. Nelson thought he'd heard 10:30. By eleven we wonder whether we had understood anything at all.

They finally arrive around 11:30. Éstefany had taken sick that morning. We don't ask for any further explanation. I decide to give her the little bear we have brought to cheer her up. It has a New England Patriots sweater and we have brought a T-shirt for it that says, "Someone at Lasell loves me." She clutches it just the way Nelson did that little Paddington Bear so many years ago. Half our group now gets in a cab; the rest go over to Mamá Chila's in Geraldo's car. It's already noon, but no one acts like we're late. We're getting used to being back in a mañana land.

Mamá's place is on the route leading from Heredia out to the airport, but it is set back from the main road, the second of three rental units on the property. It's a humble dwelling of cinder block with a corrugated tin roof, plywood walls, simply furnished. The long front room is divided into living and dining areas. A decorated live arborvitae Christmas tree stands in one corner. There is also a small kitchen area with a refrigerator and gas hotplate. I don't see an oven.

While Miriam and Roy take Éstefany to a clinic, the rest of us gather in various clusters around the dining room table or outdoors. We look at photo albums. Aunt Haydée has brought one from El Salvador, and we ad-

mire the only picture they have of Roberto as an infant. He is about three months old; his light olive skin contrasts a bit with the brightness of the cloth diaper and white T-shirt. He sits propped up on a white blanket next to his cousin César, Haydée's youngest. His ears stick out a little because his head is so small, but the round face and wistful look seem familiar.

The kids watch a home video the Cotos have brought from Panama. Mamá and Aunt Vilma have prepared a delicious meal of free-range chicken, rice with corn, and a tomato, lettuce, and heart of palm salad. We have to eat in shifts at the dining room table because there are so many of us.

In the afternoon some of us go for a long walk to the St. Joaquín Church. Nelson exclaims, "Finally I've found someone who walks like me!" We've always wondered why he saunters so slowly when he can run so fast. We can hardly believe this is an inherited characteristic. But it's obvious he and Toto have exactly the same gait.

Despite the heat, the older boys and Luis play some pickup soccer on a makeshift field in front of the church, while Tom, Derek, and I sit on a bench in the shade and watch. For Nelson, being physical like this is clearly the easiest way to bond with his father and brother. Dalila and Vilma are chatting with a woman who had stopped by the house earlier. Evidently she was Luis's compañera (comrade) in the FMLN. I hear they haven't seen each other for thirteen years. I wish I could understand what they are saying.

The day is full of surprises. Later Luis reads the investigative report for the first time. He cries when he sees the pictures of the dead guerrillas in the Honduran papers but insists that the woman pictured is not Mila. We're not quite sure what to make of that. With Roy's help as interpreter, Tom talks with him about what he and his first wife experienced in the 1980s. We get some sensational bits and pieces but no coherent narrative.

We gather that Luis was grievously wounded during a firefight. That he survived is a miracle in itself. His compañeros had to carry him on a stretcher through the mountains; his brother Reinaldo secretly sent blood. Later he was sent to Cuba for more medical treatment and rehabilitation. From this one conversation and Luis's first letter, we can gather that his and Mila's story is much more complicated than what was presented in the investigative résumé. Luis promises someday he'll write his story down so his son can better understand what happened back then.

The same problem exists in reverse. We find it difficult to answer their questions about how we came to adopt Nelson. Eva wants to know, for example, why we "chose him," but we tell her that—in a sense—he chose us, rather than the other way around. We explain that we didn't go to the orphanage to pick him out from among all the available children, and that we accepted him sight unseen—one could say, on faith. I too promise that someday I'll write it all down so they can better understand our complicated story.

Despite their efforts to include him in everything, and despite ours to comfort him, Derek is not finding it very easy to relate. He remains painfully shy. By evening he is asleep in a back bedroom, exhausted from the sheer effort of just being here. The older boys decide to go for another walk, and even though Tom and I would like to go back to the hotel, we think that is a good sign. The fathers have even managed to worry together about whether Toto and Nelson will be able to establish a brotherly bond.

Then, while the older boys are out, Eva provides an unanticipated bombshell as she announces that she and Roy are expecting a baby next summer. I don't need simultaneous translation to understand Mamá Chila's or Luis's body language as they react to this news. Eva will turn twenty next week. Roy has been her boyfriend a fairly long time and has the prospect of a good job someday, but he hasn't finished medical school yet. Eva has recently given up her university studies in order to work and save money. Will she manage to finish her schooling when she has a child to care for? Father and grandmother give the young people a lecture about the responsibilities of parenthood and everyone cries again.

Later in the week Roy admitted to me that he was really worried about becoming a father, and he asked me about what it is like to be a parent. I don't recall exactly what I answered, but I was acutely aware at the time of the challenge motherhood entails. I think I must have told him that being a parent was also a great joy. I know I tried to reassure him while cautioning him that a child would probably change the dynamic between him and Eva, but also offer the chance to deepen their relationship.

Perhaps I also ventured to say that becoming a parent unintentionally like this had its dangers. He would have to set aside some of his own immediate wants in order to give the child what it needed to thrive—his time and energy, his emotional and financial resources, and not just for a day or two but forever. If I offered advice it was simply that they should welcome the child with their whole hearts.

One of Nelson's many new cousins, Evelyn, one of Vilma's daughters who lives in El Salvador, wrote in our journal, "The feeling that fills my heart is indescribable. It feels like it is going to explode from the great sense of happiness." I was trying to identify with the joy these people must be experiencing as they met their grandson, son, brother, nephew, or cousin for the very first time. But quite honestly, the emotion that stirred most frequently within me was a profound sense of loss, the kind occasioned by parting, not reunion. This is probably the same sentiment many parents experience when they deliver their kid to college; they know full well that they are doing something for the good of the child, so he can develop as an adult to his fullest potential, yet it all comes home in a flash—now I really have to let go of him.

«   »

Four days into our stay, I slid into an emotional low. We had allowed Nelson to spend the day at the Muñoz family home in Coronado, about two hundred meters higher up in the mountains. On the one hand, we wanted to demonstrate how much we trusted the Cotos by letting him go off with his father and stepmother without us. On the other, it provided Tom, Derek, and me a little respite, allowing the three of us to act like tourists. In the morning we had enjoyed an entertaining visit to a coffee *finca* (plantation), and in the afternoon, Derek and I decided to go for a swim. When I hit the water of the hotel's pool, it was as if a dam had broken. Derek was distraught when he heard me sobbing uncontrollably and did his best to console me as we walked back to our rooms, but I think he was feeling as bereft as I.

On first learning of these developments, we had assumed it would be most difficult for Tom to adjust to the fact that Nelson had a second father who was alive, but I had underestimated how hard it would be for me to make room for a dead mother who could be romanticized and idealized, a mother who had never had to say no, at least not that Nelson could remember. I didn't doubt that he loved us, but on some level I felt threatened by this missing Mila.

Since our arrival, Nelson had naturally gravitated toward his biological family, especially his father and sisters, and he was treating me as routinely as ever. I caught myself thinking, He's hugging everyone but me; I'm just good enough to find his contact lens case, when he needs it. I couldn't help comparing the perfunctory way he was treating me to the ready embrace he had for everyone else, to whom he now extended all the sweet affection of which I knew he was capable.

Tom cried from time to time during the week, too, but he managed to bring me back from the edge on this particular afternoon, helping me uncover the good feelings about what was happening that had momentarily been buried underneath a cascade of more powerful emotions. From the moment we had gotten the investigative report and decided to go forward with the reunion, he had realized even more clearly than I that this would inevitably be a process of letting go.

Once I had stopped weeping, I could reflect on the fact that Nelson had already begun to pull away from me emotionally years before. Still, this necessary distancing seemed to be accelerating now. I couldn't help myself; I was grieving. A decade later, Nelson can write about this almost blithely:

> My adoptive parents were nervous that I would want to stay with my birth family but that never really crossed my mind. Since then I have been down about twice a year to visit them and we have become one big family. It's been truly amazing, and I'm so lucky to have had such wonderful adoptive parents who supported me all these years, especially when I went to meet my birth family.

At the time, however, I had no clue what he was thinking. He just didn't talk to me.

Looking back, I can see with some amusement that the best sign of Nelson's love for us was that he was taking us totally for granted. It probably never occurred to him that we needed reassurance. Ironically, at the same time that I was so upset and worried, I was also proud of the way he had been able to accept his birth family, readily showing all of them such affection, especially Éstefany, who clearly doted on him.

Tom and I had assured ourselves from the outset that we were prepared to share Nelson with his biological family, or we never would have embarked on this path, given their deeply felt needs as expressed so openly in the first letters we had received. Luis had phrased it in his second letter this way: "We will have to work harder and spend more time together to enjoy ourselves and make up for lost time."

We had vowed that we would help our son in whatever way we could to forge these new ties, but it wasn't yet evident how things would turn out. We had imagined that the reality of having another family might be quite seductive for our sixteen-year-old, that he might use it as an escape hatch from his difficulties in school. So we had already told him that—however things developed—we expected him to complete his college education in the United States. The choices he made later on as an adult about where he would live and work, and how he would relate to both families, would be his.

After only a few days, though, we could chuckle at some of our initial worries—that his older brother might lead him astray in some way, for example, to bars or who knows what. Toto was shy and retiring, and actually led a somewhat sheltered existence in his father's house. He was not exactly the street-smart young Latin man of our worst fears. He didn't smoke or drink. Neither did Luis, who appeared to be a hardworking family man with firm convictions.

We gathered that he had undergone a transformation during his years in Panama after leaving the guerrilla movement. At first he had led an itinerant existence, living in the mountains, working in Panama City and Colón. But things changed when he came to David in 1986 and met Miriam. With help from new friends and one of his brothers, he began to forge a new life, setting up his own business, and—under the influence of his wife and his father-in-law, pastor of a small Baptist congregation—he converted to evangelical Protestantism. For him, the unanticipated rediscovery of his missing son was clearly experienced as a kind of deliverance—as grace.

Our efforts to get Nelson to articulate his feelings during the course of our visit didn't get much of a response. After his first emotional reaction to seeing his father, grandmother, and siblings for the first time at the airport, he seemed laid back at times. Some of Nelson's maternal aunts even expressed disappointment that their nephew was not more verbally effusive. I explained that, added to his reluctance to speak Spanish, he was just like that. He was living in the moment and enjoying it, without saying much. We soon realized he was a lot like his older brother in this respect. He and Toto not only have the same gait, the same thick dark eyebrows, coffee-colored eyes, and coarse, wavy hair with a jagged hairline, but they both tend to keep their deepest feelings to themselves.

«   »

The days of our reunion were filled with simple pleasures, as well as a few group excursions, although these proved rather difficult to organize. Various groups went to the Gold Museum, the rain forest, a butterfly farm, and to the Poas volcano with its emerald-green crater lake. Its unusual clarity—one day in a hundred we were told—seemed fitted to our generally elevated mood. We attended a Christmas Eve service at the nearby Church of Maria Auxiliadora together, and gave each other presents and many hugs and kisses, but mostly we spent our time preparing and sharing meals, walking and talking, as we got to know each other as best we could in such a short time. We managed better than I had expected since we could depend on several bilingual speakers to help the rest of us jump over the formidable linguistic barriers.

The teens found they had less need of conversation. They went for walks and to a skating rink. They listened to music and danced while Nelson taught them some new moves; they played cards or pickup soccer; or they simply sat in the sun with their backs pressed against the wall of Mamá Chila's house, contemplating the tree-high poinsettia plant growing in the side yard, "hanging out" in the universal language of youth. As Eva put it in her journal entry on Christmas Day,

> Roberto, you are very special, and I don't have to speak to you very much, or know you that well, to notice this. It is sufficient enough to hug you to feel what you have in your heart. I hope that you are happy with all of this and with us—your other family—with humility and simplicity, we can bring you much of what we are accustomed to giving: LOVE.

In the course of our conversations with the adults, Tom and I gleaned more information about each side of the family. We understood that Luis and Mila had both come from the working- and lower-middle-class urban strata from which the various guerrilla organizations primarily drew their leadership cohort. In the wake of the civil war, both the Escobar and Coto families were widely dispersed, not only throughout Central America and Mexico but also in Seattle, New York, and Boston. Their socioeconomic status, as we could also discern, now covered a wide spectrum, from working to upper-middle class. Education had been the vehicle for their upward mobility.

The maternal and paternal sides of the family provided nearly mirror images. Ana Milagro, as we already knew, had been the youngest child, with six older sisters and a brother. Luis had also been the youngest, but with five older brothers and a sister. Mila's side dominated at the reunion, and the four sisters in attendance, Vilma, Dalila, Haydée, and Tita, helped me draw a family tree so I could get all the cousins straight. Dalila, a widow with two sons, proved invaluable as a translator, since—as we learned—she taught English in a San Salvador school. Marta Alicia (Tita), separated from her husband, worked as a secretary at the Technological University in San Salvador, and Haydée had worked in a factory that made sewing thread and as a domestic. When she first came to Costa Rica, Vilma had been a nanny. Later on she held a variety of factory and service-sector jobs. As they were raising a bevy of children and grandchildren, she and Mamá Chila had made the Salvadoran specialty, *pupusas*, tortillas filled with meat, cheese, or beans, and sold them on the street to make ends meet.

Given that we knew little thus far about the father's side of the family, we were surprised when one of Luis's brothers, Reinaldo, a comptroller for a Salvadoran company, showed up a few days after our arrival. He flew down from San Salvador with his wife, Ana-Doris, and son, Reinaldo Jr. They had arranged to stay in the same hotel, and over breakfast they shared more about Luis's family history and the little they knew of his involvement in the guerrilla movement. We learned that several of the other brothers were shopkeepers. Mariano, the brother closest to Luis in age, who played an important role in the family drama, owned an auto-parts shop in Zacamil, the working-class neighborhood where Luis and Mila met. This area of San Salvador is still considered a stronghold of the FMLN. His wife, Reina, sold candy, sodas, and cigarettes out of another tiny shop housed in the front room of their apartment.

From the beginning of our correspondence, both families had repeatedly expressed their pleasure that we were able to afford Nelson an "exemplary education," and we could already see that they hoped that each of their children and grandchildren could improve his or her socioeconomic situation through further education and training. We learned that several Salvadoran cousins were already college graduates—one daughter on the father's side had become a physician, and a son on the mother's side was an electrical engineer.

Recently graduated from high school and already working in his father's silk-screening business, Toto planned to take a technical degree, and Mireya hoped to do the same when she graduated from high school the following year. Like Nelson, many of these young people seem to excel in mathematics and gravitate toward technological subjects. Despite his reticence to articulate it, Nelson seemed able to handle all the people who wanted to show their love for him and—more than that—wanted him to love them in return. He was clearly happy about what had happened, basking in all the attention and feeling at peace.

«   »

Understandably, Derek was having more difficulty with the whole scene. In the first few days of our visit, he'd withdraw to a back room to sleep or read. He was reluctant to speak Spanish although he excelled in the subject at school. Luis and Mamá Chila were especially attentive to him, however, as were Tom and I. On an excursion to the rainforest the eldest Muñoz daughter made a point of sitting next to him on the bus, chatting with him in English, as Toto and Nelson were sitting together across the aisle and had begun to communicate more about their mutual interests: sports, computer design, and photography.

This particular day-trip to the Teleférico del Bosque Lluvioso Reserve, adjoining the Braulio Carrillo National Park, helped to change Derek's whole mood. Zoology is one of his passions. He got to see those fascinating leaf-cutter ants, with the smaller ones riding as guards on top of the leaf fragments carried by the army of workers. At the open-air thatched-roof hut where we ate lunch, he could admire various iridescent hummingbirds and the raccoon-like coati that came to look for leftovers. On the hike through the understory, we saw a Morpho butterfly and an inch-long bullet ant that can give a painful sting. Our guide explained which plants were edible or medicinal. We glimpsed a capuchin white-faced monkey, a toucan, and a white bat, but Derek's competitive streak got a boost when he was the only one to identify a red and blue tanager from the aerial tram.

There was one other avenue that really helped Derek out of his shell. He had a major assignment for his English and history classes on the topic of immigration due by February, and he had asked for permission to work on Nelson's story rather than choosing the history of either Tom's family or mine. Because he needed to conduct some taped interviews for this project, he had to open up to various relatives. By the end of our stay, he had begun to play cards with Fernando and kick a soccer ball around with the older boys. He gradually realized that Nelson's biological family was not trying to drive a wedge between him and his brother; rather, they wished to draw him in as a member of their family.

Miriam expressed this sentiment in our journal when she said that they felt so privileged to be able "to share in the lives of such beautiful young people like Roberto and Derek. Theirs are the lives we believe are special and will be blessed by God." Mireya also made a point of including all of us in her entry: "It has really been an unforgettable experience, incredible. Until now I had never experienced the greatness of God. I have never seen a miracle as great as this. [. . .] I feel that every one of us knows how to communicate through the universal language that is love and care that we feel not only for Roberto but for Thomas, Margaret, and Derek."

More important, Derek was the first person to whom Mamá Chila wrote after we returned home. She wanted to make sure that he knew he was included in the invitation they had extended to Nelson to return for a visit the following summer:

19 January 1998

Hello my grandson.

How are you doing? I hope that you are very well along with your family and that you are studying hard. What a joy to know that you are such a good student who studies really magnificently. I have heard that Nelson is coming here in June, and I hope that you can come with him. We would be very happy to have you come too. We have no other motivation than that we don't want you to ever feel left out, and I imagine you might feel sad if Nelson comes and you don't. Thus, I want to make sure that you know that you are invited too, and that we hope you can come. OK? I really hope that all is well with you. I close this letter to you with all my love.

Receive my kisses and hugs from your grandmother
La Mamá Chila

«   »

On the day before our departure from Costa Rica, Luis asked to write in our journal a second time. He begins his entry almost philosophically:

In our life there have been grand and sad moments that have transformed what we do and our desire to live for something worthwhile. These special moments form part of our reason for living.

Each day of my life my thoughts flew, picturing an image of Roberto daydreaming about finding us. I shivered thinking that you could possibly have been in danger due to the conditions when you disappeared, and thinking that maybe your organs could have been used, but also thinking that maybe you were adopted by a good family.

When I found out that some people had adopted you, I was happy, but I was sad at the same time because it was impossible to know where you were exactly. I looked for you. Trying to find out who had adopted you was always on my mind. I worked for a reunion because I was sure that one day God would grant me the opportunity to see Roberto, and I would recognize him out of thousands of people, and that comforted me.

But eternal thanks are to God, thanks to God for Thomas, Margaret, Roberto, and Derek for also wanting this reunion and for permitting it. When I read your letter for the first time I cried a lot from happiness and joy, and I formed an image of Sra. Margaret and Sr. Thomas—of how they were—beautiful people with a special family formed by such good feelings. Now that I know them, and we share a son, I know how human they are. I know how special their hearts are, and their goodness that is reflected in their looks.

Thanks for being how you are, for giving us in this time together—the 16 years of missed happiness—an eternity of happiness. Thank you Margaret, and Thomas thank you. Thank you Roberto for being how you are, thank you Derek for sharing and feeling part of us, and know that you are also in our hearts and that we love you. May God protect you and bless you always. I love you.

Luis Coto (José)

Only as I re-read his journal entry to write this chapter did I notice that Luis had signed himself on this one occasion with not only his given name but also his pseudonym from his days as a guerrillero—José. We had wanted to find out more about this part of his identity, but it would take several years before we could ask the most difficult questions. Only as visits back and forth bound us closer together, and mutual trust grew, could we begin to penetrate a past so fraught with pain and feelings of guilt. I realized there were some questions that would probably never yield a fully satisfying answer. Ambiguities remain to this day, yet eventually we were able to put many more pieces of his history together.

«   »

A photo that sits on my desk always reminds me of this particular part of the story. It was taken at the airport the day of our departure and captures the "miracle" that had taken place during our short reunion that Mireya had grasped so well—we were already on our way to becoming one family. The five siblings stand grouped closely together, Nelson in the rear, holding a giant pencil covered with hearts that had just been

given to him by Éstefany as a parting gift. His left arm is slung casually over Derek's shoulder, while his other arm rests on Toto's, his right hand grasping his brother's striped jersey as if to not let go of him. Their shy smiles match completely. Toto rests his right hand easily on Eva's shoulder as she stands close to Derek and clasps Éstefany with both arms in front. Éstefany is holding her bear with its red and blue Patriots sweater. A black baseball cap covers Derek's blond head, but his twinkling blue eyes are visible beneath the visor and his braces gleam in a genuine grin. His face is pale in contrast with the dark green of his sweater, but he could be taken for Eva's brother, since her complexion is also fair, complementing her green eyes. Behind Nelson's left arm, one can just make out the profile of his cousin Lucy.

The kids love this photo that has become something of a family icon. From time to time they stage the same arrangement in order to have another like it. They like to compare how they have grown and changed. In December 2004 they laughed as Éstefany took her position in front with her assorted stuffed animals, for at thirteen she was so much taller that she practically blocked the siblings who stood behind.

A large contingent of Cotos and Escobars accompanied us to the airport on December 28, 1997, and they stayed until we emerged from the terminal over an hour later to board our flight. We were surprised as we walked across the brightly sunlit tarmac to see them all still standing there, strung out along the chain-link fence at the far side of the field, waving and blowing kisses as we climbed the stairs—and, no doubt, until we completely disappeared from view as the plane lifted into the clouds.

PART TWO

Their Stories

FOUR

Putting the Pieces Together, 1952–1992

MISSING PIECES: BOSTON, AUGUST 2005

We have invited Mamá Chila; Nelson's siblings Eva, Toto, and Éstefany; and his niece, Daniela, to come from Central America to join us for a week of celebration surrounding Nelson's graduation from Wentworth Institute of Technology. Their visit to Boston comes at an opportune time. Since my return from Central America in February, I've managed to draft the first three chapters of this book—our part of the story—something I'd been promising the children I would do for years.

When we first met, Eva had posed the question, "Why did you choose Roberto from among all the available children?" Our answer then—"Well, it didn't quite happen the way you may imagine"—couldn't satisfy her justifiable curiosity. Added to the complexities of international adoption, our rather unusual experience seemed impossible to explain fully in 1997. Now, I have decided not to wait to finish the book. I will give her and Toto each a copy of the first draft to take home with them, since Chapter 1 holds all the explanation I can muster.

It was as difficult for Nelson's biological family to comprehend why we had adopted this particular child as it was for us to understand what they were telling us about their experiences in the 1980s. At first, having nothing else to go on, we had simply accepted the storyline of the investigative report, but as soon as we met, it became clear that there was much more to it.

Although the core truth was certain—their missing Roberto was our Nelson—some of the specifics remained hazy. Beneath the unanimity occasioned by our reunion, we sensed there ran an undercurrent of disagreement among members of Nelson's birth family, who shared nei-

ther the same experience of nor even the same perspective on the political turmoil of the 1970s and 80s. To our surprise, however, Luis, Mamá
Chila, and Mila's sisters all agreed on one thing—the dead woman pictured in the Honduran paper was not Ana Milagro.

During that reunion week, we saw Luis cry while reading the investigative report. He was also eager to place his actions in a somewhat different light. The day after we arrived, he had taken Tom aside to talk in
the street in front of Mamá Chila's house while the women prepared a
meal and the children kicked a soccer ball around the yard. Back in our
hotel that evening Tom recorded everything he could remember of this
initial conversation, for which Eva's boyfriend had provided simultaneous translation. Much of the information Luis offered us was confusing.
Dramatic subplots suddenly took center stage—a nearly fatal shooting,
power struggles within the revolutionary command structure, betrayals,
murder, and suicide.

Not only were there many more characters than we had suspected,
but the action spread across the Central American map and beyond:
El Salvador and Honduras, of course, but also Nicaragua, Costa Rica,
Panama, and Cuba. Luis later insisted, in an interview I arranged with
a colleague in the Spanish department when he attended Nelson's high
school graduation in June 2000, "I want my story to be told, not just for
Roberto but for other young people."

The familial narrative that I construct in this chapter is based on
many informal conversations with members of the Escobar and Coto
families since 1997, and on videotaped interviews with Mamá Chila
and Luis when they visited us in Boston in 1999 and 2000, respectively.
Then, on December 24, 2004, when we were visiting the Coto family in
Panama, Luis surprised us by hosting a testimonial luncheon for a gathering of about forty family members and friends at which he offered an
entire master narrative of his life. We have that on audiotape, and the
next day I was able to ask some follow-up questions with his three adult
children present. Added to this are the more informal conversations I
had with family the following January and February in both Costa Rica
and El Salvador.

Members of the family have also provided me with personal documents: letters, newspaper clippings, and photos. These, as well as other
primary and secondary sources to which I will refer, have helped me
place the story of Luis, Mila, and their children into the much broader
picture of the Salvadoran conflict. I have relied on the work of investigative journalists and historians to better understand the familial ac-

counts, but I write neither as a journalist nor a historian would, so I have sought to understand rather than to corroborate their testimonies. Like the old puzzles that my grandfather cut with a jigsaw, there are pieces that have been irretrievably lost. Even after assembling what everyone can remember or was willing to tell and setting those "facts" within a historical framework, gaps remain.

«   »

Before I begin writing this chapter, however, I'm eager to find out what Eva thinks about something I've only recently discovered: a connection that might help us find a few of those missing pieces. The day before Nelson's graduation, I have a chance to sit down with her. "See this woman?" I point to a photo on the first page of an online article that was posted in February. Only days after my return from Central America, President George W. Bush had announced his appointment of John Negroponte—the ambassador to Iraq—to the newly created post of director of intelligence. The headline was a teaser—"Negroponte Draws Criticism South of Border"—but the accompanying picture was what really drew my attention to this article among the many reactions to the news of the appointment.[1]

A middle-aged woman rests her chin on her left hand and looks sadly but firmly at the camera. Behind her sags a blue and white banner—the flag of Honduras—with sketched portraits of the disappeared and detained superimposed on its fading colors. The man in the center wears one of the flag's stars in the middle of his forehead like a bull's-eye. In his shirt and tie, he appears to be a white-collar worker, a young man trying to make a living for his family. Under what circumstances had he disappeared? To his right one can see the face of an unidentified young woman with long dark hair swept back from her round face. She could be any twenty-something who had gone missing in those days. For me she stands in for Ana Milagro.

Although Eva is looking at the picture too and trying to read the caption, she doesn't react immediately. I point to the woman in front of the banner more emphatically, explaining, "She's the coordinator of COFADEH, the Honduran human rights organization that conducted the investigation about Roberto. When I was going over the original documents this past summer in order to write the first part of the book, I found her name on all the correspondence. She's the person who appealed to the Honduran Court of Minors for access to the adoption records, the one who found the newspaper articles and sent the information to Pro-búsqueda in El Salvador."

I hardly allow time for this to sink in before clicking on another web page. "It has never occurred to me before, Eva, but of course, COFADEH has its own site. See these lists? They're still trying to find out what happened to the 184 Hondurans and Salvadorans who are known to have disappeared there during the 1980s. I checked; your mother isn't listed. Her case must be considered closed. But this Berta Oliva might know something more now about what actually happened in May 1982 than she did a decade ago. Eva, my Spanish isn't good enough, but you could contact her"—I catch my breath, and end the sentence with question intonation—"if you think it's a good idea?"

Eva gazes at me pointedly, and her eyes seem to be asking, Don't you know better than that? Her look makes it clear she doesn't want to open any new investigative avenue. Then she says sadly, "Margaret, you know I don't always want to be digging up the past. And thinking about what happened to my mother is just too hard for me. Do we really need to know exactly what went on in Tegucigalpa, whether my mother is the dead woman pictured in the newspaper or not?" I respect her resistance and let it go.

« »

For a moment, though, I have to return to the article that got me started on this track, for it resonates with another unanswered question—not what Berta Oliva might know now, but what John Negroponte might have known then of the episode involving Mila and baby Roberto. At the time of his previous confirmation hearings, Negroponte's years as ambassador to Honduras (1981–1985) were reopened to public scrutiny. This article recalls how his appointment to ambassador to the United Nations in 2001 was delayed six months over what he knew of the source of the funds being funneled to the anti-Sandinista contras operating out of Honduras, and what he knew about human rights abuses being committed by the Honduran military in the 1980s. Then September 11th changed the equation, and his confirmation was rushed to a positive conclusion.

This time, documents Negroponte had declassified when he briefly left the diplomatic service for the private sector in the 1990s were being made public because of a Freedom of Information Act petition. They showed not only that Negroponte knew of the Iran-contra connection but also that his involvement in the "paramilitary operations against Nicaragua" was a "role that normally would be reserved for the (CIA) station chief."[2] Ironically, this involvement was a boost to his résumé for the intelligence post.

Above all, this article makes clear that human rights activists "south of the border" had long since drawn their conclusions about his involvement in their "dirty wars." It cites a 1993 human rights report prepared by a law professor and issued by the Honduran government, for example: "They used outlawed methods to kill [. . .], and it is absolutely impossible to believe that a diplomatic mission such as that of the United States was unaware of the situation."[3] It is no wonder that Negroponte's elevation to a position at the pinnacle of U.S. intelligence had met with such a strong response from Oliva, among others.

This news appeared in Salvadoran papers too. Dalila sent me several clippings from *La Prensa Gráfica*, including one in which Oliva is quoted more fully: "What an outrage! The United States of America has invented a position to reward a nefarious personality in the history of Central America."[4] Another article blames Negroponte outright on account of his identification with U.S. policies and his known connections to Gustavo Álvarez Martínez and other generals: "Driver of the doctrine of national security that the U.S. applied in the eighties, Negroponte has been linked to generals who took part in coups, with violators of human rights, and with death squads in various Central American countries including El Salvador."[5]

All that is offered here is guilt by association, but as if in answer to my unspoken question, the headline of this second article asserts, "Lo sabrá todo, todo" (He Knows Everything, Everything). In another article that appeared at the same time in Britain, Mrs. Negroponte reacts to a similar insinuation: "I want to say to those people: Haven't you moved on?"[6] For those families who lost loved ones to the U.S. national security doctrine of that time and place, the answer is, of course, a resounding "no." Stories remain to be told. This is just one of them.

FORMATION OF THE VANGUARD: EL SALVADOR, 1952–1972

Our story begins just a little over twenty years after the 1932 *Matanza* (slaughter), with the birth of Luis Noé Coto Amaya during the rainy season. The seventh of Adrián and Estebana Amaya de Coto's children was born July 6, 1952, in the village of San Ildefonso in the department of

San Vicente. Four and a half years later, on the second day of 1957, Ana Milagro Escobar Angulo was born in the city of San Salvador to Héctor and Lucila Angulo de Escobar. The youngest of eight, she was nicknamed Anita, but later on, the reference to "miracle" suggested by her second given name must have seemed more apt. "Mila" stuck. I wonder: did the fact that each was the youngest child in a large family make them mature more quickly? What set them on the path that transformed them into José and Iris, revolutionary compañeros who were willing to set aside concerns for their own safety and that of their families in order to fight for what they believed in?

In his 2004 testimonial, Luis vividly recalled for us the grinding poverty of his childhood: "Everyone had to work just to make ends meet. One day I was sent with my older brothers to clear a field of boulders. We labored all day in the hot sun, all six of us. It was backbreaking work. At the end of the day, I saw with dismay that we'd cleared only half the field. I thought to myself that there must be some way to improve oneself so that one would not have to work like this the rest of one's life."

The task he had to perform that day must have seemed overwhelming to the eight-year-old. Yet, instead of despairing, it infused him with the desire to change things. In the economy of his master narrative, at least, the experience marks an early end to childhood naïveté. Whether he arrived at his ambition to rise above the circumstances of his birth in exactly this way is beside the point. We can be sure that Luis's determination to find a way out of poverty took firm root at an early age.

Although they had little formal education, Luis's parents hoped they might give their children a chance at a better life by moving to San Martín, a town about thirty miles from San Salvador and just off the Pan-American highway. During my 2005 stay with the family, I stopped there with Dalila Escobar and some staff from the nongovernmental organization Save the Children, after we had seen several of their early childhood development sites in the countryside.[7] Although San Ildefonso is in a different department, it occurred to me that the site of Luis's early childhood might be a lot like the villages I visited that morning in Cuscatlán.

I imagine a rutted dirt road, washed out in the rainy season, and a trek of several kilometers each day for Noémi—the only daughter—to fetch drinking water from the place where you have to ford a silt-filled river to get up to the village; cows bar the way as they stand in the mud alongside women washing clothes. On the steep hillside, houses with dirt floors and thatched or corrugated tin roofs provide basic shelter, or none at all when an earthquake or flood unleashes a mudslide. Each classroom of the elementary school overflows with over forty children to one teacher. During recess the kids laugh as they run around, kicking up the white dust in the schoolyard, and a skinny dog that has been taking a siesta wanders off.

The streets of San Martín, brimming with activity among the whitewashed and tiled houses and colorful market stalls, must have been an exciting change for an impressionable young boy. Luis evidently maintained the fire in his belly and took advantage of every opportunity the town afforded. He not only attended but also graduated from high school. This would still be considered an unusual achievement today, since many children born in rural areas drop out of school in the first few grades. Luis also got practical training as a tailor.

«   »

One evening during my stay in San Salvador in February 2005, I was sitting with two of Luis's older brothers in the back of Mariano's apartment while his wife, Reina, sold cigarettes and candy out front to a man and little boy, who were happy to find her convenience store open at that late hour. I had prepared my questions in Spanish and gotten Mariano's and Reinaldo's permission to tape our conversation, but I was a little nervous since I remembered from our 1999 visit that the Coto brothers were notably taciturn.

"What was Luis like as a teen?" I asked. They remembered that their youngest brother was very serious, and that he was willing to work hard to realize his dreams. "He always wanted to improve himself," Mariano stated. Reinaldo expanded a bit: "He was quite young, but he had the ambition to set up a business making men's trousers. Only he ran right into the economic realities in our country. He learned the hard way that there was a monopoly on fabric, and it was only sold to certain people." Those realities included the fact that the oligarchy that controlled the land also held the economic levers of power. Luis discovered early on that there were social barriers to his aspirations, but he was not deterred.

Timing played a decisive role in determining his future. A revolutionary vanguard was beginning to form in El Salvador in the late 1960s as the economic situation worsened in the aftermath of the so-called Soccer War. A long-simmering border dispute had boiled over in July 1969 after several bitterly contested games. The conflict lasted four days and took about four thousand lives before the Organization of American States arranged a precarious ceasefire. Afterward, the Salvadoran econ-

omy simply could not absorb the estimated one hundred thousand returning refugees—approximately a third of the Salvadorans who had settled over the years on small plots just across the border in Honduras.
The dispossessed joined the cohorts of un- or underemployed.[8]

Issues of political power became enmeshed with resentments over
economic and social inequalities during these years. Unions were growing in strength, including the teachers' union, ANDES (Asociación Nacional de Educadores Salvadoreños). Luis witnessed street fights that
broke out between the police and union organizers in San Martín, but
he told us that it was the words of certain activist teachers in his school
that had an even greater impact. Yet he emphasizes that he was no different from other kids who chaffed against the curfews imposed by the government: "Many of us felt the need to actively participate in the growing
conflicts over economic issues and in the demand for social justice."

«   »

At first Tom and I were under the mistaken impression that Luis
had been influenced by liberation theology and its "preferential option
for the poor," but we learned that was much less important for his trajectory than developments taking place at the same time within the Salvadoran Communist Party (PCS).[9] Since the 1930s when it was outlawed,
the PCS had remained a clandestine wing of its legal political front that
continued to contest elections. In the summer of 1968, party members
disagreed about the wisdom of the Soviet-led Warsaw Pact invasion of
Czechoslovakia. They clashed the following year over support for the
Salvadoran government in its war with Honduras. The party's secretary
general, Salvador Cayetano Carpio, formerly head of the bakers' union,
broke abruptly with the PCS and began to develop his own clandestine
group, beginning with a band of six followers. He argued that an entirely
new party was needed to provide leadership for an armed struggle that
would issue forth a prolonged "people's war."[10]

Carpio rejected *foquismo*, with its emphasis on the rapid military
overthrow of a repressive government by a small revolutionary cadre—
a popular doctrine among Latin American socialists since the 1959 Cu-
ban revolution, despite its subsequent failure in Guatemala and Peru
and the annihilation of Ernesto (Ché) Guevara's guerrilla force in Bo-
livia. By contrast, Carpio believed one must first recruit and educate an
extended rear guard, then build coalitions with peasants, and finally organize the masses until a popular front could rise up in a general insur-

rection within one's own country.[11] As his group grew and began to take on a more public role around 1971, it took the name FPL-FM (Fuerzas Populares de Liberación—Farabundo Martí), thereby stressing its connection to the martyr of the 1932 insurrection. Carpio became "Comandante Marcial."

In the early 1970s the FPL was promoting the organization of secondary school pupils as well as university students and sponsoring secret gatherings to enlist new adherents. Luis told us that an older cousin, whom he admired because he was a medical doctor, brought him to his first meeting: "I learned more about the exploitation and misery of the workers and peasants. At the beginning the FPL had very good ideas and exhibited high moral values. I was attracted to their ideals and the Marxist-Leninist theories that supported them. I too believed that we had to free our people from a repressive government. Now I began to see a way to do this."[12]

As part of his indoctrination Luis had to learn more about socialist theory, but also about how to use weapons. There was no doubt that the *lucha* (struggle) they were preparing for would be an armed one. He was still working as a tailor and even dreamed of going to college, but once he became a member of the FPL, his studies only served as a front for his political activities. "Being a guerrillero was a full-time job," he stated quite simply. He took the pseudonym José. With the exception of the cousin who had recruited him, his nom de guerre was kept secret from friends and family.

TWO WEDDINGS, TWO IDENTITIES:
EL SALVADOR, 1972–1976

The fraudulent election of 1972 proved a turning point for all the nascent guerrilla organizations. A center-left coalition had clearly won the contest, but the election results were overturned and the military installed Colonel Arturo Armando Molina as president. Outrage at the massive fraud that had been perpetrated roiled the National University in San Salvador. This time it wasn't indigenous peasants or trade unionists but largely middle-class students who experienced the heavy hand of political repression. Government troops occupied the campus in July 1972; the faculty was disbanded and the rector sent into exile. It remained closed for two years.

Some members of the political parties with which the guerrillas had earlier broken became disillusioned with the electoral process at this point. Frustration at their political exclusion led to more protests on city streets and in the countryside, accompanied by brutal repression by the Molina regime, including the use of paramilitary death squads. This in turn fueled the expansion of the revolutionary movement. Marcial never-theless argued that there would still need to be a long process of coali-tion building between the largely urban, middle- and working-class mil-itants, who had come either from the universities or the trade unions, and the mass of Salvadoran peasants.

Since the FPL was intent on organizing in the campo, José was sent to the countryside to recruit and train members of the newly created peasants' union, the UTC (Unión de Trabajadores del Campo).[13] Af-ter only a short time, however, he contracted typhoid fever from drink-ing contaminated water and was forced to return home. His mother had moved to Zacamil, a working-class district in the capital. She could not afford proper medical care for her son, but as his condition worsened, a relative who worked in a hospital managed to get Luis admitted. He was twenty years old; a prolonged convalescence gave him time to think of other things besides his mission.

«   »

Meanwhile, Mila's mother, Lucila Angulo, had left her alcoholic husband, Héctor Escobar, and—thanks to her father's generosity—owned an apartment in Zacamil. She was living with her eldest daugh-ters, Vilma and Haydée, and her youngest, Mila, who was fifteen and had finished ninth grade. There were young children in their household, Mila's nieces and nephews, but no husbands. Mila was helping out at home and taking classes at an institute. Her older sisters thought she was learning to be a seamstress, so they bought her a sewing machine to sup-port her aspirations. While Mamá Chila, Vilma, and Haydée were at work, Mila took care of the children. Once the university reopened in 1974, Mila told her family she was taking karate lessons there at night. Mamá realized much later that this was probably a cover; she must have been going to political meetings.

Luis saw Mila for the first time in Zacamil as he walked from his mother's place across the field between the apartment blocks to visit his grandmother, who lived in the same building as the Escobars. They be-came "romantically involved," as he put it, without expanding on this part of his narrative. Her family can't say much about their romance ei-

ther. Yet these four years between 1972 and 1976 were when all the decisive moves occurred: Luis approached Mila, they fell in love, he introduced her to the FPL, she joined, and they decided to get married and
to commit themselves to the revolutionary movement full time.

Her sisters only remember that they were "definitely a couple" for
about two years before they married, but they thought the wedding took
place in October 1975. Haydée had to go to the registry to get a copy of
the wedding certificate in order to establish the exact date for me. Their
memories had been off by a whole year—it was November 11, 1976.

Luis insists that he and Mila fell in love when she was fifteen, not
long after they first met. That would have been in 1972. As neighbors
they certainly had opportunities to get together without anyone taking
much notice. In addition, as it turned out, they were both attending
the same school at the time, the Instituto Nacional General Francisco
Menéndez.

Mamá Chila told me she did not know that the institute was a place
where the guerrillas actively recruited. Accusations along these lines
were made publicly by October 1980, when *La Prensa Gráfica* carried
a photograph ostensibly showing the institute's graduates being given
weapons training. The participants are wearing bandanas to hide their
faces.[14] Luis admits that they were being prepared both "physically and
mentally for the lucha." We can be sure Mila was learning something
besides sewing.

«   »

Politically, there was a great deal happening during these four years,
and Luis and Mila were certainly involved. By 1973 Luis, in his role as
José, had been assigned to drive Marcial around San Salvador and had
therefore met him several times in person. Things were kept so secret
that he did not realize that the man in the backseat was his *comandante
jefe* (commander-in-chief) until a compañero filled him in.

Around that time, another small militant group emerged, the ERP
(Ejército Revolucionario del Pueblo). At first Marcial had not been interested in working with the group because of its distinctly Christian
base and its push for immediate armed insurrection; he continued to
take the long view and emphasized the importance of enlisting the peasants. Nevertheless, in 1974 the FPL forged some rudimentary ties with
the ERP. The following year the ERP abducted a well-known industrialist and killed another man in a botched kidnapping. And in a bloody dis-

pute over strategy, one of their leaders, the internationally renowned poet Roque Dalton, was purged.[15] After his execution one faction splintered off and re-created itself under a different name, the RN (Resistencia Nacional). The incident serves here as a reminder of how internal power struggles were often brutally resolved within such militant groups.[16]

The year 1975 also brought more violence to the countryside, as well as to the streets of San Salvador. One incident took the life of Mamá Chila's father, Salvador Ramón Angulo. She first told me about it in January 2005, as the thirtieth anniversary of his death approached.

In 2003 Mamá and Vilma had been able to acquire some land in Santa Bárbara de Heredia, Costa Rica. When I visited them in January 2005, they were still putting the finishing touches on their house, but they were happy to be able to call a home their own. Before this they had moved eleven times from one rental property to another. We were sitting on the back patio with Eva, who had agreed to help me with translation as needed, since I was doing my best to conduct the interview in Spanish.

Mamá spoke very respectfully of her father, although she also laughed when she told me, "He had sixty children. And I can name about forty-seven of them!" Angulo was the manager of a large hacienda, La Normandía, in Usulután department, near the Pacific Ocean, the heart of the cotton-growing region. "He was in charge of the payroll for several thousand laborers," Mamá explained. "One day in February he was called out to the farm on a ruse. When he discovered his boss was not there, he headed back to town, but he was ambushed."

When I mentioned the incident a few weeks later to Haydée, the family "archivist," she rummaged in her papers and showed me a yellowed clipping—the front-page story that had appeared in *La Prensa Gráfica* at the time. It shows a dramatic picture of her grandfather's Jeep riddled with bullet holes, and inset photos of Angulo and his son, Oscar, who—though seriously injured—had been rescued. I could read that the motives for the attack remained unclear as the payroll money had not been stolen, and the criminals were evidently never identified.

Mamá Chila was nevertheless convinced they must have been leftists who associated this "honorable man" with the wealthy landowner for whom he worked. In her recollection there had been three attackers; five were reported. It makes little difference. The perpetrators got away, and, as the newspaper account puts it, the seventy-three-year-old "died of his wounds."[17] After that, Lucila Angulo had little sympathy for the guerrillas. I have to wonder how Mila—already training as an FPL militant—reacted to her grandfather's murder.

« »

Less than six months later, in July 1975, a band of several thousand university students marched in protest from campus toward central San Salvador. Army troops lay in wait at an underpass; a volley of gunfire erupted. No one knows how many were actually killed; estimates range widely from six to thirty-seven. Some were wounded, and among those arrested some "disappeared." The FPL and ERP leaders agreed on a combined response. As the two groups jointly occupied the Metropolitan Cathedral the next day, another student demonstration was broken up violently elsewhere in the city and deaths were reported.[18]

Capitalizing on the public outcry in the wake of these incidents, the largest of five Salvadoran mass organizations emerged at this juncture, the BPR (Bloque Popular Revolucionario). Like the other mass organizations it "drew together already existing groups and their already active memberships into something new."[19] The BPR's strength rested on its strong peasant base, but it also included some urban poor. ANDES, the teachers' union that had been active in the vanguard since 1968, joined forces with the new bloc, which had covert ties to the FPL and thus provided it with a vital link to both intellectuals and student activists. The key figure among the ANDES leaders was the former teacher Dr. Mélida Anaya Montes. She quickly advanced to second in command in the FPL and was thereafter referred to by her pseudonym, Ana María. Both she and Marcial were to play a significant part in the story of Mila and Luis.[20]

The day after their civil wedding at Mila's home, a beloved compañero, Roberto Siprían—for whom their third child was later named—conducted what Luis termed a "wedding at arms." The couple pledged their love and loyalty to the revolutionary movement and vowed to give their lives, if need be, to reach its goals. The two weddings emphasize the double life they were already leading by November 1976. On the one hand, they were Mila and Luis, students and—as it says in their *cedulas* (personal identity cards)—small merchants. On the other hand, they had assumed the names Iris and José as guerrillas of the FPL. "Because we were entirely dependent on each other and were always in great danger," Luis emphasizes, "we forged a strong bond at the outset."

CLANDESTINE LIVES: EL SALVADOR, 1977–1979

The couple's subversive activities had to be carried out clandestinely. Reinaldo Coto recalls that soon after the wedding, Luis and Mila "simply dropped out sight," but he thought little of it since he himself was preoccupied with his university studies. Both families evidently accepted the fact that "business" took the couple away for months at a time. In reality the pair had not gone to Guatemala as Mila's sisters thought, but into hiding in the capital. More than a year later, as Mamá Chila remembered, her daughter showed up with a baby girl in her arms—Eva.[21]

At his December 2004 testimonial, Luis told us for the first time more about their dangerous life in the urban underground:

> We participated in many actions around the city and stayed in safe houses with weapons caches. Once, one of the compañeros in our cell was captured, but he did not reveal our hiding place. Mila's first pregnancy was a particularly difficult time for us. One firefight we knew about moved us deeply. Our beloved compa Eva [Elizabeth Ramírez] died after a shootout with government troops [in Santa Tecla]. The guerrillas fought bravely for eleven and a half hours, but when they finally ran out of ammunition, they wrote on the walls in their own blood our slogan—"FPL Revolution or Death." Then they committed suicide. They didn't want to be taken alive to be tortured; someone might reveal the whereabouts of others of us.
>
> On the last day of 1977 our daughter, Eva Nátaly, was born. We named her for this martyred compañera who was our hero. But the danger wasn't over. Not long after that, we heard the police were coming to search the safe house where we were staying. Some neighbor must have suspected us. Mila was able to escape with Eva before the police came, but I was under orders to remain there. Miraculously, when the police did come, they didn't really search the house. They would have found weapons. We felt lucky to have survived that whole period.[22]

In 1977 what were widely regarded as fraudulent elections led to the installation of another general, Carlos Humberto Romero, as president. The defeated opposition candidate mounted a protest vigil, attended by tens of thousands of supporters. The numbers of his supporters began to dwindle after he left the country for exile in Costa Rica, but several thousand demonstrators were still gathered in the Plaza de la Libertad on February 28th. Without provocation, the army attacked them. The exact number of dead and wounded was disputed. The government admitted to only eight deaths. Other sources claim that hundreds were killed or wounded, and as many as five hundred arrested.[23] The government subsequently declared a state of siege. In May, the priest who had said mass on this occasion was assassinated.

« »

In other parts of the country, the blood of priests was also being spilled. Not long after the February massacre in San Salvador, Father Rutilio Grande was assassinated near the town of Aguilares. He had been ministering to peasants in the spirit of liberation theology. The government viewed Jesuits like Grande as supporters of the guerrillas. Most of them had come to El Salvador from abroad. The death squad known as UGB (Unión Guerrera Blanca) saw it as their special duty to rid the country of these "communist subversives" and issued an ultimatum that the remaining forty-six Jesuits either leave the country or be eliminated. All these developments occurred shortly after Oscar Arnulfo Romero was named archbishop, and they proved to be the catalyst for his transformation from a man thought to be sympathetic to the oligarchy to a champion of the poor and an open critic of the regime.[24]

By the end of the year constitutional guarantees had been suspended, allowing the military "virtual *carte blanche* to pick up anyone it remotely suspected of being subversive in word or deed."[25] The following year, 1978, brought no relief. In the capital, the Fuerzas Armadas (Armed Forces) and its regular police arm, the Policia de Hacienda (Treasury Police), as well as paramilitary death squads came increasingly into play on the government side.[26] However, despite curfews and the constant threat of extrajudicial killings, the government could not stop the mass organizations from mounting more marches and demonstrations. Escalation among the clandestine guerrilla organizations took the form of direct attacks on army installations and kidnappings for ransom.[27]

In the countryside, clashes between guerrilla groups and death squads were also increasing. ORDEN (Organización Democrática Nacionalista), for example, had been organized in the 1960s as the rural arm of a multilayered National Guard and trained in anti-insurgency techniques with the help of the CIA and Green Berets. After 1974 it began to act as a separate paramilitary force. By 1978 it had greatly expanded in the campo. Its core members were given special treatment and weapons with which they could protect their own small landhold-ings or carry out search and destroy missions.[28]

At the beginning of the year José participated in an urban cell largely devoted to actions against army installations, but Iris was reassigned to an administrative collective under a comandante called Filo. She was put in charge of organizing the trips for foreigners who were coming "from all over the world to offer their expertise to the FPL," according to Luis. "She arranged for airline tickets and visas and was entrusted with large sums of money." He was still hiding out in safe houses throughout the city, but Mila needed to blend in, so she and baby Eva were living with her sister in the middle-class neighborhood Jardines de Miralvalle (Gardens of Valley View) in that pretty yellow and red house with its pro-fusion of allium, helaconia, and roses that Dalila showed me.

« »

Historians disagree on the extent to which other countries fanned these first flames of the Salvadoran conflict. We know from Luis's testi-mony that the guerrillas argued among themselves about how much out-side aid they should accept: "There were always strings attached." Cuba played the most significant role at this early stage, supplying not only Soviet-made guns but also experienced combatants to train and lead some of the first military-style attacks. Luis gave a negative example that proved a turning point for him:

> A Cuban woman was put in charge of an operation I was involved in. My collective was to bomb an army installation, but she botched the whole raid; the bomb went off ahead of time, wounding many of my compas. When her gun did not even work, I countermanded her or-ders; we retreated. I still think I did the right thing to save the lives of my remaining comrades, but I was punished for my insubordination. Our dear compañero, Roberto Siprián, was similarly punished for dis-obeying the order of a superior. He was transferred to a cell in San Vi-cente where he later died heroically. We named our third child Ro-berto because we admired our friend so much.

After this debacle, José was sent north to Chalatenango department to fight for control of the territory that would become an FPL stronghold during the twelve-year civil war. But the guerrillas were not yet well or-ganized there, and firefights with the Fuerzas Armadas, ORDEN, and various death squads were common. During 1978 and 1979 he operated in and around many villages north and east of the lake now called the Embalse Cerrón Grande, including Las Vueltas, San Antonio Los Ranchos, and San José Cancasque. In his testimonial, Luis highlighted another near miss:

> One time three of us were traveling on a bus. It was stopped on the road to the next village, and army officers began a search. The sergeant came right up to my seat and looked me in the eye, but left without uncovering the weapon I had hidden under some sheets. It was a miracle. The living conditions in the field were difficult, and I was separated even more from Mila and Eva, who stayed behind in San Salvador. Our marriage suffered, even though we were allowed to visit each other every two weeks or so. During this time Mila became pregnant again.

Separating couples into different revolutionary cells, but allowing them to see each other "every fifteen days," was evidently a regular FPL practice.[29]

About a month before the birth of their second child, Ernesto Arnoldo (Toto), in San Salvador on June 4, 1979, five leaders of the BPR were arrested, including the FPL representative and its secretary general, Facundo Guardado. The left mounted another collective response to demand the release of these important political prisoners, occupying the Metropolitan Cathedral in San Salvador as well as three embassies. By May 9th they had been joined by thousands of protesters outside the cathedral. When the police and National Guard troops fired point blank into the crowd, dozens were killed. The BPR leaders were eventually released, however, and Guardado continued to play a key role in the highest echelon of FPL political leadership. He also figured prominently in Mila and Luis's story.[30]

A little over a month after Toto was born, the Sandinistas in Nicaragua ousted the dictator, Anastasio Somoza Debayle, after a final offensive that lasted only six weeks. It had begun with a general strike that unleashed a national insurrection, exactly the scenario the FPL hoped to duplicate in El Salvador. They took heart from this victory by Daniel Ortega's FSLN (Frente Sandinista de Liberación Nacional). As the Salvadoran conflict was accelerating at this point, the Sandinistas allowed the FPL leadership to take cover in Managua and maintain training camps on Nicaraguan territory.

The summer and fall of 1979 brought important developments inside El Salvador, as well. By this time Archbishop Romero was regularly speaking out for the poor and against military and death squad violence in his homilies. On August 6th he issued a pastoral letter in which he openly supported the right of the people to self-defense. Then, on October 15th a reformist military coup headed by a group of young officers overthrew the regime.

This junta made up of three civilians and two military men garnered immediate support from the United States under the Carter administration, but it failed to make the promised agrarian or other reforms. Moreover, the cycle of repression and protest, followed by even more government repression, was repeated. For example, in late October another peaceful demonstration in the capital decrying earlier state violence resulted in an attack by security forces that left an estimated sixty-five dead and hundreds more wounded and detained. By January 3, 1980, a day after Mila's twenty-third birthday, the first junta had fallen apart when all three civilians resigned. A second replaced it.

«   »

By the end of the 1970s, "poverty and inequality in the rural areas and in the cities had increased dramatically, the balance of payments was showing a structural deficit and a rapidly growing armed movement was gaining increasingly widespread popularity among the general population."[31] Moreover, despite the second junta's promises, human rights violations on the part of the government and its allies actually increased. It is variously estimated that there were one thousand to two thousand civilian deaths due to right-wing violence in 1979. This number jumped wildly to about 10,000–12,000 in 1980 and 12,500–16,270 in 1981, the two years that proved most crucial for Mila and anyone associated with her.[32]

Luis was far away from the gruesome scene in San Salvador but hardly out of danger in Chalatenango department, where counterinsurgency measures were also under way. In December 1979 his group was directed to take a village at the Honduran border near Arcatao. José was put in charge of the nighttime operation. When I asked Luis during an interview in June 2000 to tell us more about this part of his story, he just broke down. We had to stop the taping. After he had calmed himself, he could only make the following general statement: "The life of a guerri-

llero was difficult and involved a lot of sacrifices. I had hoped to transform my own life, and—beyond that—the social and economic power
structure in my country."

For the testimonial luncheon in 2004, he was prepared to give a
fuller account of what happened that night:

> I suddenly found myself face to face with a member of La Escuadron
> de la Muerte. The man was holding a child in front of him as a human
> shield. I couldn't fire; I raised my hand to signal that he should let the
> boy go. He used this moment of hesitation to shoot, and I was actually
> saved by my involuntary gesture. The bullet grazed one of my fingers,
> deflecting the shot so that it lodged close to, but not directly in my
> heart. I was gravely wounded, but conscious. I called off the attack. My
> compañeros made a makeshift stretcher out of wood, carried me out
> of the village to a nearby stream, and administered first aid. I begged
> them to look after my two children if I died.

Luis was quite clear about which group his foe had belonged to—
the Squadron of Death. Its members were drawn from the security forces
working in concert with the military and accounted for the largest proportion of right-wing violence at this point. They could be easily identified because they wore "special masks and vests bearing the group's
name." It is said that as part of their atrocities, they would often carve the
"initials E.M. into the flesh of their victims."[33]

José's compas managed to transport him first to a field hospital
in Aguilares in the department of Cuscatlán—the town where Father
Grande had been murdered—then to the capital, where he was admitted to a metropolitan hospital under a different assumed name. It was a
dangerous ploy.[34]

> It took them three days to transport me on foot out of the hills farther
> south to Aguilares to one of our secret field hospitals. As it turned out
> the doctor was a friend of my cousin [who had gotten me involved in
> the FPL], and he was able to get word out to my family. My brother
> Reinaldo immediately sent blood. But those who were treating me
> did not realize that the bullet had caused an aneurism. As some days
> passed, I began to feel as if my blood vessels were going to explode.
> My condition was critical, and I needed a series of tests and treatments
> that could only be done in a proper hospital.

Luis concludes his gripping narrative laconically: "After about three months, I was well enough that a doctor could perform the first of three open-heart surgeries. Both families gave me a lot of support at this time."

WATERSHED: EL SALVADOR— COSTA RICA—NICARAGUA, 1980

Mamá Chila had taken a central role in their lives by now, as Mila and the two children were living with her again in Zacamil. It must have begun to dawn on Mamá that her son-in-law was involved in some dangerous business. It is hard to imagine that the Escobars had no inkling before this that Luis and Mila were revolutionaries. It was safer, of course, not to know, but they must have been suspicious. After Luis was wounded, it became increasingly difficult for the couple to maintain their secret.

First, Dalila went to the hospital to give blood and discovered that Luis was there under an assumed name. Further, the sisters had all noticed that Mila always wore a key around her neck and sometimes carried a locked bag. When we were having lunch at Dalila's house one day, she and Haydée suddenly offered this anecdote about what happened next: "One day when Mila was taking a shower she left the key where someone could find it. Mamá decided it was time to see what her daughter was hiding. She found materials of the FPL and money in the bag. Mila had to fill out some kind of financial forms. We couldn't tell what position she had in the organization, but it was clearly a responsible one. We knew that having those papers placed us all in great danger." Soon thereafter, Mamá confronted her, and Mila admitted that she and Luis were guerrillas. When Luis was released from the hospital, Mamá Chila nevertheless unhesitatingly took him in.

« »

Commentators tend to view 1980 as the watershed year in the Salvadoran conflict, as ever-increasing repression and violence on the right helped to unify the left. It also marked the beginning of more intrusion by outside powers, including the use of large-scale U.S. military aid to shore up one government junta, then another, and training and arms supplied to the guerrillas by Cuba via Nicaragua.[35]

The new daring of the revolutionary forces was underscored by a startling press conference held by the most important clandestine leaders on January 9th, just a week after Mila's twenty-third birthday. Marcial and Ana María evidently felt confident enough to reveal their identities in public. One almost whimsical account describes how Marcial, "a courtly gentleman," escorted Ana María, "an elderly woman with a slight stoop and vigorous opinions," to a "comfortable chair."[36] The two FPL leaders then made the ominous announcement that a coordinated military command structure for the armed opposition had been formed.

Two days later the left declared a similar unification of all the popular organizations, which immediately showed their strength by organizing a demonstration on the anniversary of the Matanza, attended by a crowd estimated at anywhere from one hundred thousand to three hundred thousand. This proved to be the high-water mark for the legal mass movement. According to one commentator, it "posed a greater threat" to the regime at this point "than did the military capability of the guerrilla groups."[37] Predictably, the army opened fire on the demonstrators, leaving some fifty dead and approximately 250 wounded.

As the second junta tottered, the regime lashed out at whatever group it considered its enemy. On February 18th the library of the Jesuit private university, UCA (Universidad Centroamericana José Simeón Cañas) was bombed.[38] Five days later the attorney general, Mario Zamora, was murdered shortly after Major Roberto d'Aubuisson denounced him on television. That same month the Fuerzas Armadas, together with ORDEN, unleashed a campaign of terror against peasants in villages throughout Chalatenango, producing a flood of internal refugees in a country that is roughly the size of Massachusetts. Some peasants escaped into Honduras, where they were crowded into huge refugee camps.

Finally, the government began to implement the first stage of an agrarian reform, but a state of siege was simultaneously declared that sent even more forces into the countryside to maintain order.[39] By March, constitutional guarantees had once again been suspended, and a third junta had to be formed, this one with Christian Democrat José Napoleón Duarte as a member for the first time. Ironically, he had been the moderate presidential candidate of the opposition coalition that had actually won the election of 1972. Eight years later, however, most of his supporters from the center had moved much farther to the left. And despite this superficial change in the regime, the campaign against the Jesuits continued unabated.

On March 22nd the National Police surrounded the UCA campus

and threatened the priests living there. In the homily he delivered at the Metropolitan Cathedral the next day, Archbishop Romero appealed directly to members of the Armed Forces to stop the killing. His words were an inspiration to some, a gauntlet thrown down to others:

> Brothers, you are part of the same people and you kill your brother *campesinos*. Before an order to kill given by a man, the law of God must prevail that says, "Thou shalt not kill." No soldier is obliged to obey an order that is against the law of God. [. . .] In the name of God, and in the name of this suffering people whose cries rise up to the heavens every day more tumultuously, I beg you, I beseech you, I order you in the name of God: Stop the repression![40]

Many Salvadorans hoped the *monseñor's* appeal would be heard. Instead, the very next day, while celebrating mass in a small chapel on the grounds of the Hospital of Divine Providence, where he lived, he was slain by a gunman.[41]

Reinaldo Coto's wife, Ana-Doris, took me there only a few weeks before the twenty-fifth anniversary of Romero's assassination. I wrote about it in my journal. *She volunteers at this cancer hospital. We first spend time with some of the terminal patients, who smile wanly in response to her cheerful inquiries. To one frightened young woman—newly admitted and far from home—we give a headscarf. "They are sent here from all over the country. No other clinic will treat such hopeless cases," Ana-Doris explains to me later. On the way out she stops to talk with a young man she knows who is softly playing his guitar. He has come back for more chemotherapy but seems upbeat about his prognosis. Then, one of the nuns takes time to show us the chapel and unlock the humble two-room dwelling where Archbishop Romero resided nearby.*

On this day, the chapel is empty but filled with sunlight. A vase of bright flowers stands in front of the altar and on the wall behind hangs a small photograph of the priest who was killed in this unlikely spot. His house nearby is as he left it, except two murals featuring Romero adorn its outer walls. A bust of the archbishop—by a Boston artist, our guide tells me—stands out front. One room contains little but the hammock in which he slept when guests required his bed; the other is furnished with only a cot, desk, and typewriter. His personal effects—glasses, appointment calendar, pens, and the vestments he was wearing when he was murdered—are on display in a vitrine in the front hall. Through my tears I can still make out where the bullet pierced the left pocket of the white shirt, dyeing it forever with his blood.

« »

Archbishop Romero's murder outraged the international community. Americans began to take more notice of the deepening crisis in El Salvador, and some congressional leaders even called for an investigation and a halt to military aid. As if enough blood had not been shed, at Romero's funeral on March 30th, a bomb went off at one corner of the plaza and then gunfire erupted. The crowd of mourners, estimated variously as between thirty thousand and eighty thousand, ran helter-skelter.

A poignant photograph that appeared in *La Prensa Gráfica* the following day shows thousands of shoes that were left behind in the ensuing stampede.[42] Sandra Benítez captures the chaos in her novel *The Weight of All Things*. In a single opening sentence she indicates the indeterminate origin of the bombs and first shots, but also touches the reader with the randomness and crushing finality of the shot that kills a single mother, whose death strands her young son Nicolás:

> Later after the bombs went off, after the monstrous black clouds they sent up dissipated in the gentle breeze, after the shooters, whoever they might have been, pocketed their stubby handguns and vanished into the crowd, after the police ceased returning fire and attempted instead, with their superior presence, to control a multitude run amuck, it would be clear it was a bullet to the head that killed her.[43]

Once again, sources vary in their estimates of the dead and wounded—twenty-six or thirty-five dead, 200 or 450 wounded—but most agree that these twin events carried weight and symbolic power beyond any numbers.[44] Luis assured us that FPL fighters admired the archbishop's courageous stand against the government and mourned his death. Those who joined the movement in the two years after 1980 often trace their willingness to risk their lives to the impact of Romero's assassination and its immediate aftermath. One couple that lost a son in the stampede at the funeral joined the guerrillas after returning to their home in the area around the Guazapa volcano.[45] More and more Salvadorans of all stripes began to share the view that the pattern of repression could only be broken by force and that "revolution was a positive and viable alternative."[46]

«   »

Against this backdrop Mila began to arrange for Luis to flee El Salvador. In some respects they were lucky, because as Iris she knew how to get people secretly in and out of the country. Although Luis now downplays the significance of his position within the organization—"I never had the ambition to gain power in the movement; I did not want to stand out"—by April 1980, he had been with the FPL for nearly a decade, almost from its beginning.

As José, he had recruited others and provided weapons training. He had even been put in charge of operations in Chalatenango, despite his earlier insubordination.[47] It was surely in the FPL's interest to try to get this twenty-eight-year-old seasoned fighter rehabilitated, so that he could return to the front when they unleashed the general insurrection. If his medical condition made that impossible, they could use his expertise in some logistical capacity.

Barely a month after her husband's first operation, Mila was able to have Luis flown to Managua, where he could get additional medical care. He was almost too weak to travel. "He almost didn't make it to Nicaragua," her sisters agree. His brother Reinaldo remembers taking him to the airport: "Luis didn't return for fourteen years, not until two years after the peace treaty was signed and a general amnesty reassured him that it would be safe. He wanted to finally come to visit our mother's grave."

By this time Mila must have known perfectly well that if she were found out, her family would be targets of death squads or the Treasury Police. She acted to protect her two young children. Two years earlier, she had persuaded her eldest sister to take a job as a nanny in Costa Rica. At the beginning of 1980 Vilma had married a Costa Rican citizen and thus regularized her visa status. Now she asked her mother to come with the five children she had left behind in El Salvador.

Instead, Mamá Chila was entrusted with the lives of three other grandchildren that the family must have considered much more vulnerable: Eva, twenty-eight months old; Toto, an infant of ten months, still drinking from a bottle; and Haydée's eldest, René. The family was worried about what might happen to René in the current situation because he was a little rebellious, and they knew twelve-year-olds were being re-cruited on both sides of the conflict.

Mila was clearly concerned about her children but still optimis-tic when she said good-bye to Mamá, who remembered her daughter's words exactly: "It will all be over in about a year. Then you can come back." Mila's optimism seemed justified. After all, more and more peo-ple were participating in the mass movement, and the various armed revolutionary groups were beginning to cooperate. She may even have anticipated that they would unleash a so-called final offensive. They did eight and a half months later.

For her part, Mamá Chila was less sanguine, but she was prepared to do all she could to protect these grandchildren. Firefights between the FPL and government troops made the trip north through Chalate-nango and then Honduras especially dangerous. Mila had a different plan. Because another armed guerrilla group already held the south-eastern department of La Unión, she figured the family would have a better chance of safe passage that way. Mamá would have to cross the Gulf of Fonseca by ferry into Nicaragua and then proceed overland to Costa Rica.

Mila's calculation proved prescient. On May 14, 1980, shortly af-ter Mamá's departure, as many as six hundred women, children, and el-derly were killed as they fled the fighting in Chalatenango by trying to cross the Sumpul River into Honduras.[48] Both Salvadoran and Hondu-ran troops were involved in this massacre, which also figures in Benítez's novel. A Brooklyn-born priest who visited the site a day later tried to de-scribe the horror: "There were so many vultures picking at the bodies, it looked like a black carpet."[49]

Fearing a repeat of what had happened in Nicaragua in 1979, the U.S. House of Representatives approved $5.7 million in military aid for the Salvadoran government at the beginning of April, just around the time Luis was spirited out of the country. When Mamá left with her grandchildren, the die had been cast on the other side too. On April 18th the FDR (Frente Democrático Revolucionario) held its founding cere-mony after the guerrillas and the popular organizations of the left and left-center agreed to join in a coalition of twenty popular organizations, political parties, labor federations, and four of five armed groups. By May 22nd these same four groups announced full coordination of their military operations, and a month later they called for a massive general strike on June 25–26 that proved about 80 percent successful. As one commentator has noted, "By the second half of 1980 the stage was set for civil war."[50]

«   »

Mamá Chila escaped with the children, but their life in Costa Rica was not rosy, according to Vilma: "I had married just to get residency. My husband, Eduardo, was abusive, but separation was impossible. He threatened to report us to immigration authorities if I left him." In June, Luis was well enough to travel to Costa Rica to visit his children, and when he saw the conditions they were living in, he insisted on bringing Mamá, Eva, Toto, and René back with him to Nicaragua at once. He and Mila had many contacts, and they could be sure the children would be safe since the FPL operated in Nicaragua under the protection of the Sandinista government.

By June the family group had gotten settled in an FPL training camp outside of Managua. José was given some new administrative duties. Then suddenly he was shipped out to Cuba for another operation. For some reason, the surgery to remove the bullet lodged near his heart could not be performed, and three months later he was back. Mila was allowed to visit them for a few days in late August. The couple had not seen each other in almost five months.

Eva vividly recalled the suitcase of clothes and toys her mother brought, but also their tearful parting: "We both cried and cried as she hugged me good-bye. I never saw her again." Eva was not quite three, but the psychological trauma must have seared these emotionally charged moments of separation into her memory: "I can also remember that my parents argued loudly in front of me." Mamá Chila has confirmed Eva's recollection that an argument took place. Luis speaks only generally of the fact that he and Mila "sacrificed our marriage to the revolutionary cause."

Their estrangement probably began earlier, for they had been together only sporadically since Eva's birth. Enforced separation, compounded by the anxiety produced by Luis's nearly fatal wounding, had surely put an extra strain on their relationship during the previous year. It is not hard to comprehend that as the immediate threat to his life began to recede, their solidarity with each other could break down. I can't be sure that they made up after the marital spat Eva witnessed, but we do know that during these few days their third child was conceived.

On August 29th Mamá Chila addressed a carefully worded letter to Dalila in San Salvador; Mila may have carried it back. Mamá first apologizes for not being able to write since her departure four months earlier and explains that she is now living with the children in an isolated spot, somewhere outside of Nicaragua's capital. She doesn't know exactly where they are. She is worried about the situation of her daughters and grandchildren left behind in El Salvador.

Mamá wants to reassure Cony, Vilma's daughter, that "Dios" (God) will arrive in December, although it "depends on when the current situation ends." This may be coded language to promise the little girl she would be reunited with her mother in Costa Rica by Christmas if all went well. She then advises her own daughters not to leave any of their money in a bank account. Mamá tells them to "invest in a business, buy some real estate, or send it to me" so that they would have a little nest egg when they made it out of the country. In the meantime, she is laying her own plans:

> It is necessary to think about tomorrow. I plan to return to Costa Rica, and I'll let you know when. Mila says that I should leave her children here so that they [Mila and Luis] can come to see them when they can. For this reason she thinks Haydée and Tita are angry with her. But tell them they shouldn't be angry because the only solution will be this one: I will raise these poor little children like my own since they [Mila and Luis] really cannot take care of them. Ask our Lord that the situation will be resolved soon.

Twice Mamá Chila alludes to her hope and prayer that the escalating conflict will soon be over. In fact, what historians have defined as the civil war proper was just beginning. Lucila Angulo did not foresee that it would be twelve years before she could return to her home country or that she would never see her youngest child again. But this wise woman seems to have known already that Mila and Luis were fooling themselves in some profound ways, and that she would be the one to raise Eva and Toto. As Eva put it, "Mamá Chila became both my mother and father."

Not long after Mila's August visit, Luis was sent back to Cuba for open-heart surgery. Even with this third operation, the bullet could not be removed. Mila, pregnant again, was back in El Salvador living with her sister Haydée in the family's Zacamil apartment. The country was sliding rapidly into all-out civil war, and Mila, as Iris, was evidently needed there. She was given no chance to see her mother, her husband, or her children again.

After Luis was sent to Cuba, Mamá Chila grew particularly disturbed by the way René was being treated. He had been a big help to her when she fell and broke her leg. However, as soon as he turned thirteen, the guerrillas separated him from the younger children, and because the boy "didn't obey their commands, they treated him very poorly, punished him and insulted him."[51]

She resolved to leave as soon as she could. Approximately three months before Luis returned from Cuba after a prolonged convalescence, she rejoined Vilma in Costa Rica, taking Eva, Toto, and René with her. The two women took whatever jobs they could find to sustain themselves, Eduardo, and the eight children they were caring for—factory work, domestic work, even selling pupusas on the street.

« »

By August 1980, after a second general strike had been thwarted, there was agreement among the Salvadoran left that armed struggle was necessary and inevitable. Even more members of the mass organizations were joining the militants. Then in early November, after the government had launched an offensive in Morazán that left several thousand dead and created as many as twenty thousand refugees, all five armed groups created a single umbrella organization. They retained the 1932 martyr's name in their new appellation—FMLN (Frente Farabundo Martí para la Liberación Nacional).[52] While each group within the FMLN kept its own separate identity and structure, they nevertheless achieved a loosely unified military command. The FDR was considered its political wing.[53]

November 1980 also marked Ronald Reagan's election to the presidency of the United States and Duarte's appointment as head of a reorganized junta in El Salvador. The indiscriminate killing did not stop. Of the roughly twelve thousand who died that year, "two-thirds [were] at the hands of the army and security forces," according to one source.[54] A second source speaks of 750 killings per month in 1980; another puts the figure for urban victims alone at fourteen thousand.[55]

In a brazen attack, five of the FDR's executive committee members, and a man with whom they were meeting, were assassinated on November 28th. Public opinion in the United States was only briefly re-aroused, however, when four North American churchwomen were brutally murdered on the night of December 2nd as they left the airport.[56] President Carter, who was still in office, suspended military and even economic aid pending an investigation.

The year ended with the dissolution of the third junta and the formation of a new one, this time with Duarte as president. But fear of the state governed the lives of many Salvadorans. Decapitated bodies were being dropped at the garbage dump on the outskirts of the capital in the middle of the night, and corpses with mutilated faces to disguise their identity were being left by the side of the road. It is generally agreed the "darkest moments for human rights in El Salvador were between 1980 and 1982. Thousands of civilians were tortured, made to 'disappear,' and died at the hands of the military, security forces and paramilitary death squads."[57] Between March 1980 and March 1982, as many as twenty-five thousand may have been killed. This was the world into which our son was about to be born.

NEW BABY, NEW MISSION: EL SALVADOR, 1981

On January 3, 1981, just a day after Mila's twenty-fourth birthday, there was another high-profile killing. Two American consultants and the head of the Salvadoran Institute for Agrarian Transformation were murdered while having coffee in the Sheraton Hotel in downtown San Salvador. The act seemingly signaled that violence on the left would escalate, though it was later proven to have been carried out by a right-wing commando that wanted to further undermine agrarian reform.[58]

Only days later the FMLN military command did act. Comandante Marcial read the "General Order No. 1" on Radio Venceremos (Radio Liberation), which called for another general strike and roused all sectors of society to revolt. José may have been uplifted as he heard these ringing words on the radio while recuperating in Cuba:

Decades of suffering and more than 50 years of military dictatorship are about to be eradicated forever by the thrust of popular combat. At this historic moment, which is crucial to the destiny of the Salvadoran and Central American peoples, the DRU [Direccion Revolucionaria Unificada] of the FMLN, which is the general command, calls on all the people, the workers, peasants, students, teachers, employees, democratic sectors, progressive soldiers and officers, religious sectors, everyone, men and women, the combatants of the regular and guerrilla revolutionary units, the militias of the revolution and the combative masses to immediately begin the military actions and the popular insurrection to achieve the triumph of the revolution. [. . .] The time for the revolution has arrived. The time for liberation has come. The definite victory is in the hands of this heroic and courageous people who for so many years have shed their blood to obtain the right to be free, to enjoy democracy, real independence, social progress, sovereignty and self-determination. [. . .] United to fight until the final victory! Revolution or death, we shall win![59]

The popular insurrection that was supposed to be the prelude to this "final offensive" failed to materialize, however. Instead, a high-intensity military phase in the overall struggle began. It would last for more than three years.

Predictably, on January 14th the United States resumed military aid to the Salvadoran government.[60] Four days later, a congressional delegation reporting on both military and death squad atrocities urged a halt to the aid, but after Ronald Reagan came to office at the end of the month it was expanded. As one of his administration's first foreign policy moves, the State Department issued a white paper in late February that described the Salvadoran conflict as being entirely directed from Moscow via Cuba. The thesis was soon discredited, but the United States government continued to prop up its side in what the Reagan administration narrowly viewed as just another proxy war in the contest with the Soviet Union.

At the beginning of March the world federation of socialist political parties, Socialist International, offered the services of former German chancellor Willy Brandt as a mediator. President Duarte rejected this initiative, and the military buildup began. The U.S. government announced that it would send twenty more advisors, for a total of fifty-six, and $25 million more in military aid, in addition to the $69 million previously approved. Congress, at least, demanded a certification process every six months to show that the Salvadoran government was making progress on human rights.

The government responded by launching a major counterinsurgency campaign in the northern departments. At least fifty civilians, mostly women and children trying to flee across the Lempa River into

Honduras, were massacred by Salvadoran and Honduran troops using helicopters that had been supplied by the United States. Under pressure from their northern neighbor, the two Central American countries had signed a peace treaty the previous October, setting aside their earlier dispute in favor of such coordinated military actions in the contested border areas.[61]

«　»

On May 22, 1981, the day Mila gave birth to Roberto Alfredo in the Maternity Hospital in downtown San Salvador at 2:05 p.m., the political-diplomatic commission of the FMLN-FDR proposed dialogue for the first time as a way to find a solution to the conflict. What would have happened to Mila and her baby if the government had not rejected its proposal? Could eleven more years of civil war have been averted?

Later that month, the Socialist International tried again on the diplomatic front, offering another moderate, Canadian New Democratic Party leader Edward Broadbent, as a mediator, but Duarte also rejected this initiative. Meanwhile, on May 26th the FBI reported that its investigation had directly tied members of the Salvadoran National Guard to the murder of the four American churchwomen the previous December, but this announcement made no difference in the basic thrust of U.S. policy.[62]

Much of what Mila was doing during these few months remains obscure. Only a few family members had any regular contact with her, and she may have deliberately deceived them about her intentions. Haydée claims that she wanted out of the movement. We do know that she became a wanted person. Her picture—without her name—appeared in the newspaper along with other FPL guerrillas. No wonder she didn't venture out much after Roberto's birth. His birth certificate shows that she waited until mid-July to go to the city hall in Mejicanos to register him.

Mariano Coto seems to have played an important role as a sounding board during these tense months. He still runs the same small auto-parts store in Zacamil that he had then. Haydée remembers that he came over every day with milk for Mila to help her keep up her strength. He would sit with her in another room to talk, and Haydée could not make out what they said.

The Escobar sisters feel sure that Mariano was involved either with one of the mass organizations or perhaps directly with the guerrillas, because he was the one who first put Mamá Chila in touch with FMLN activists in 1992 when she began to hunt for Roberto. During my conversation with him and Reinaldo in February 2005, Mariano insisted, "Mila did not confide any secrets in me. I was under the impression that she was going with the baby either directly to Costa Rica to rejoin Mamá Chila and her other children, or possibly to Nicaragua first to see Luis."

He was the first person to mention that Mila's picture had appeared in the paper, however. He told us that when we first met in January 1999. At that time, his wife, Reina, had looked tearfully at Nelson as he played chess with her youngest son, Sergio, and remembered, "I changed little Roberto's diaper just before Mariano took him and Mila to the bus station. We had kept her hidden for a while and were the last members of the family to see her alive."

By 2005 their memories of those earlier times were clouded by a fresh grief. In the midst of our conversation, Mariano exclaimed, "Nothing has changed in our country for the better. Now it is criminal gangs that roam the streets and shoot innocent people instead of the Fuerzas Armadas. But nothing has changed, nothing." Less than a year before, on March 13, 2004, while his father sat in the seat beside him, Sergio was shot dead by some carjackers in Zacamil.

Before Reinaldo and I left that evening, Mariano asked me for a picture of Nelson and Derek to keep, handing me the card that was passed out at his son's funeral. On the back there is a picture and words of archbishop Oscar Romero: "Each person has something akin to a secret room in the depths of his being where God comes to talk in a low voice and where that person decides his proper destiny." On the front one sees a photo of the handsome twenty-year-old and a final salutation from his family that could apply as well to Sergio's Aunt Mila:

> It is impressive how death surprises us, with no regard for age, social status, or creed. Each person decides what to do in life. The path of God is full of love, justice, and truth. The just person practices these three things, but also denounces injustice and fights to create conscientiousness in others. Until we meet again, Sergio.

« »

The day after my conversation with Mariano and Reinaldo I spent time in several newspaper offices in San Salvador with Ana-Doris, slowly turning the pages of the bound copies that constitute their archival records. In one instance we waited in a hot, gritty room with the printing presses while the staff looked in vain for the missing October 1981 volume. I was hoping to find that photo of Mila.

While her sisters had confirmed Mariano's story, no one could say for sure which newspaper, much less which month or day. I didn't find it then, but I learned a great deal more about what was going on during the weeks leading up to Mila's departure from El Salvador. I had a few pages photocopied, and I wrote furiously in my notebook. Later journal entries reflect some of my reactions to the headlines, ads, and articles that caught my eye.

I am struck by the number of ads in El Mundo *placed by families pleading for information about their "disappeared" husbands, sons, and daughters. Not a day passes without several such personal ads. On August 10th, for example, a mother reports the curious disappearance of her twenty-two-year-old daughter who had just returned from the United States, where she had supposedly received medical treatment.*

I am also surprised at the number of human rights organizations that were submitting public appeals. On September 17, 1981, pictures of student "detainees," age twenty to thirty-one, are displayed on a single page in the same newspaper. "The Salvadoran Commission on Human Rights demands their release." Two days later there is a picture of a fifteen-year-old girl who has simply "disappeared." [63]

On September 23rd "The Salvadoran Committee of Families for the Liberation of Political Prisoners and the Disappeared" places a prominent full-page ad urging the release of another large group of young people. The name of the head of this organization and his personal ID number appears at the bottom of the page. Two days later a "Mothers of the Disappeared Committee" takes out a similar ad. Four days later yet another denounces human rights abuses and demands "respect for the rights of unions" in the same paper. But these appear side by side with appeals to young men to join the Armed Forces. Strange juxtaposition.

I could also see that by August 1981 the FMLN had launched a second offensive, in which economic sabotage was added to its strategic arsenal. As I wrote down that the U.N. High Commissioner for Refugees reported 305,000 people who had fled El Salvador in the first half of the year, I thought of how many individual stories lay behind the statistic.

Many of them, I knew, lived in huge refugee camps like La Virtud or Mesa Grande in Honduras.[64] Others, like Mamá Chila, Eva, and

Toto, had been able to get to Nicaragua or even Costa Rica, where they scraped by. Still others, like the boy in Graciela Limón's novel *In Search of Bernabé*, made their way laboriously through Guatemala and Mexico and got smuggled into the United States, which announced it would deport twelve thousand of them in July. A few were helped when they got to the United States by organizations like the American Friends Service Committee, and some churches helped refugees get to Canada in a kind of modern-day underground railroad.[65]

In September, the founding of the ARENA party (Alianza Republicana Nacionalista) under former military man Roberto d'Aubuisson was headline news. He formally announced he would stand in the next legislative elections, to be held the following March. D'Aubuisson had been second in command of the intelligence system during General Romero's presidency and was founder of the right-wing death squad UGB (Unión Guerrera Blanca). This group had been largely responsible since 1977 for the campaign against the Jesuits, and d'Aubuisson was also thought to have planned the assassination of attorney general Mario Zamora. Moreover, former U.S. ambassador Robert E. White was already openly postulating a direct link between the former major and the assassins of Archbishop Romero.[66] My notes continue.

On September 15th the pages of El Mundo, Diario Latino, El Diario de Hoy, *and* La Prensa Gráfica *are all filled with photos of the Atlacatl Brigade, an elite, "rapid reaction" force trained in the infamous School of the Americas.*[67] *They can be seen giving a simulated attack on terrorists to a cheering throng at the Estadio Flor Blanca (White Flower Stadium) in San Salvador, a chilling yet evidently crowd-pleasing demonstration that was organized as part of the 160th anniversary celebration of the Salvadoran republic!*

On the first of October, the armed opposition formally announces its willingness to have the government of Panama negotiate the conflict. The next day the Salvadoran government bars the FBI inquiry into the murder of the North American churchwomen. No reason is given. Then on October 3rd the front pages show the results of the guerrilla bombing of the Social Security Building in the center of San Salvador. By October 7, 1981 the headlines and front-page photos are taken over by the state visit of President Duarte to Washington, D.C. He can be seen posing with a smiling President Reagan, secretary of state Alexander Haig, and Ted Kennedy. President Duarte stresses the need for the United States to send more logistical equipment and rejects any idea of negotiating an end to the conflict.

«   »

Haydée can almost pinpoint the departure date of mother and child, because in mid-October she sold the family's apartment in Zacamil and moved to Soyapango, taking Mila's sewing machine with her. After spending some days with Mariano and Reina Coto, Ana Milagro probably climbed onto the bus with the baby in her arms on October 10, 1981. She was twenty-four and tiny Roberto Alfredo not yet five months old.

I note that on this same day the Sandinista leader, Daniel Ortega, read a "Proposal for Peace" to the U.N. General Assembly that had been prepared by the Salvadoran guerrilla movement. It called for negotiations without prior conditions. I can't help but wonder what would have happened if this call had been heeded instead of Duarte's pleas in Washington for more military aid. Of course, as long as the guerrillas held the upper hand militarily, the Salvadoran regime would continue to reject any such overtures, even though the governments of Mexico and France had recognized the FMLN-FDR as a "representative political force" in August.[68]

It is not reflected in the Salvadoran newspapers I read, but I know that during the preceding months, the Armed Forces had not even been able to dislodge the guerrillas from the Guazapa volcano region, less than fifty miles north of the capital, despite multiple attempts. And offensives in Chalatenango, Morazán, San Vicente, and Cuscatlán had all failed to achieve their objectives.

I can see that on October 9th the government simply announced the end of their campaign in Chalatenango department, while predictably rejecting the latest negotiation offer by the armed opposition. For its part, Washington seemed bound to support Duarte, who was still viewed by our government as a moderate caught between the right and the left, despite the fact that he was giving the military and its related death squads free reign.

Approximately five days after Mila and Roberto left San Salvador, the guerrillas made a dramatic show of their strength by blowing up the Puente de Oro, the main span across the Lempa River between San Vicente and Usulután departments, the most important bridge in the country. This was generally considered another major military victory for the FMLN. In the meantime, Mila had not turned up in either Nicaragua or Costa Rica. Instead, unbeknown to her family she had taken her baby and joined two younger women along with several compañeros in safe houses in the Honduran capital.

We know the pseudonyms of at least two other women in the cell— Rosa and Blanca—and just a little more about this collective because another compa, identified later as María López, visited them at the end of 1981, but this woman returned to El Salvador long before their kidnapping of the industrialist the following spring. According to López, the two other women both came from the department of Cabañas and had lost their families in the massacre at the Lempa River in March 1981.[69] They had been recently recruited at the refugee camp La Virtud, where they had hooked up with two guerrilleros and been allowed to follow them into this cell. She describes the two girls as newlyweds, experiencing the hardship of clandestine activity for the first time but still full of revolutionary fervor. Blanca was expecting a baby in January 1982 and Rosa in early May.[70] The two must have looked up to Iris, who was already the mother of three and had been an FPL member for about eight years.

DISAPPEARANCE: HONDURAS—
NICARAGUA—EL SALVADOR, 1981–1982

From October on we know almost nothing of Mila and Roberto except what was reported by the Honduran newspapers after the shoot-out in May 1982. Luis's narrative for these seven months only complicates the matter. When he returned from Cuba to Nicaragua the second time, he found his children gone and himself reassigned to the section that his wife had been working in previously, the one that organized visits by foreigners who now came to the training camps in Nicaragua to instruct new recruits. He met her superior, "Comandante Filo," for the first time.

The plan was to send José to Honduras, but first he was given permission to visit his children in Costa Rica. Luis bumped into Mila's comandante again there, since Filo was organizing a solidarity committee in Costa Rica to raise money for the FMLN. Luis evidently found out that Mila was going to be sent to Honduras around the same time he was. Luis tells it this way: "Even though we were not going to be in the same cell, I asked Filo for permission to see my wife and young son when I got to Honduras, but my request was denied. He gave no reason."

By late 1981 José had arrived in Honduras. The timeline of the narrative Luis constructed for us remains somewhat vague. In his 2004 testimonial, he emphasized that his immediate superiors at the time, Comandante Filo and Comandante Esteban (Facundo Guardado), both refused to let him see his wife and child, despite repeated requests.[71] He resented their refusal, but obeyed orders. Whatever the purpose of the operation, things evidently did not go well. In early 1982 Esteban, who was in charge of multiple FMLN cells in Honduras, was captured and imprisoned by the Honduran government; José was sent back to Nicaragua while other operatives remained in Honduras, Iris among them.

"The FPL—in contrast to other groups—kidnapped typically only in order to have leverage to trade prisoners," Luis insists.[72] Because Guardado was a member of the FPL high command and also represented their group within the combined political leadership of the FMLN-FDR, the group was understandably anxious to negotiate. Comandante Ana María was in charge of all such trades, according to Luis, and if—as it was rumored among the guerrilleros—she and Esteban were intimate, she had all the more reason to make whatever arrangements she could to obtain his release.[73] The FPL's need to have someone important enough to trade for Guardado may have been the reason for the abduction of the lumber company executive, Jacques Casanova, by Iris's group on March 10, 1982.

«   »

It evidently took several months for the FPL to arrange the terms of a prisoner exchange. It seems safe to assume that the Honduran military leader, General Álvarez, who was also in charge of FUSEP, played a central role in any negotiations. And while we have no proof, we cannot exclude the possibility that his mentor, the U.S. ambassador, referred to by some as the "pro-consul" of Honduras, was informed.[74] Finally, a trade was arranged, but according to Luis, instead of a quiet one-for-one trade, Ana María agreed to let the Honduran police force eliminate the FPL cell that was holding Casanova.

All three women in the cell had small children. Blanca's baby girl was about four and a half months and Rosa's only about two weeks old at the time of the shoot-out. As we now know, Iris's Roberto was exactly three days shy of his first birthday. A dramatic armed action in which the Cobra battalion appeared to ferret out not just one, but two safe houses

on the same day, and managed to eliminate all the guerrillas while res-
cuing a hostage and three small children, made good propaganda for
Álvarez's special police force. According to Luis, the Honduran police's
knowledge of the cell was no accident, nor due to superior intelligence:
"They [the guerrillas and their children] were betrayed by Ana María."

I have reflected on the fact that this explosive claim that challenges
conventional portraits of Ana María may or may not be true, but Luis
does seem to have been in a position to know, for he had been reassigned
to the inner circle of the command structure when he returned to Nicaragua from Honduras. He had already been involved in administrative
work when he came back from Cuba the first time, so he was well aware
of the widening fissures between the top FPL leaders by 1982: "The original principles had been compromised and people began to struggle for
power within the organization." These factors disillusioned him, but he
still revered Marcial, to whom he now became personally attached.[75]

> When I returned from Honduras, I began to work directly for Coman-
> dante Jefe Marcial. There was an ideological struggle going on be-
> tween him and the second in command. Comandante Marcial sus-
> pected that Comandante Ana María was about to betray him and the
> whole movement. He asked me to spy on her, so I took a position as
> her bodyguard. This was right at the time when she was responsible
> for the fate of my wife and child. The day after the shoot-out in Tegu-
> cigalpa she told me to my face that Iris and the others had been elimi-
> nated in exchange for Comandante Esteban, and that there wasn't any-
> thing I could do about it. But she also promised that the organization
> would find my son and see that he was taken care of.
>
> I was shocked that she would betray our compañeros like that and
> openly admit responsibility for the death of Mila and the disappear-
> ance of Roberto. I was filled with hatred for her, but I disguised my
> anger and only told Marcial privately that I personally wanted to kill
> her. He replied, "José, no. The commando will take the proper action
> for what she has done." A few days later I was released from my duties
> as her bodyguard. After what had happened in Honduras, Ana María
> could no longer trust me. After that, I assumed a strictly logistical
> post, working at first with the person who after 1983 became the head
> comandante of the FPL, but later on I was with the small group
> that remained loyal to Marcial right up to his death the following
> year.

While they remain contradictory, the Honduran newspaper accounts of 1982, as well as the version offered in 2001 by Pro-búsqueda's book *El día más esperado*, begin to make more sense to me in light of Luis's claims.[76] The Hondurans may well have had all the information they needed, including the pseudonyms of some of the guerrillas and the location where Casanova was being held. They could storm the first safe house, knowing the hostage was hidden below, and shoot to kill the other adults. The police must have also known in advance that the guerrillas were well armed and that they had children living with them. It remains a miracle that the little ones were not caught in the crossfire. The newspaper reports establish without a doubt that Roberto was in the first house, but where was his mother? There are differences of opinion about what actually happened to Mila.[77]

FISSURES: EL SALVADOR—NICARAGUA—
COSTA RICA—PANAMA, 1982–1992

Mamá Chila received several messages from her daughter right before and then after Mila left San Salvador, but she didn't know where she was. A man within the revolutionary front whose name Mamá didn't know delivered the letters personally. He usually came back and collected her reply a few weeks later, but the third time—she thinks it was in February 1982—he didn't return.

Mamá told me she had a premonition that something bad was going to happen. Then there was the unexpected telephone call. No one can say for sure exactly when it came, but some think it must have been the day of the shoot-out in Tegucigalpa. Mamá and Vilma were at work, so Vilma's husband, Eduardo, took the message. "Tell Mamá to take care of the children," Mila supposedly said. One version has it that she actually told Eduardo she would call back. But they heard nothing more until they learned that Mila was dead. No one knows for sure whether Mila made the call to Costa Rica that day from the second house before being killed. Some prefer to speculate that she was allowed to make a call after she was captured, although to me this seems unlikely.

Reflecting on the fact that none of them had seen her in a long time, I can't help thinking for a moment that Mila might be the woman in the newspaper photograph after all, whose face is entirely hidden from view. But then I have to concede that even to me, the woman doesn't look like the photographs of Mila I've studied so carefully. Nor does the description sound right—"quite young, almost juvenile in appearance, short, fair-skinned, with long, straight brown hair." Mila was the eldest woman in the group at twenty-five and, after bearing three children, probably not juvenile in appearance. I decide this figure lying in the pool of blood must have been one of the two younger women, perhaps Blanca, whose nom de guerre suggests she might have been very fair.

The question of what happened to Mila on that day is rendered even more complicated by a 2003 Pro-búsqueda report that cites "unnamed" Honduran sources not included in the investigative report of 1997 or even the 2001 book, *El día más esperado*.[78] These sources identify the three victims of the shoot-out in the first safe house as Olga, Alex, and Néstor, clearly noms de guerre. Luis knew the men and was able to identify Néstor as one of those in the photograph of the shoot-out, but the other man pictured is unfamiliar, and his sources had told him Alex got away. The name Olga is a mystery, as it does not belong to any of the women whom we had previously associated with the cell. I am forced to imagine how FUSEP might have extracted these three names from members of the cell who were captured later on in the second house. Or did some informer provide them in advance?

« »

Luis is firmly convinced that his wife was taken alive in the second safe house along with Alfredo, the guerrillero with whom she had worked for some time and whose pseudonym had been given as a second name to their son Roberto. The partners may have been tortured and killed soon after. He also says he heard from other compañeros who had been in Honduras at the time that her body had been "dumped in the middle of the road in a sack." But we don't know their source of information and can't verify any of this.

These same people misinformed him concerning the whereabouts of the baby, after all. Luis says he was told, "Your little boy was taken away from the shoot-out by a woman who was later arrested with two kids. Everyone else was killed." That point at least confirmed what Ana María had told him—the whole cell had been wiped out. Sacrificed—but for what? he asked himself.

Another story circulated among the Escobar sisters—Roberto was being taken care of by some Nicaraguan nuns.[79] In reality, none of them knew exactly what had happened to Mila or her baby, and none of them enjoyed the sense of safety or had the necessary resources to hunt for the child, whom they firmly believed had survived. They worried that he could still be killed and his organs sold.

Luis was in turmoil. The couple hadn't seen each other since August 1980. He had never seen Roberto. He wasn't even sure the boy was his, for guerrilleros had also spread a rumor that Mila had hooked up with another compañero while he was in Cuba the first time. One thing he was sure of—he had to get out. He was disillusioned by the direction the FPL was taking and bitter about the death of his wife, but he remained loyal to his jefe, Marcial, who represented the purity of the original belief structure to which he had signed on a decade before. He bided his time.

The period of high-intensity conflict, with the guerrillas regularly initiating campaigns, continued throughout 1982 into 1983. There had been some dramatic victories for the FMLN, like the destruction of about 70 percent of the Salvadoran Air Force at its Ilopango base on January 23, 1982. President Reagan responded quickly, circumventing congressional debate by releasing $55 million in defense equipment to the Salvadoran Army by executive order. In late May the elite Rámon Belloso battalion launched an offensive in Chalatenango directed primarily against civilians who were seen as collaborators. Hundreds were killed, and at least five thousand fled, ending up at the Mesa Grande camp in Honduras.

Despite such successes, the U.S. government frankly thought that the Salvadoran Army was losing the war. While much of its urban network had been lost to death squad counterterrorism by 1983, the FMLN was operating at will throughout the countryside, where it understandably had the support of many peasants who had suffered from government reprisals. Marcial had famously described the Salvadoran revolutionary situation by stating, "The people are our mountains."[80] By this time the guerrillas controlled about a fifth of the country. They began to rely on larger fighting units, and they were less dependent on outside sources, as they could now arm new recruits with captured weapons.[81]

«   »

Historians don't know as much about what was going on at this time in the inner circle of the FPL in Managua, where—by contrast—things were falling apart. The unexpected assassination of Comandante Ana María on April 6, 1983, and the suicide of Comandante Marcial a week later remains a murky minor episode in most accounts of the Salvadoran civil war, usually relegated to a few sentences or a footnote giving the bare facts.[82] Marcial was in Libya at the time of Ana María's brutal stabbing, but he returned for the funeral. Since it had occurred on their territory, the Nicaraguans were in charge of the investigation. At first the Sandinistas accused the CIA, but eventually Comandante Marcelo (Rogelio Bazzaglia) and three other FPL militants admitted to the crime and were convicted.[83]

Conventional wisdom places Marcial at the center of the plot to kill Ana María, and his subsequent suicide is usually interpreted as a sign of his guilty feelings. Tommie Sue Montgomery is one of the few who puts forward a more nuanced version of this thesis while also accepting the premise of Marcial's guilt. According to her, the murder-suicide was really the result of a classic power struggle in which Ana María's group had already won. Marcial, whom Montgomery calls too "rigid and dogmatic," could not stand this defeat.[84]

José was as close as one could get to both these figures during that crucial year. Luis agrees at least in part with Montgomery. He, too, believes Marcial saw he was losing a theoretical battle and finally recognized that the divisions within the organization he had founded were insurmountable. But understandably, Luis views Marcial's position far more positively.

Colored, no doubt, by his personal history in the movement, Luis maintains that the second in command was "too enamored of the Cubans and too dependent on the Sandinistas." Ana María was willing to compromise ideology in order to hammer out a more unified strategy with the other armed groups, whereas "Marcial remained true to the FPL's core beliefs." But Luis also thinks that Marcial had an added motive: to see that Ana María was disciplined for what had happened in Tegucigalpa the year before. Yet, interestingly, he still does not think that Marcial actually ordered the killing.[85] The struggle for power evidently lasted many months, as those Luis calls "opportunists" jockeyed for position.

Days after Ana María's funeral, Marcial was brought to the place where a few of his loyalists were being held, José among them. Luis explains that they were basically "under house arrest and were surrounded by the Sandinista army. Comandante Marcial was not willing to compromise his ideals, and he was depressed." Rather than stand trial or be summarily executed by the new guard—as Roque Dalton had been in 1975 by the ERP—"he preferred to commit suicide." His followers saw this not as an admission of guilt but as an act of realism and courage. José was one of the security guards stationed in the next room when his jefe pulled the trigger, described in one account as "a shot to the heart at 21.30 hours."[86] Luis still speaks of it with deep emotion:

> Before Marcial went into the next room to destroy his papers, the co-mandante jefe spoke to me and handed me a sealed letter—his ideological last will and testament. When we heard the gun shot, we rushed in. I held him in my arms. He didn't expire immediately. We were allowed to take him to a hospital, but by the time we got there, he had died. With him the heart of the FPL was dead!

Most of what went on in Managua during the investigation by the Sandinista government was kept tightly under wraps. Only when a new splinter group of Marcial loyalists went public in December in El Salvador did the FMLN issue a general statement specifically condemning Marcial for Ana María's murder. In any case, the old guard had been eliminated. A new group of leaders took over, and there was greater unanimity from then on. A few of those who had remained loyal to Marcial formed their own faction, calling it the Salvador Cayetano Carpio Revolutionary Worker's Movement. But the FMLN would not accept them. The others had long since chosen sides when they named their April 1983 offensive after the slain Ana María.[87]

In the end, I think that the victors still get to write their version of the story. In this internal drama, Marcial's faction—with which José so closely identified—lost out in the contest over strategy and leadership. I think it unlikely that those now in positions of power within the FMLN party would confirm what Luis asserts. These claims are his, not mine, and I have purposely not sought corroboration. I only want to convey the way this man, with whom we now stand in close relationship, saw his place in history as it was unfolding.

After Marcial's death, Luis believed that the new people in charge would want to get rid of him because he had been so close to Marcial: "They wanted to do it in a quiet way that would not arouse any more suspicion about their motives. I was directed to go back to El Salvador on my own, where I was supposed to link up with a new contact, but I was convinced this man would betray me." Luis did not join the new group or the ones that splintered off from it. Instead he used this opportunity to walk away—to shed his identity as José. Luis went to Costa Rica first to see his children, but he did not stay for long. Vilma says that whenever he visited them in the next few years, "he was always looking over his shoulder, always worried that he might be found out."

«   »

By mid-1984 Luis had gone to Panama. He lived in the mountains and took odd jobs, then worked in construction and on a cruise ship. By this time in El Salvador the period of high-intensity conflict was subsiding; a new phase in the struggle had begun, in which political strategies took primacy. The toll of the preceding four years had proved costly— at least five thousand combatant and fifty thousand civilian deaths. Prisoners and disappeared numbered in the untold thousands, and 468,000 Salvadorans had been displaced within their own country. An additional 244,000 refugees were said to be living in Mexico or elsewhere in Central America, and another half million were in the United States.[88]

Luis finally settled down in David, Panama, a place where he felt he could make a new start. Eventually he was able to establish his own small business, stenciling T-shirts. He began by firing them one at a time in the kitchen stove. After the war, his brother Reinaldo helped him get the business on a more secure footing, sending machinery and inks from El Salvador and arranging for Luis to get further training. In 1988 Luis married a Panamanian, and when their daughter, Jennifer Éstefany, was born in November 1990, he belatedly tried to unite his family by bringing Eva and Toto to live with them.

Family harmony remained an elusive goal. Eva was thirteen and rebellious; she missed Mamá Chila and her friends in Costa Rica and didn't think it was right that she had to do child care and housecleaning in the morning while her stepmother worked as a pediatric nurse, then go to school in the afternoon. And Eva had never really bonded with her father. After three years she had had enough of fighting with him. One morning she and Toto started to sneak out of the house, planning to return to Costa Rica. Luis told us how he awoke to the sound of the taxi they had called and confronted them. Eva remained firm and left that day, but Toto decided to stay.

Scattered as they were and in need of reconciliation, the members of this extended family followed the events in El Salvador from their various vantage points and wondered when the civil war would be over. Mamá Chila clung to her idée fixe—that as soon as it was safe, she would hunt for Roberto. Miriam also told us that Luis put aside some of his meager earnings each week in a jar, money he planned to use to do the same.

«   »

The Duarte inauguration to the Salvadoran presidency in July 1984 was seen by some as a breakthrough for a U.S.-backed policy of supporting elections, but it took another five years of missed opportunities, failed judicial and economic reforms, and a military stalemate before there was real movement toward peace. In January 1989, the FMLN offered to participate in the next elections if they could be postponed until September, but the government refused. The violence briefly accelerated rather than abated when, on October 31st, leaders of the national federation of unionized workers were brutally murdered. And on November 11th— the same week we were riveted by the images of East and West Germans embracing as the Berlin Wall opened—the FMLN launched its final strategic counteroffensive.

The front came from the countryside back to San Salvador. Dalila, Haydée, Tita, and their eight children experienced fierce combat in the streets of Soyapango and the aerial bombardment by the Air Force that followed. Although the guerrillas held parts of the city for over a month, the populace was war-weary and not at all prepared to rise up. Many of the guerrilla groups had mistakenly counted on a popular insurrection sweeping them into power. Surveys showed that by this time 63 percent of the people wanted a negotiated settlement.[89] Nevertheless, the FMLN resisted an immediate cease-fire.

The needless bloodletting on both sides was not over. In the early hours of November 16th, Ignacio Ellacuría, SJ, the rector, and the other Jesuits living on the UCA campus, along with their housekeeper and her daughter, were shockingly murdered.[90] It is no accident that negotiation only became a real option when U.S. aid finally faltered after this last atrocity was proved to be the work of the Salvadoran Armed Forces. Moreover, the imminent collapse of the Soviet Union obviated the international context that had been used to ideologically justify U.S. participation in the struggle in the first place.[91]

The political landscape in Central America was being reshaped in many ways. In December 1989 the United States invaded Panama, ousting Manuel Noriega, and the following February Violeta Chamorro's coalition trounced the Sandinistas in Nicaraguan elections. In El Salvador, as it became clear that no side could win militarily, and as international support began to wane, negotiations were finally taken seriously as the only option to end a conflict whose cold-war framework was rapidly disintegrating. By mid-November 1991 the FMLN had finally ceased its military hostilities, and the following April constitutional reforms were agreed upon. On January 16, 1992, a peace treaty was signed in Chapultapec Castle in Mexico City, officially ending the civil war.

The Truth Commission report published a year later by the United Nations paved the way for a general amnesty. Twenty-two thousand complaints, including extrajudicial executions, forced disappearances, and the use of torture, were registered with the commission during its three-month investigation, 85 percent of them against government security forces or their agents. The remainder could be attributed to various commandos of the FMLN. While the investigation covered the period from 1980 to July 1991, a full 75 percent of the complaints concerned human rights abuses that had occurred between 1980 and 1983.

After 1992 the various groups under the FMLN umbrella began the process of reorganizing themselves into legitimate political parties. The FPL was the last to formally dissolve itself. It joined with another group and retained the old acronym, FMLN, to contest elections. Its last secretary general, Facundo Guardado, ran for the presidency in 1999, losing in the second round to ARENA's Francisco Flores. After that electoral loss, Guardado faced corruption charges in Nicaragua that prevented him from seeking office in El Salvador again. He went into exile.

One historian summarizes the end of the bloody twelve-year conflict this way: "Instead of winning power, they [the FMLN] won the right to compete for power in a democratic setting."[92] This outcome, while on the surface positive for both sides, strikes me as a Pyrrhic victory, for the cost was so high—around seventy-five thousand dead out of a total population of three million, and at least a quarter of the Salvadoran people displaced!

Of the 13,600 guerrillas who fought for the FMLN, it is estimated that 30 percent were women, and of the roughly one hundred thousand people in the rear guard thought to have lent support in the field—everyone from tortilla grinders to radio operators—as many as 60 percent were. But the Truth Commission report, whose figures are based on the official complaints filed during its investigation, registers only 5,239 women as murdered, disappeared, tortured, kidnapped, badly injured, or raped during the war years.[93] Given the high participation rate of women, I find this an unbelievably low figure. And I feel certain that Mila was not counted.

Una madre joven, calmada,
fuerte,
Ana Milagro,
"Iris," mi flor favorita.

Tú veías solamente la pobreza de la patria
los asesinatos, las injusticias.
Tú luchabas
fuerte,
pero la vida de una guerrillera es
peligrosa, solitaria.
Tú te fugaste a Tegucigalpa
Robertito en los brazos.
La casa se llamaba seguridad,
pero nada es seguro,
Milagro,
"Iris," mi flor favorita.

¡Pobre madre!
La policía hondureña te mató.
Tu sangre enrojeció la solería.
Tú lloras
fuerte,
pero mira, milagrosamente
tu hijo vive todavía
Robertito
Ronny
Nelson
Roberto
Vive.
Él sonríe cuando él escucha tu nombre hermoso,
Milagro,
"Iris," mi flor favorita.

—MARGARET E. WARD

A mother, young, calm,
strong,
Ana Milagro,
"Iris," my favorite flower.

You only saw the poverty of the country
the killings, the injustices.
You were fighting
strongly,
but the life of a guerrillera is
dangerous, lonely.
You went to Tegucigalpa,
little Roberto in your arms.
The house was called safe,
but nothing is safe,
Milagro,
"Iris," my favorite flower.

Poor mother!
The Honduran police killed you.
Your blood reddened the floor.
You were crying,
strongly,
but miraculously
your boy is still alive
Robertito
Ronny
Nelson
Roberto
lives.
He smiles when he hears your lovely name,
Milagro,
"Iris," my favorite flower.

FIVE

Imagining Mila

NEW HAMPSHIRE, SUMMER 2007

Since I drafted Chapter 4, Tom has retired, and we have moved to our home in New Hampshire. Derek graduated from Macalester College in May and is working in North Carolina as an endangered species intern, and last August Nelson left a job in the IT department of a local bank in order to start his own business. His degree is in management of technology, and he now designs administrative software systems, as well as creating web-based marketing strategies tailored to the needs of small businesses and start-ups. With the help of one Salvadoran cousin, he worked on a project to bring such systems to small businesses in Central America using donated laptops and open-source software. He's living with some college friends in Auburndale now, less than a mile from where we lived for nineteen years on the Lasell College campus and about half a mile from the church basement where World Adoption Services had its offices, and where this whole story started for Tom and me in 1983.

In terms of this project, the most important development has been that Nelson and his sister Eva, joined occasionally by Toto, Éstefany, Derek, and Mireya, have begun to tell this story in their own way, using a weblog that Nelson initiated. He commented there on his transition to independent living:

> It's strange to think how much has changed in our lives since we moved here [to Auburndale from Wellesley, Massachusetts]. When I moved in [to the president's house] I was just starting the first grade. Now I am all grown and on my own. Half the time I spent here I had no idea I had family looking for me. The other half I spent visiting them, and some of them came here to visit me.

When Eva came with her eight-year-old daughter, Dany, in December 2006 to spend Christmas with us, I asked her and Nelson if I could interview them. I explained how I wanted to concentrate in this chapter on their mother and give a voice to the one person who had been silenced forever by these events. It was already December 31st when we got around to it—Eva's twenty-ninth birthday—and only two days before what would have been Mila's fiftieth.

It was also the last day of Eva's visit, and a friend was waiting impatiently for them to finish with me so they could all go out for New Year's Eve. Nelson was slightly amused by my retro technology—a micro tape recorder—the same one I had used in Panama, Costa Rica, and El Salvador two years earlier.

Eva had always been reluctant to broach the subject of her mother, but this time she seemed to understand why I needed to talk about her. The friend agreed to wait, and we three sat together for nearly an hour. I asked them to tell me what they thought about Mila's motivations, how they had imagined their mother as they were growing up, and, of course, what they thought about her now. And I shared some of my thoughts. Our conversation proved to be a catalyst.

Soon thereafter the two of them began their blog, *Ana's Miracle* (www.anasmiracle.com). When Tom and I returned from a trip near the end of January, Nelson told us about it, and I quickly read the entries they had already posted. It took my breath away. For Eva, especially, it was as if something that had been bottled up for too long finally had found a way out. She posted first on January 16th:

> I have to start talking about how hard it is to lose someone you love, even when you are only three years old and are not aware of a sense of loss. You suffer, and it hurts deep in your heart. Growing up without the guidance and care of a mother is a really tough task. You always feel there is something missing, there is something gone. You always feel you need something in your life but you don't realize what that thing is. There is a lonely feeling that stays with you no matter if you are happy or sad . . . It is something more, something not understandable.

Nelson had introduced their goals in his first entry on January 13th this way:

> The other day I saw the movie *Freedom Writers*. It's a story inspired by the real lives of Long Beach, California, teenagers during the early

90s. The film was really good and it made me think about my own family and our story. In the movie the students kept diaries so that they could write about their life experiences. This made me want to write down some of my own experiences. [. . .]

I'm writing this blog with the help of my siblings to tell our story. We want to write our thoughts and feelings about the things we went through. We also want to help my mother [he means me] as she writes a book detailing the events that brought us all together. We have been through so much over the years and we are so lucky to have found each other.

This year marks an important year for our family and our story. It was twenty-five years ago that I was separated from my birth family and this coming Christmas it will be ten years since we were reunited. A lot has happened during that time, and it has not always been easy, but now we can look back and reflect on these incredible events.

My birth mother's name was Ana Milagro Escobar. Milagro is miracle in English and is the inspiration for the name of this blog. This is our story—this is Ana's Miracle . . .

In her introductory post, Eva also reflects on the central question in their minds:

WHY?
Wondering why has been a deep thought during my life, and now I know it is a question without an answer. However, it is the most important question we have asked ourselves . . . I guess this is the reason why we are telling our story. So maybe we can understand, and make others to understand what we went through. How after all, it has become a MIRACLE . . .

As my brother said, Ana Milagro is the name of our mother, which means MIRACLE. If you think about it, a miracle is full of power, full of hope, full of blessings, and I like to think that this is the legacy she gave to us, and this is her story, the story of a MIRACLE . . .

When Nelson went to Costa Rica again in May 2007, he and Eva recorded their first video blog. It was one day after the twenty-fifth anniversary of Mila's disappearance. The comfortable way they have with each other, and the ease with which they address their unknown viewers, amazes me. I have to recall that they now look back on nearly a decade of relationship with each other, and as "digital natives" they are much more comfortable than I with this technology that connects them to perfect strangers in an instant. As I watch their video, I notice how Nelson looks fondly at Eva on his right, but from time to time also glances to the left, as if he were looking at the portrait of Mila that is posted there, where she seems to watch over the proceedings.

In the dossier that accompanied the investigative report we received in the summer of 1997, there was a 3 ½ × 5 enlargement of this portrait, copied on an 8 × 11 sheet of paper. For the first time, we read Mila's full name that appears in oversized capitals immediately below. When Nelson saw it he wept. We found out later the original was only a small black and white passport-sized photo, perhaps one that had been taken for her identity card when she was fifteen.

Mila's long black hair has a wide middle part and is pulled tightly against her head and drawn back behind her ears, revealing a round face with a straight nose and full, shapely lips. Dark eyes peer out from thick brows. The photocopy accentuates the shadows on the right side of her cheek and under her nose and chin. Her eyes appear deeply set, as the right eyebrow cannot be distinguished from the eye socket. There is no trace of a smile around her mouth or in her eyes. She is looking slightly to the left as if something were happening nearby that she was quietly observing. That observant attitude reminds me a little of Nelson.

We first saw a softer version of this same portrait at the reunion in December 1997. Mamá Chila had it hanging on the living room wall of the house in Heredia where she was living then, a tinted 8 × 10 enlargement. Haydée, who has the original picture, arranged to have a similar enlargement made for her nephew and sent it to him from El Salvador soon thereafter. I bought a silver frame for it, and since then it has stood on Nelson's bureau. This enlargement is the one he scanned for the blog. The artist has lightened Mila's skin tone a bit and tinted her lips a pale pink. The hank of thick dark hair showing behind her head on the left side has strangely disappeared, and a fanciful bright pink blouse added. The sharply outlined V-neck of the blouse and the missing hair draws even more attention to the severity of Mila's gaze. Her finely arched brows show up, but the observant eyes are still dark and impenetrable. She appears to me to be someone who has already found her own inner strength—someone capable of making her own judgments and keeping them to herself.

«   »

The blog reveals that Nelson is taking a much broader interest in human rights as he completes his third decade of life. He comments there, for instance, on a visit to the Holocaust Museum in Washington, D.C., on the humanitarian crisis in Darfur, and the war in Iraq. But it is what he has to say about adoption that has blown me away, for instance in his post on March 13, 2007:

> Growing up as an adopted child was not always easy. The most difficult emotion I have *ever* had to deal with was the uncertainty that

came from being adopted. I imagine that most, if not all, adopted persons go through a similar experience sometime during their life.

Perhaps in my case these feelings might have been harder to deal with. For my parents did not even know my birthday, never mind how I came to be [orphaned]. Today I could not imagine my life without my adopted family, but back then having them was not enough.

There is just something about your birth mother / birth father that you can never forget or completely let go of. You want to know what they look like, if you look like them, and what kind of people they are. But most importantly you want to know: Why was I given up?

To this question there is no easy answer. It is something that I struggled with and watched my adopted friends struggle with. Some were more vocal than others, but you just knew even the quiet ones were thinking about it too. You wonder how can the people who gave you life simply give you away? Well I'm sure it's never that easy, and I'm sure they never forget either.

I used to sit at night staring out of my window wishing I could just see my mother. I thought if I could just see her, she would make everything better. These feelings never went away, no matter how hard I tried to fight or ignore them.

In the first video posting, he reminds Eva—and me—that when his family found him, he lost his biological mother for the second time, because up to then he had always imagined her alive:

One of the toughest things for me, though, was when I found out about my family, it meant that I would never meet my mother. And she was the one person I had always wanted to meet. You don't think so much about having brothers or sisters, not even a father. [. . .] But you just know you have a mother. That's the one person I dreamed about. So losing her as I found you was really hard for a long time. [. . .] [With this blog] we want to honor her; we want to remember what she gave up, what so many in my family gave up.

«   »

I think I always sensed Nelson's deep need for this other mother and feared I couldn't compete with a figment of his imagination—the perfect person who could bind all his wounds, "make everything better." But to discover now the extent to which he was fixated on his missing mother as a child has been a painful eye-opener for me. Whether he knew it or not, he was kind to keep these thoughts to himself for so long. As a teen he could have pitted this imagined figure against me and torn my heart in two with angry words. But sometimes he inflicted wounds on me by keeping his feelings to himself.

One Mother's Day sticks in my mind quite vividly. I think he was eleven. His sullen silence brought me to tears. I felt crushed by the weight of something I could not fully articulate, and it didn't help that Tom thought my reaction overwrought. Preoccupied with my keenly felt certainty that I had lost the little boy who had seemed to love us unconditionally, I did not appreciate how much he was suffering too. I realize now that had he wanted to share his feelings with us then, it might have been even harder for me to bear than his silence.

Given what has happened to our family in the past ten years, though, I can now listen with greater—although never perfect—equanimity when he writes of his childhood longings for his birth mother and tells of his grief at her disappearance, experienced ironically at the very moment when the rest of his biological family was so unexpectedly found. At least I can better appreciate why this portrait of Mila brought Nelson to tears the night we first shared the dossier with him and Derek.

Over the years, I have tried to find ways to create a connection to his other mother, a person I can never know. I have thought about her a lot, and I have read about women caught up in somewhat similar circumstances, such as *Audacity to Believe*, Sheila Cassidy's account of being captured and tortured in a Chilean prison after the Pinochet coup, and Margaret Randall's *When I Look into the Mirror and See You*, which provides the testimonies of two women who were among the few to survive disappearance in Honduras in 1982. Fiction has been helpful as well, such as Nicaraguan writer Gioconda Belli's novel *The Inhabited Woman*, about a middle-class woman who gets involved in a Latin American revolution, and Julia Alvarez's *In the Time of the Butterflies*, about three sisters in the Dominican Republic who resist the Trujillo dictatorship.

A plethora of recent studies on women's roles in the Salvadoran and other revolutionary movements have provided me with a sociological and historical framework to think about Mila.[1] One thing seems clear: the majority of the women who got involved in the leadership ranks of the FMLN in the late 1970s tended—like her—to be urban and better educated. Age also had something to do with it. Teenagers without children were more likely to join the militant groups, as they were more oblivious to the risks involved and more likely to embrace an idealistic view of the future. Those who had children or became pregnant when they were already guerrilleras believed that they were sacrificing to give the next generation a better future.

Looking at the various photos that accompanied the investigative report and the ones given to us by family members has also helped me bridge the divide, for I always try to imagine what Mila was doing and thinking at that moment, and what she would have said if we had been sisters or compañeras, and she had confided in me. Of course, I have also talked with her sisters, with Mamá Chila, with Luis and the children about her, and I have reflected on everything they have said. The memories they cherish and the visions they harbor don't always mesh neatly with what I have read, or with my own idea of her. She remains elusive, but I feel compelled to offer this patchwork—what I've learned about her from her family and from my reading about other women in similar circumstances, held loosely together by my own emotions.

There is so much one cannot know, yet I feel this necessity to not privilege the voices of all those who remain, leaving her alone without one. I think every adoptive mother probably has some kind of internal dialogue with the other mother. In our case, this imagined relationship has been magnified as Nelson has gradually revealed to me his singular focus on this missing mother. I have felt a similar need to fill an empty space for myself, to explore through the power of a reconstructed voice how Mila might have come to make the decisions she did.

While much of what I present in this chapter is based on what I have learned about Mila from her family, neither her true motivations nor what actually happened to her in Honduras can be verified. I have to go out on the thin ice of my imagination, but my attempt to know her and honor her mirrors my son's desire, for she will always be a part of him that is missing and that he misses.

« »

Derek was the first to try to think through Mila's experience. As part of his seventh-grade English history project on immigration that was due soon after we returned home from the first reunion, he was required to write two papers, one based on historical research, the other using his imagination. He read Tommie Sue Montgomery's entire book on the Salvadoran civil war among other sources for the first paper. But his fictional account of Nelson's story—as we then understood it—was told from Mila's point of view, an extraordinary choice for a twelve-year-old boy. He clearly had more emotional distance from her than his brother, and he must have realized that making Mila the first-person narrator would lend his writing real drama.

As I re-read the piece now, I am still struck by the way Derek tried to deal with the question of Mila's motivations by imagining her mental state right before the shoot-out that takes her life. It is the question each of us has asked ourselves repeatedly. Why would a young woman in her twenties do what she did, risking her own life and that of her child? Interestingly, Derek solves this dilemma, by visualizing Mila as not entirely comfortable with her assignment in the safe house in Tegucigalpa. He also concentrates on her just cause. She is on the side of the defenseless, the unjustly mistreated and poor.

Understandably, he couldn't quite grapple with her role as a kidnapper or her complicity in the violence, and so he preferred to imagine her, Job-like, imploring a personal God with the same question her children now ask—why?

> No one is safe in El Salvador. It is a horrible thing that no one can hide from the military. They come and take anybody; they don't care who it is. They torture or shoot them. Why God, are men such savages? Why?
>
> My name is Ana Milagro Escobar. [. . .] I am fighting for the rights of the people. I guess I will just have to get used to assignments like this. Every once in a while one of us goes to the market for food. We are told to look like an ordinary family, and so I guess Roberto makes it look even more like one.
>
> I cannot wait until this war is over and the senseless killings are put to a stop. The people deserve economic justice, and they deserve land. They deserve all that is being withheld from them. When I think about all this, my head starts to hurt, and I get really angry. So I lie down and rest awhile. Staring up at the ceiling, I say to myself, "Why God? Why this hurt? Why this pain to all who deserve none of it? Why do you not punish those who are inflicting this suffering? Why?"

After Derek's Mila reveals what happened on May 19, 1982, she explains the aftermath as well, including our adoption of the orphaned Roberto a year later, and the way the civil war ended. Derek thus imagines her having a heavenly overview of the political and familial events that transpired after her death. The Mila he constructs expresses disappointment that her dream of a better Salvadoran society was not realized, but she seems pleased that Roberto is happy with his "adoptive family in America."

Derek could thus conclude the story with the point that meant the most to him, but stated in her voice: "He has an adoptive brother too. I am glad that he is growing up well in a place I could have only dreamed about." By comparison, in his history paper Derek gives a more objective treatment in his own voice of Nelson's "interesting and unusual immigration to America," ending with an utterly realistic rendition of their brotherly love:

> Without my brother, Nelson, I would have a dismal life. He makes me laugh. He helps me with things I do not understand on the computer. He and his biological family make ours a culturally diverse family. He is nice most of the time, but sometimes he pokes me, tickles me, slams me on his bed, or teases me by calling me "Blanco," which means "white guy" in Spanish. But overall Nelson is a great kid, and I am proud to call him my brother.

« »

After re-reading Derek's essays, and after listening to Nelson and Eva talk about their mother, I realize the extent to which Mila is a presence in all of us. A poem I wrote for an assignment in an intermediate Spanish class in the fall of 2004, "Mi flor favorita" (My Favorite Flower), placed as an epigraph to this chapter, bears that out. It reveals that I have often thought of her as someone I can address directly. The poem plays on the idea that we might have something in common. After all, she chose my favorite flower as her pseudonym. The poem remains one-sided, however, as only my voice can be heard. Now I want to risk imagining how she might respond to me.

I hear her say, as if in answer to the poem's refrain, that she loves flowers too, like Tom and I do. Only once did she live in a place where she could cultivate her own garden. That was when she was living with Dalila, when Eva was just a baby; the sisters had a beautiful pocket garden out in front of their little red and yellow house. But I must understand; she was on the run, hardly daring to go outside. I hear her confirm my suspicion, though. She loved the roses and helaconia there, but blue irises had always been her favorites.

Oh, tell me all about it, Mila! I am eager to hear your voice that suddenly seems to ring true, if only in my mind. I want to ask you so many

things. What were you like before you met Luis on that day by the apartment block in Zacamil? In the photos we have of you, you look so serious. Why were you not smiling like a carefree teenager? The only Mila
I have gazes at me with those unfathomable eyes from photographs,
but I can distinctly hear her toss back one of my words as a question.
Carefree?

Yes, I already know from talking with your sisters and your mother
that life was not exactly free of cares. You couldn't escape the fact that
your family had been touched by tragedy when you were only six. I saw
the portrait of your older brother, René, hanging above Mamá's bed in
Heredia. You could never forget that your Papá had been negligent, leaving a loaded gun like that around the house, and he couldn't forgive
himself. He drank a lot and took his feelings of guilt out on all of you.

Then, not long after René shot himself accidentally, Vilma got into
trouble. She was only seventeen when she got pregnant the first time.
Your parents were scandalized. When the man denied being the father,
they sent her to your grandparents' house. They took care of the baby so
Vilma could go back to work. Later she got married and had another girl
and twin boys in quick succession, but her husband was no good. He was
an alcoholic too.

In 1971 your eldest sister had another baby girl, Martha Haydée.
Vilma suffered a lot during and after that pregnancy since she had injured her back, but she had to get right up and start working again. It was
fortunate for her that you had just finished the ninth grade and could
stay at home and look after the children while she and Mamá went to
the factory. They say you loved the children and tried your best. Haydée,
for whom the baby was named, often brought her boys over to Zacamil
too. Her eldest, René, reminded everyone of your brother, but your favorite was her little Jorge. I imagine all those kids were a handful.

When Martha was not quite one year old she got really sick. She was
coughing a lot because the house was very damp. One day, she fell out
of bed. You told your sisters later that you put her in the sink with water
to get her to respond. When that didn't help you took her to the hospital.
It must have been awful to see her turn blue and to feel so helpless. Were
you frantic? Did you run all the way? They called Vilma at the factory to
come quickly. The doctors said that the baby had congested lungs; a few
days later she died.

I can imagine all your sisters gathered around to comfort Vilma at
the burial—Dalila, Haydée, Tina, Tita, even Inés. And, of course, Mamá
was there. None of them blamed you, but that must have been small

comfort. Not long after that Vilma decided to get a divorce, and Mamá left Papá for good too. Luckily your maternal grandfather was a generous man. He had given Mamá some money to buy the apartment in Zacamil.

You had a roof over your heads—Mamá, Vilma with her children, and you—but you were still poor. The women in the family stuck together, but I imagine you sometimes longed to get away from all their demands. After Nena was born, Vilma quit her factory job because of her rheumatoid arthritis; she could take care of her own kids. You didn't wait long to act on your ambition to get more education and forge a life of your own. That's when you started taking courses at the Instituto Nacional General Francisco Menéndez.[2]

« »

I am looking again at the photos we have, all taken in the early 1970s when you were fifteen, sixteen, seventeen. I see only one that suggests you might have had some carefree days as a teen. You are standing next to Vilma on a beach, by a lifeguard tower with a thatched roof. You look as if you had just been in the ocean. But both of you appear subdued. Your hands are clasped a little awkwardly in front, as if you were pulling nervously at a finger. Maybe this was taken soon after the baby died. Kneeling in front of you, Haydée is the only one with a broad smile as four of the children are gathered around her.

Almost all of the other photos show you with your nieces and nephews. In the earliest, labeled December 1972, you are caught in what looks to be an outdoor corridor of the apartment house. You're standing in the shadow, with your face in the light, but still indistinct, brushing your hair out of your eyes. You watch Jorge toddle along well ahead of you, but you look worried. Will he fall? In another I see you holding him securely around the knees at the top of a flight of stairs against a background of cinder block. Your hair is wound in a loose topknot. The camera angle accentuates the length of your slender legs that stretch down three steps in front. Other photos show you indoors sitting on a couch with Vilma's youngest, Nena, and Haydée's daughter, Eugenia. In one you are caught in profile, revealing how your thick hair is held in place simply, with a barrette. You are giving the little girls a sidelong glance, smiling faintly.

Finally there is a series of six photos all taken the same day in October 1973. In these you are either standing or sitting in front of the apart-

ment block in Zacamil. You have your little nephew Jorge in your arms, on your lap, or you're holding his hand while he toddles across the uneven ground. In another, four other nieces and nephews sit or stand nearby while you hold Jorge in your arms. In these photos your hair is the same as in the formal portrait, pulled tightly back from a visible center part. In the last you are standing alone in a dusty field with only a few uncut grass tufts. One can just make out the corner of a building and a utility pole in the background, emerging from a bank of overgrown bushes.

«   »

We have an enlargement of this last photo. In it, the apartment block has disappeared entirely, and one cannot tell what the pole is doing in this otherwise wild, unkempt place. Mila, by contrast, is neat. She looks the way her sisters described her to me—very natural with no makeup. She stands comfortably straight with her arms hanging loosely at her sides, dressed in shorts and sandals. A silky short-sleeved blouse nearly covers her white shorts. It is loosely belted and clings to her body, accentuating her small, firm breasts and boyish figure.

The enlargement allows me to make out how tired she looks, though. No wonder, I think, with all those kids to look after and training as a militant at night. Here, too, Mila's eyes completely disappear into shadowed sockets. Her figure is that of a sixteen-year-old, but not her face. Had you met Luis by then? I can't help asking. I know it must be so, but understandably, Luis has kept the details to himself.

Mila had known him for about a year by the time this photograph was taken. She met him by chance in Zacamil, but they must have recognized each other right away because they were both going to the same school. I hear her say that Luis wouldn't have spoken to her otherwise. He wasn't shy, just very careful about choosing his friends. It must have been clear to her from the beginning that he sympathized with the popular movement, as did most students at that institute, but he didn't reveal how deeply he was involved until much later. He wanted to be sure that she had developed the right consciousness first.

Her sisters were right. Luis had recruited her into the FPL, but her political education was the responsibility of others. Being in the non-clandestine mass movement was one thing, joining a clandestine revolutionary organization another. It takes a long time before an individual is deemed ready. I imagine that the more she learned about the goals of the FPL, the easier it was to love Luis, but these were two different tracks she was on, although they were happening at the same time and were related. Her political formation didn't interfere with their growing intimacy.

I can even imagine she would meet Luis out in the brush in the photo, behind the apartment blocks. Or they would go out for a coffee after their courses at the institute and discuss things. He was nearly five years older. That meant a lot. She could learn from his experiences. He was serious too, but different, not as patient as she. I think she must have been attracted by his fiery passion for the people. And he was handsome.

Under the circumstances Mila would not have wanted Mamá to find out that she was getting serious about an older man any more than she wanted her family to know she was becoming a guerrillera. She managed to keep their relationship a secret from her family for nearly two years. It proved to be good practice for her later life in the underground.

«   »

You told them you were taking lessons so you could become a seamstress, and your sisters even bought you a sewing machine; Haydée still has it. It made some sense because Luis knew tailoring. Maybe you thought you could start a little business of your own someday. But first you had to see that the economic structures were changed, and that the repression of the regime was stopped. Several of your sisters think that you did everything because you were under Luis's spell, but I can't believe that is true. He was no *brujo* (sorcerer). I think you had a mind of your own. You just kept quiet about things. Luis liked the fact that you were so calm and centered. You could keep a secret. He knew that you would make a good militant.

During my visit to San Salvador in February 2005 I noted the following in my journal: *We're gathered around Mila's sewing machine on Haydée's porch, myself and three of the Escobar sisters, trying to make sense of the young girl for whom they had purchased it. "As a child she was happy, obedient, shy, and not adventurous at all," they insist. Tita emphasizes that as a teen she was very serious and responsible, but "quiet and shy. She didn't talk very much. She was very attractive, very feminine. She wasn't a flirt, though; she had no boyfriends."*

Being the youngest sister and taking care of all those kids, you had long since taken on adult responsibilities and were mature for your age; your sisters confirm that. You must have been willing to risk a lot to be with Luis and to make a difference for your country by his side. But I imagine you were determined not to make the same mistake Vilma had. You didn't even introduce Luis to the family until you were sure he wanted to marry. One thing puzzles me, though. Did you not comprehend that you might have to risk your life?

I once again hear her answer in the affirmative. Of course you knew being a revolutionary was dangerous, but when you're young, you don't think so much about it. You may even be fearful at times, but you don't really believe you'll lose your life. You always have your ideals in mind. Maybe it didn't sink in until you saw someone drop to the blood-spattered street during a demonstration. Others you knew disappeared. I can imagine that from then on, you had no illusions.

When Luis thought you had attained the right consciousness he admitted he was already in the thick of things and revealed his nom de guerre to you. By then your own commitment was deep enough. You must have believed you were involved in something so important that it would be worth any sacrifice. And you were probably hopeful then too, because the various groups were beginning to work together to create a real mass movement. You told your family that you were learning karate at the university. But you were actually preparing to be Luis's partner in every way.

You needed to complete the necessary weapons training so you could be placed in the same urban commando with him. By then, everyone knew you were a couple, your families and the people in the FPL responsible for your training. You didn't get married right away, though. Mamá still thought you were too young. Then your grandpa died, and you were all in mourning. Finally in 1976, Mamá gave her permission. But you waited until November. It was a tense time. You already knew that you might have to go into hiding right after the wedding.

«   »

I turn to one other picture I have of Mila, the only one in which she and Luis appear together. His brother Reinaldo had his copy scanned and sent it to us electronically after my visit to San Salvador in 2005. Creased by years of handling, the two figures are nonetheless distinct. It shows Luis Noé and Ana Milagro on their wedding day. When the children first saw it, they teased their father about his polyester leisure suit, his mustache, and the bouffant style of his dark curly hair. And each of them remarked that except for the mustache, the resemblance of the father to his son Roberto is striking. The newlyweds stand apart, each staring at the camera, just the trace of a smile on Luis's face, but none on Mila's.

Perhaps they are standing in Mamá's apartment where the civil ceremony took place. Mila seems to be grasping a railing. Luis's jacket is

open, revealing a sporty polo shirt with dark trim and open neck. One arm hangs at his side; the other is placed on his hip so that he is not standing quite straight, accentuating the fact that in her high heels, Mila is a bit taller. Here she shows the feminine side that her sisters described to me—she "never wore pants," according to them. Her princess style dress drops softly from a high waist to just below the knee, revealing trim, almost athletic calves. The material is light, a small flowered pattern on a white background, and the dress has wide, three-quarter-length sleeves. I wonder whether she sewed the dress herself, whether some of the flowers I can't make out are irises.

For the first time, I see Mila wearing glasses. Is she the source of Nelson's myopia? She has a nice watch on—perhaps a wedding gift—and drop pearl earrings. For once her hair is not parted and pulled back, but cut shoulder length and styled softly around her face. Most striking to me is the way the two are standing so far apart, not touching each other.

I can't help contrasting their stance with our favorite wedding photo, where Tom is standing behind with his arms encircling me, our hands entwined. I try not to read too much into it—I've been told that not smiling in photos is simply a cultural difference—but they still seem very grave for such an occasion. What were they thinking about? Did they already anticipate how little life they would actually have together? Mila is wearing a shoulder bag, as if they were ready to leave.

In fact they were, and not for a traditional honeymoon. The next day, as Luis has told us, they participated in a second ceremony, in which another oath bound them even more tightly together "till death." He did not describe this in detail, but I can imagine the scene quite well. I picture Iris and José in a safe house, surrounded by a few trusted compañeros and compañeras. I start with the wedding photo, for the look on their faces seems to belong in another costume.

For this occasion I see them both wearing pants, José in used fatigues, a cap with a star on his head, a little like Ché Guevara's. Iris prefers a bandana. I have removed the jewelry and tucked her hair gently back behind the ears. The glasses remain. She'll need them if she must shoot, I think reluctantly, for I have to remind myself that there is a reason this solemn ceremony is called a "wedding at arms."

The two mentors I've assigned Mila in my imagination look on proudly. Their charge has come a long way in her political formation these past three years, they agree. She has completed her politico-military course and been tested. Now Iris can rightfully take her place in an urban commando with José. Much will be demanded of her in the future, but they are confident that this young woman is strong and ready to commit herself totally to the revolution. Although José participated in an initiation ceremony years before, he wishes to renew those vows with Iris by his side. Each of them carries a gun to underscore their willingness to take up arms. I'm not sure whether they are assault rifles or machine guns, an AK-47 or an M-16.

The standard of the FPL is raised and their arms presented. After a brief speech, their beloved compañero Roberto Siprián—the person for whom they will name their third child—administers the oath of allegiance:

> Compañeros, the FPL has gratefully received Iris's application to be a full member of the organization. You know that "the FPL defends the interests of the working class and of the [Salvadoran] people and whoever is committed to these aims must be ready to defend them as the most important undertaking in their life."
>
> Iris, "do you swear to remain faithful to the interests of the working class and of the people, and to defend them with your own life or that of someone dear to you?"
>
> Do you swear to "always remain on the side of the poor and humble, loyal to them and never to oppose them?"
>
> Do you want "to remain faithful to the FPL and bear the slogan 'Revolution or Death' with honour, in the conviction that the people in arms" will attain the victory?[3]

I imagine her answering each question in a calm, clear voice: I do so swear. I am ready to defend the people with my life or that of someone I cherish. And her husband echoes each time, I do. I am. At the end of the ceremony, Siprián reminds them again of their duty and warns them what will happen if they should stray from their commitment to it. If they remain faithful, "the people would reward them," and if not, "the people would call them to account."[4] The couple puts down their arms; Iris and José embrace.

For a moment I am mesmerized by my picture of them in this other guise, and by my certainty that Mamá Chila was right when she gave me her considered view of Mila's actions: "At first we criticized Luis because we thought he had made her join the FPL. But no one can oblige you to do this kind of thing. My youngest always hid her feelings and opinions, but that didn't mean she didn't have any. She always observed very closely what was going on around her. I think she felt strongly that there should be equality for everyone in our country and that the oligarchy had to be overthrown."

Dalila seemed to agree with this conclusion when she wrote in her first letter to Roberto, "I admire [your mother] because she had enough encouragement [courage] to take the arms and fight for her cause; she was an idealist woman and she died. She offered her life because of her ideals. I didn't have the encouragement that she had." Toto concurs, as he wrote in his first blog post on February 13, 2007:

> [My mother is one of those people] who no matter if they will make a difference or not they try and they try. Against all odds no matter what they might risk or lose, they keep following those strong feelings. So this is something I won't forget about my mom, Ana Milagro Escobar. She had strong feelings that moved her to pick up arms and fight for others, fight for her cause, fight to try to change her world, and fight to give us a better life. That is one thing that made her such a strong woman and that I would never forget about.
>
> I too would like to help others as she did, and helping others was indeed her cause. Even though they [my parents] didn't change the world, they got a chance to make things better for us—a chance to try and make a better world and a chance to give us the opportunity they never had. That means a lot to us.

« »

Redirecting my attention to the Mila in my mind, the one who seems to answer me, I ask, What happened after your wedding at arms? Did you two have to go underground right away? What was that like? I have heard Luis talk of your activities, but as a woman and from what I've read about other women in the movement, I think you must have experienced things a little differently.

I asked Luis about this, and he cut me short. He told me it wasn't difficult for a woman to be a guerrilla, that it was "just a matter of having the right consciousness." But I have read that some women were upset that compañeros talked about equality but didn't really mean what we call gender equality. I've also read that the FPL discouraged couples, because if one person died, the other might abandon the cause. My imagined Mila interrupts my questioning quite forcefully this time.

Admittedly, it was hard for you to cut off all contact with Mamá, your sisters, and your closest friends. But I can hear you answer calmly that you just did what you were expected to do. You confirm what Luis has told us, that you were passionately in love, but that passion was all mixed up with your love of country and your belief that armed struggle was the only way to radically transform Salvadoran society. I think you must have been looking for solidarity more than equality, and Luis has emphasized that you had that at first.

I can't forget that José had been in the vanguard. He was already a trusted combatant. You must have felt that you still had to prove yourself. Yet, you were accepted as his equal and placed in the same urban cell. It may have been the case later on among combatants in the rural campsites that the FPL didn't want fraternizing, but in the urban commandos at the beginning, there were other couples like you. I've read how another couple, Eugenia and Javier, lived for two years together in hiding in San Salvador and raised their daughter in a safe house, believing that she was a part of their collective too.[5]

Luis had already been involved in some armed fights in the city before you got married. Things were getting too dangerous for him. When you chose the date for your wedding, you knew he would have to reassume his incognito very soon. You went underground in early 1977, about the same time as Eugenia and Javier. They were in a parallel cell of midlevel leaders. I know your friend Eva was placed in a different one, and the sacrificial manner of her death set an example for you. When you first heard about the shoot-out in Santa Tecla, did you weep or hide your grief at your personal loss?

Maybe you realized around this time that in comparison to your political sophistication, you were not prepared for the intimacy of marriage. Your older sisters describe you as pretty reserved, a homebody, young and naïve. You'd never even had a boyfriend before you met Luis. You probably knew what you didn't want, because you had seen your parents' marriage break apart because of alcoholism. Vilma's too. You must have been glad that Luis didn't drink at all; alcohol wasn't tolerated in the FPL. I wonder if you even thought much about having a child. No, I imagine you were preoccupied with the struggle.

I have even read that sexuality was a taboo subject for a lot of Salvadoran girls your age. One just didn't talk openly about sex, not even with older sisters who already had kids. Maybe you didn't understand how to protect yourself. In any case it wasn't very long before you did get pregnant. That must have been in April or early May. Even though it was a very difficult time, as Luis has admitted, and you had no contact with your family, you were overjoyed when your daughter was born at the end of the year. She was fair like Mamá, with green eyes and curly hair. You remembered your martyred compa when you named her Eva.

Of course, you hadn't realized that as soon as you had a child, it would change the role you were asked to play in the clandestine struggle. Instead of bringing you closer to your husband, it would keep you apart. But you both knew that you had to do whatever your leaders told you to do, whether you liked the assignments or not. Luis was opinionated and rebellious at times; later on he paid for that by being sent away to Chalatenango. That made it even harder for you to see each other, although in theory the FPL let couples meet once every fifteen days. And when you did, you only wanted to make love, not war.

The Mila in my mind smiles just a little at the "hippie" turn of phrase I have just used. I wonder whether I am right about this, whether what I have just imagined provides an answer to Eva's exclamation to me: "I could understand that they had one child, but given the dangerous circumstances they were in, how could they go and have three!" She wrote about this in a blog post on January 19, 2007:

> One of the things that really bothered me the most since I lost my mother is the fact that Mom and Dad had kids even though they knew they were at risk and their lives were in danger. I used to wonder: Why if I know my life is in danger would I have children? OK, let's say that one child is the legacy of the marriage, but two? And then three? I thought that it was irresponsible of them. Especially since they were actually fighting in the field and part of something really difficult in the middle of the war. And again I wondered WHY? For so long I blamed my parents for our separation. I blamed them for losing my little brother [. . .]. For years and years of seeing my Grandma quietly suffering and for not being there. [. . .] None of this made any sense for me during all my childhood. It took years and years for me to understand . . .

I know Eva would not now wish away her two younger brothers for the world, for in another post she writes about each of them with such great tenderness and insight into their personalities.

«   »

I also want to ask Mila whether in these urban safe houses women were left to do only what was considered women's work—cooking and cleaning and child care—while the men took part in armed actions. This time I imagine she might answer by lecturing me. Everyone was needed for the lucha. As the theory of a broad mass movement and a protracted struggle took hold, the inclusion of women across the board became necessary. Roughly 40 percent of the FPL members overall, 30 percent of the combatants, and 20 percent of the leadership were women, right up to the top echelon with Comandante Ana María as the equal of Comandante Marcial.

Some people think this was a mostly peasant movement, but in the case of the women, the urban component was important. Some were women who had been abandoned and had migrated to the city with their children in search of employment. Some women were pushed into the movement by the escalation of violence against their own families or friends. They knew someone who had been tortured, raped, disappeared. They joined in self-defense.

Others were pulled into it by their own growing political consciousness. They had enough schooling and could read the newspaper and the political pamphlets. They could see what was going on. Most joined the insurgency at a very young age. A lot of the women in the various leadership ranks were born during the 1950s. In the late 1970s when the repression was escalating, they were relatively free of family obligations and were ready to assume huge risks.

I interrupt this train of thought with a rhetorical question. That's probably why you were prepared to join while your older sisters didn't even think of it. In part, your involvement was an accident of birth order, wasn't it? I don't wait for a reply; an answer in the affirmative seems obvious.

Back to my original question, I realize you were assigned to a small cell, and each person was a compa. Luis has told us the way you had to depend on each other utterly. You all had to know how to fight, women and men alike. Nevertheless, I sense your willingness to acknowledge my suspicions. We both know a patriarchal society doesn't change overnight and that the attitude of individual men can differ.

As a couple everything changed for you quickly. Only a little over a year after you got married, you had a child to take care of, and after the shoot-out in Santa Tecla, things got very difficult for all the urban guerrillas. Luis told us about it, but I wonder how you felt that day when your cell was tipped off that the Policia de Hacienda was going to raid the safe house you were in.

It seems that José no longer thought of his pledge to willingly sacrifice the ones he loved, but only of your safety. You were able to get out of there with Eva but soon found out there had been no raid. Still, it wasn't safe to go back. The police were surely watching that place all the time. I wonder whether you were grateful you had escaped. Or were you resentful that you had become separated for naught?

I can imagine you slipped back into your old identity as Mila pretty easily and discovered you were even more useful to the movement that way. By then the FPL knew you had organizational skills. They gave you greater responsibility. It was important logistical work. You told the family that Luis was in Guatemala on extended business and went to stay with Dalila in the little red and yellow house with the beautiful garden.

«   »

Before the Mila in my mind and heart can elude me, I venture another question. Of course, this was much later, but how did you react when you learned that José had been badly wounded up north? You must have been alarmed, but I feel sure you had to remain absolutely calm in the face of this new danger. You couldn't just go running off to be at your husband's side. Any move you made could endanger everyone in the family. You had returned to Mamá's flat in Zacamil by then since you had both Eva and Toto. By the time you found out, Luis was already at the secret FPL medical facility in Aguilares. He was a valued combatant and surely they would take care of him.

You yourself had been involved in secret operations for two years and were well versed in the ways of the organization. You knew a lot of important people too and how to arrange false identities. When it became clear he needed surgery they couldn't perform in the field, you must have realized they would bring him to San Salvador, where you had connections. You were able to get him into the hospital under another false name. But he needed blood transfusions. So you had to risk your families discovering what you were doing. I imagine you thought saving his life was worth any risk.

Your sisters have told me what happened next. You left the key you wore around your neck where Mamá could find it. With your training, it is hard to believe you would be so careless. Did you do that on purpose? I imagine Mamá didn't have to say much. She let you know with her eyes—the way my mother used to—that she did not like the choices you'd been making. But despite her disapproval, you could trust her. Whenever you needed Mamá Chila, she always came through. She cared for Luis when he was discharged from the hospital. And one can't forget that she saved Eva and Toto. The children are right about her. She is the true heroine of this story. Eva wrote about her on January 25, 2007:

She is such a strong woman and at the same time the most caring woman I've ever known. To look into her eyes is to look at a whole life filled with suffering and sadness. Every mark on her face shows she is old, but even so, she is young at heart. This woman has been through too much, so that the sadness never goes away, even if she is happy. So small and delicate, she has done any kind of work just to support her family. She's got an incredible wisdom given by God. Always a leader, always the center of the family, she is always there for us. She means the whole world to us. She has many daughters and sons because everyone loves her.

She didn't give me life, but I don't think the kind of love she has for us could possibly be named. She loved us like a mom and she loved us like a grandma. For all these years she took care of us, suffered, and worried. She worked for us and gave us all material things she could give, but her most important gift was her unconditional love. She showed us the right and wrong, she was an example of how to be a good person, she made us the people we are today and she made me the woman I am.

Never afraid, she never gave up in any situation in her life. She never gave up looking for my brother either, and in this story she is the angel God sent to earth to take care of all of us. She is an example of a person who never forgets and never abandons anyone in the family.

She used to talk about Roberto a lot. The thing she worried the most about was if he was with someone who loved him. It was what she really cared about, because she always said she has a lot of love for him. So she wondered all the time: Where is Roberto? Is he loved? Finally one day she announced she was going to El Salvador to look for him, even though she knew it was risky. She started the journey with my aunt's help and went to knock on every door of people she could possibly remember my mother being involved with. A lot of them were slammed in her face. . . . One day, her reward came unexpectedly. Years and years of wondering where he was, if he was OK and what kind of boy would he be, finally ended for her.

Every day I wonder how is it that this tiny and old woman could have been so strong and never broke down. So calm and quiet, I never saw her crying . . . just once . . . the day she knew Roberto was alive . . . that day she changed. Let me tell you she became a different person then. Certainly her sadness was still there but extraordinarily she was happy, and you could see it in her eyes. They were never the same anymore. Somehow she got strength from somewhere, and it seemed

to me like she started all over again. It was like she could breathe
again and release part of this pain in her heart. All the effort and pain
through all of these years gave her a reward—she had lost a daughter
but then she recovered her grandson.

«   »

All the attention I'm paying to what the children are now writing on
their blog is just postponing the inevitable, shielding myself for a time
from thinking too much about the scenes that come next. I am reluctant
to imagine the couple's estrangement, even though Luis confirmed it.
By the time they saw each other in the Nicaraguan training camp, intimacy could be briefly restored, but their solidarity was broken. In one of
her first posts, Eva described it this way:

> After thinking a lot about what I should write next, the day I saw my
> mother for the last time came to my mind. A lot flashes through my
> mind; the vision I have is so blurry. I do remember that day . . .
> I've never talked about it before to anyone, maybe because I didn't
> trust my memory. But now it seems to flow in my mind and makes
> sense after all. Oh God, I was just three years old . . .
> I have the feeling I hadn't seen her for so long the day she came
> [to visit us in Nicaragua], the last time I saw her. I remember she was
> in a rush, kind of nervous, maybe anxious, but looking at her was like
> looking at an angel. I couldn't have been happier to have her back.
> I remember her bringing a lot of presents for me, my brother Er-
> nesto, and for my Grandma too. At that time, there was just the two of
> us siblings. I remember I loved all of the presents, but all I wanted was
> to be with her. However, she was having a conversation with my father
> and they seemed to be very serious about it. Their faces had an expres-
> sion of anguish that I couldn't understand at that moment, and now
> I think that maybe they knew they were not going to see each other
> again . . .
> After that, all that I remember is my mom packing her bag the
> next day . . .
> She got a perceptible sadness in her eyes, a sad look that will never
> fade from my memories. Even so, she was calm and peaceful, with a
> peace that only someone who is doing the right thing can have . . .
> She comes to me and hugs me for so long. I don't remember the
> words she said to me, but I do remember her looking at me with such

love. I can say it was with the love that I use to look at my beautiful daughter nowadays, as if you were looking at the most precious treasure you could have. My brother Toto was standing there; interestingly enough, he was calm as well. He wasn't crying, but he had those puppy dog eyes [. . .]. Maybe because he wasn't aware of what was happening and was trying to understand, or maybe it was just a preview of his strong but calm personality.

I wish I could remember more about her. After watching her say good-bye, all I remember is that I cried, cried from the deepest part of my heart, like I am crying now. I remember all I could say was: "Don't go, Mom, don't go . . ."

After re-reading Eva's post, I dare not conjure up the argument that she remembers her parents having at this time, something she and Mamá had mentioned to me when we talked about it two years ago, but the specifics of which have faded. What could such a little girl, not quite three years old, grasp of her parents' emotional turmoil anyway?

I can't help wondering, though, whether the argument was a purely personal matter or partly political. Had each already begun to doubt the efficacy of their struggle, not admitting it to the other? Mila, perhaps you were upset at the thought that Luis might further injure himself by making love, but you could just as easily have been mad because you found out he believed the rumors he had heard about your infidelity with another compañero while he was in Cuba. Was Roberto conceived before or after your heated exchange?

My questions hang in the air unanswered, unanswerable. My Mila remains silent on this score. I have to admit, it is easier for me to picture her as a daughter, sister, and mother than as a wife and lover, and easier to think of her as a victim of violence than as a person who herself was willing to use violent means to achieve her ends. I try one more question. What was in your heart and mind when you kissed Mamá and the children good-bye? A fainter but still distinct voice seems to reply that her heart was aching. Eva was clinging to her and wouldn't let go, as if the child knew this was it.

You surely realized that you were not likely to see her or Ernesto again soon. Toto was still such a baby, barely walking. He needed you. But unless you were willing to abandon your vital work for the FPL in San Salvador, you could not be with them. You weren't ready to do that yet. You were still committed to the cause, although no longer as optimistic as when you had asked Mamá to take the children out of harm's way. I imagine you doubted now that everything would be over "in a year or so." But you may still have trusted that you would find some way to be together. I know that you wanted Mamá to stay in Nicaragua, for now, so you could see the children whenever your comandante would allow it.

It wasn't so clear what would become of your marriage under the circumstances. It had been hard enough to arrange this meeting, and there had been too little time. Why had those compañeros spread lies about you? Were they purposely trying to drive a wedge between you and José? Why? Somehow, I am sure that you left feeling confused, sad, and hurt, but nevertheless determined to carry on with your work.

«   »

It is a little easier for me to think about what it must have been like for Mila when she discovered back in El Salvador that she was pregnant again, at a time when urban militants were being found out and killed daily. She was living in the Zacamil apartment with Haydée and her family. One revolutionary recalls the period this way: "People were being killed a lot then. You'd wake up in the morning and somebody would be dead in the street. You see, around this time the guerrilla movement was just getting strong." If the security forces thought someone was a guerrilla, or knew the whereabouts of one, "they'd drag the person away for investigation or they'd just shoot him in the street."[6]

You may have been a little frightened and perhaps even angry about the vulnerable position you found yourself in. Luis was back in Cuba—so far away and in no danger, although you knew his health was fragile. Haydée has told me this third pregnancy was difficult for you, and it took you longer to recover. It wasn't anything serious, though. You weren't depressed. Surely you were relieved that Roberto Alfredo was another healthy baby. It isn't hard to imagine that when you looked into his sweet dark eyes, you knew you wanted to keep this child with you at all costs.

All this time you still got your assignments from Comandante Filo, but you had to discharge them alone. You no longer experienced the comforting solidarity of living in a revolutionary cell or being able to share things with Luis every few weeks. You only had your own conscience to guide you.

Just once, you articulated your doubts and confided in Haydée. You were arranging for Cubans, Russians, Libyans, and other foreigners to get into the country illegally. You told her this wasn't what you thought you were going to be doing when you joined. "I want to find a way out; I want to live with Mamá and my kids in Costa Rica. That's my dream. I don't think this war will end very soon. Can't you see the so-called final offensive earlier this year was just the beginning?"

This account comes from Haydée, whose word I trust, but I'm not certain of you, Mila. Perhaps you did intend to go to Costa Rica, now that the baby was born, and your plans got scratched when the FPL suddenly shifted you to a different task in another country. Or were you just trying to make your family believe that you were disillusioned and wanted to get out of the movement, throwing up a smokescreen before disappearing on a top-secret mission to Honduras? Both of these scenarios seem plausible and possible to me.

I wonder about Roberto's birth too. He was born in the Maternity Hospital in San Salvador. How did you dare have the baby there instead of at home with the midwife who had always attended Haydée? I find myself answering my own question this time. Remember, Mila's photograph hadn't appeared in the paper yet. She must have been confident that the cover provided by her apparently normal existence was sufficient. Perhaps the difficult pregnancy made her want to give birth in a hospital.

I have seen Larry Towell's photograph of newborns labeled "Maternity Ward, San Salvador, 1986." They're crammed two to a box, lined up head to toe, toe to head, but enjoying the body warmth and all sleeping peacefully. I can well imagine Roberto as one of these swaddled babies in a cardboard container instead of a crib. The photograph on the following page is much harder to focus on.

It too relates to maternity. The mothers of the disappeared, in their distinctive white scarves imprinted with the word "CO-MADRES," stand in an office with a single poster of a young woman on the wall behind them. They are displaying dozens of albums with photos of the bloodied, disfigured faces of their slain sons and daughters, so many pictures of the disappeared and abused that the women who are standing there are half covered by these awful pictures. What chance did the little ones on the previous page have of escaping the fate of their older brothers and sisters, I ask myself.[7]

«   »

And while I am thinking of photographs—can you have known that your picture appeared in the paper on the very same day you brought

Roberto into the world? Did you read the paper that day? I wonder how long you were in labor. Now I have to smile at my questions, for I feel certain you must have been preoccupied, although Roberto didn't appear on the scene until mid-afternoon. You might have heard about the publication the next day; Luis's brother Mariano had seen it and recognized the peril. Luckily it did not provide a good likeness. But how did you react in your weakened state? Did you panic or keep your head? Haydée recalls only that you weren't feeling well and therefore didn't go out much after the birth.

Now I know I was on the wrong track when I searched only the September and early October 1981 issues of those newspapers in San Salvador in 2005, hunting for the page of photographs that Mariano, as well as Dalila and Haydée, had described to me. I had wrongly assumed this turn of events had immediately precipitated your departure for Honduras and thus came up empty-handed.

« »

It seems worth a second try in the Library of Congress, where one can more comfortably undertake a wider search. On our way from Boston to Florida in February 2006, Tom and I stop for a few days in Washington. Each of us is sitting at a microfilm machine in the Hispanic Reading Room in the James Madison Building, going back through whatever Salvadoran newspapers are available for the year of our son's birth, page by page. Finally, Tom finds what we are looking for, something which fits their story. He can hardly believe his eyes, though, when he comes to the front page of the right-wing newspaper *El Diario de Hoy* in San Salvador, and notes the coincidence of date, Viernes, 22 de Mayo de 1981, Roberto's birthday.

Up to now, all we have found are pictures of individual captured "subversives," or sometimes two at a time, with a caption identifying them by their family names. I see a photo of two women, for instance, each holding a rifle with the ERP banner between them, reportedly captured February 16, 1981, and implicated in various kidnappings and assassinations. I assume that torture extracted their given names, which appear in the caption. Even more numerous are the photos of disappeared young people placed as ads by their families, the kind I had seen by the dozens already during my earlier search.

This is different. The headline announces, "Detienen Otra Mujer Terrorista" (Another Female Terrorist Detained). The news about a spectacular capture appears in other papers, but here it is featured in a front-page article. No photo of the captured woman is shown, but in the middle of the page, we see a grid of small photos found in her house. The pictures purportedly show various "collaborators of the clandestine FMLN-FDR." The last sentence of the caption harbors a thinly veiled threat: "The detainee can provide information about their activities."

The woman is identified as Ana Margarita Teresa Gasteazoro Escolán, nom de guerre, Monica, thirty years old, accused of "conspiring against the security of the Republic." She is said to be facing a "military tribunal," after having been "detained by the National Guard." I have read about what the Guard did to their "detainees." I feel certain she was tortured after her capture, but could Ana Margarita have revealed Ana Milagro's identity? I think not. That was the whole purpose of their pseudonyms, I remind myself. Monica may have known Iris, but not Mila.

Ana Margarita was evidently a top-level operative of the FMLN in charge of national and international propaganda efforts. A letter supposedly found in her house and mentioned only in *La Prensa Gráfica*, shows that she had very close ties to Marcial and infers that an internal struggle was already going on in the FPL.[8] The many audiovisual and print materials uncovered by the raid are enumerated in *El Diario de Hoy* article in great detail—for example, a thirty-one-page document outlining all the FPL's propaganda plans, including use of radio and films. What is most interesting for me, however, are the number and range of Monica's international ties.

Multiple instances of supposedly nefarious contact with the Socialist International are cited, beginning with her clandestine attendance at an international youth festival in Cuba in 1978. I am particularly astonished by the fact that a stay in Bonn, Germany, is made to appear extremely suspicious. Her contact there was with the SPD (Social Democratic Party)—the party of former chancellor Willy Brandt. To me, a professor of German who thinks of the SPD as a party of the center, this sounds pretty innocuous.

Similarly, Monica's visit to the Latin American Bureau of the British Labor Party youth branch is held against her, as well as a trip to Canada paid for by the women's group of the NDP (New Democratic Party). Tom grew up in Manitoba and was a member of the NDP, a mainstream, socialist-leaning governing party in that province; we know it was no more radically left-wing than the German SPD at the time. As I recall, Ed Broadbent, its leader, had been suggested as a mediator for the Salva-

doran conflict after Willy Brandt had been rejected. The government always refused; even these moderates were suspect because they could be
labeled "socialists."

Monica's international contacts might be a reason why she had a
photo of Iris in her house. The small square photos are arranged as if
they had been kept in an album. We can make out three rows of young
people, seven in each row, eighteen men and three women. Could the
one with the round face, long hair, and visible center part be Iris, the
second from the left in the top row? It is hard to tell by looking through
the microfilm machine, and on the photocopies the individual faces are
even less distinguishable. We can't be absolutely sure it is Mila, but we're
inclined to think so. At least it demonstrates that this kind of thing was
going on—a group of photos of FPL guerrillas published in the paper,
without names, just like the family had told us.

« »

Tracing the publication of the photo back to the day of our son's
birth helps me make sense of other things I do know. It could explain
why Mila waited two whole months before registering Roberto, preferring to pay a fine rather than risk being recognized by some official who
would surely turn her over to the National Guard. As it turned out, the
late fee was waived. I have seen that written on his birth certificate. Perhaps, with all her medical contacts, Mila was able to produce a doctor's
affidavit to attest she had been too sick to come to city hall.

Turning the clock forward again to August or perhaps September
1981, I imagine Mila taking a deep breath. So far, she has not been recognized. First her sister Haydée, then her brother-in-law Mariano and
his wife, Reina, have hidden her in plain sight. She feels stronger now,
and Roberto is nursing well and growing. She has written her mother
a letter. She is either waiting for her next assignment or looking for a
chance to escape.

We have only one baby photo of Roberto; it was taken around this
time. He's still not able to sit up by himself, so he is propped up against
the back of a big basket or possibly a carriage or bassinet, disguised completely by the white blanket with pale yellow trim that has been thrown
over it. He almost disappears into all that whiteness since he too is all in
white—dressed only in a plain undershirt and diaper. His strong arms,
round face, and sturdy legs are visible, but his feet are hidden. His cousin
César, Haydée's younger son, a year or so older than Roberto, has placed

his arm around the back of the basket in a protective gesture. I study Roberto's face. The photograph is small and there isn't much to go on. He's just a baby—round face, dark hair, dark eyes, a lighter skin tone than now; he hadn't been exposed to the sun much, I am thinking. But the widow's peak already visible on his hairline might be called a recognizable feature.

When were you notified that you were needed in Honduras? Was it before or after you wrote to Mamá Chila in late September? Had you really intimated to your comandante that you wanted out of the FPL, as your sisters now claim? If so, was that the very reason you were sent on such a mission—to put your loyalty to the test? Did you worry about what might happen to the family if you refused, or did you weigh that against the danger you and Roberto would face if you went? Did you have any real choice in the matter?

I have to wonder whether there was any way out for Mila at this point. How much was she told in advance about the mission? She certainly knew that it was dangerous to travel to Honduras. Did those who sent her have any idea she would assist in a kidnapping months later? Iris hadn't been involved in that kind of thing before. Why was she chosen?

I try turning over different scenarios in my mind. Perhaps Iris's comandante enticed her with the prospect that she would be able to see José in Honduras. Perhaps she thought that they could reconcile and figure out their next steps together. Or did she just want one last chance to defend herself, now that there might be the opportunity to introduce Luis to Roberto in person? He would see at a glance that the child was his. I don't know; I can't hear her voice any longer. I don't get any answers to these questions.

«   »

The only concrete testimony we have is the letter Mila addressed to Mamá Chila on September 23, 1981, about three weeks before the date the family proposes for her departure from El Salvador. Dalila gave me a copy when I stayed with her in 2005, and her eldest son, Juan Carlos, translated it.

The children like to read what their mother says about each of them. They can see how she cared for them, how she wanted to be with them and believed someday she would be. They can even laugh when she scolds her own mother and says she's heard that "Toto is a crybaby and is drinking too much coffee." They can appreciate that their mother had a mind of her own as she voices strong opinions. She was the youngest Escobar sister, but she clearly wasn't a "crybaby" herself, and she didn't want her children to be. Here for once, instead of mere imaginings, I have Mila's authentic voice—clear, strong, unafraid:

September 23, 1981

Dear Mamá,

I hope that when you receive this letter you are in good health as well as everybody around you. Mamá, the person who carries this letter will ask about the kids and how he can help you. I want you to tell him everything that the children need. I will stay here in the meantime. I don't know how long, but I hope that you can understand my situation. I want to see my children more than anything, but right now I cannot.

I could only send you some of the things you asked for because as you know my economic situation is difficult.

On a different note I want you to explain why you left Nicaragua and what you told those people. Finding out that you are there [in Costa Rica] was for me a great surprise because I don't know your reasons. Can you tell me where Luis is? I haven't seen him since I was there [in Nicaragua].

Some people are telling me that Toto is a crybaby and is drinking too much coffee. Please don't make them spoiled kids. Remember that they are with you for now, but they will be with me again one day, and you know how I am with them.

I want to let you know that Haydée is going to move into her own house in October and we are thinking about selling the apartment. Dalila says not to sell it, and Tita says sell it to buy a house instead. My advice to you is to sell it and have the money sent there because here [in El Salvador] the situation is getting worse every day. It [victory] is not going to be as soon as we thought. Maybe it is going to take two years or more, and for that reason it is better that you sell the apartment and try to start over there [in Costa Rica]. Even we [in the movement] don't know how the situation is going to be, and if my sisters left the country they wouldn't have anywhere to go. However if you are there they will have somewhere to go in an emergency. Dalila might move in when Haydée leaves because if not, we will lose the apartment.

Regarding the power of attorney, I advise you to do it there with help of a lawyer. Then send it back to the country [El Salvador]. I don't advise going in person because it is too dangerous. Passing through Honduras is too risky. They let you go in [to El Salvador] but do not let you go out again. Something bad could happen. Everybody who goes inside the country is checked and interrogated. I want to tell you that some female cousins of Haydée's midwife came back here, were taken out of their house, were raped, and killed. For that reason it is better that you do not to go to El Salvador, although I know you want to see your daughters. But it would be far worse being so close, but dead.

Try to solve the problem about the apartment staying there. Come to an agreement with them [your other daughters]. You can call them by phone or write to them, but don't let them know where I am, because that could be risky. Please tell Vilma the same. She should not write things that could compromise me, because every letter coming into or out of El Salvador is read. The same goes if you call by phone. Be careful because the risk is with your daughters who are there [El Salvador].

Tina called 5 months ago and she said that she had written several times to Vilma, but Vilma didn't answer. Even more she thinks that the letters never were received because of the situation of the country. I explained to her that you were fine, and I told her not to worry. I promised I would write to you, but I don't know if her letters were received.

Tita says that Raulito of Andreita [Andreita's son] wants to buy the apartment. He wants to get a loan. We told him that you wanted 8,000 *colones* for it. I think that is a very good deal. If you still find someone who wants to buy it, sell it. Please do what I tell you because you know better than anybody that I am always truthful with you. Even if you do nothing with the money but spend it on food that money is still yours.

Lupe of Andreita [Andreita's daughter] came to ask for clothing and shoes. She said because you always brought her cloth and shoes she misses you. Andreita also came. She has become a fat woman and asked us to send her regards to you. They still live in Tierra Blanca ["White Land"]. Alicia lives in La Santa Lucia, and she rents a house there with a young man and Yolan. She wasn't able to get to the United States. Isabel of Andreita is pregnant. Lupe was looking for a job because Roque's salary is not enough.

I am sending you photos of the baby. His name is Roberto Alfredo. Tell the kids that he is their little brother. I trust God that they meet him soon. Tell me what Eva says about her father, if she misses him, if she still remembers me. I am fine, although I had some problems because of the childbirth but it was nothing serious. The baby looks like Eva.

I will see if I can send you money monthly so tell me what you need and how much money you spend. I sent you some things inside of the suitcase. If you need the suitcase then take it, if not send it back to me because I can use it.

The things which I am sending are:

3 panties for Eva
socks for Toto
1 pan and spoons
2 blankets
1 lotion
1 soap
1 talcum powder
1 blouse for you (Dalila sends it)
underwear for you
1 pair of shoes for you (Tita sends them)
3 towels
2 pair of pants for René
2 shirts
socks
handkerchiefs
shoes
1 jacket
other things

Now I must say goodbye to you.

The daughter who misses you so much,
Mila

P.S. Send me Vilma's phone number. I will see if I can call from time to time in order to see how you are. If Luis should call Vilma's mother-in-law, she shouldn't tell him where you are. She should tell him that you left for El Salvador.

«   »

When I asked him what his first wife was like, Luis stated simply, "She was a good mother." We can see this in the letter. Mila was trying in every way she could to be the best mother to her children under extremely difficult circumstances. Eva reflected on that in a post on February 21, 2007:

> I have to say that I've never understood much about the purpose of being a mother. As we are developing as mother or parents, we are discovering ourselves as well, and it makes our task even more difficult. We have to handcraft this person and decide what is right and wrong for our children while at the same time for ourselves. This brings me to the purpose of this blog and to talk about my mother. If you think about what I just said, it is inevitable to think about what our mother did for us. Maybe she regretted not being able to see us grow up every day, maybe she didn't enjoy looking at us sleeping, maybe she missed a lot of birthdays, but I have no doubt she loved us with this unconditional love. I can assure you she sacrificed herself for us, and now as a mother I totally understand her decisions. As young people, we used to judge our parents and expect them to be perfect, but the truth is that there are not perfect parents, just parents full of love and that was her love, a love like no other . . .

Mila's letter also demonstrates that she was not sentimental. She knows who she is and what she can and cannot do. She knows that she is part of something larger than herself. This is the "we" of the letter. She is relying on her revolutionary network, on the trusted messenger who has delivered the letter and will bring back the longed-for information about what the kids need. She will stay where she is until she has gotten that. But she implies she will not be there—wherever that is—much longer, and that she may have need of the suitcase. Even her sisters, especially the ones arguing over what should happen with Mamá's apartment in Zacamil, don't know her whereabouts and should not know. She remains clear-eyed and forthright about the reality of her personal situation, both economic and strategic. And she doesn't want to be compromised:

> I want to see my children more than anything, but right now I cannot. [. . .] Remember that they are with you for now, but they will be with me again one day, and you know how I am with them. [. . .] I could only send you some of the things you asked for because as you know my economic situation is difficult. [. . .] I will see if I can send you money monthly so tell me what you need and how much money you spend.

It doesn't sound as if she is going to be able to join them soon.

To me, the Mila of this letter comes across as honest and not devious, but also as hard-nosed and decisive. She asks her mother to explain why she left Nicaragua, where Mila felt sure the children would be safe. She asks for reasons. She doesn't hesitate to use the imperative repeatedly with Mamá Chila and by implication with her sisters. Other parts of the letter seem almost matter of fact: the list of items sent, for example, so Mamá can check to see that all had arrived, and the details about the arrest and rape of women they knew. Mila does use the words "risk" and "risky" repeatedly. She has a realistic view of the dangers now that the Salvadoran conflict is an all-out civil war. She thinks that it is likely to be a prolonged struggle.

By means of this letter we also learn that she has not seen Luis for over a year and does not even know where he is. At first she seems to want to know: "Can you tell me where Luis is? I haven't seen him since I was there." I wonder when she last heard from or of him. "Tell me what Eva says about her father, if she misses him," she writes, then poignantly adds, "if she still remembers me." The postscript makes it clear, however, that Mila wants to keep him from finding out where the children are. Only with regard to her husband is her voice ambivalent, leaving me confused. Perhaps she was too.

«   »

Reading Mila's letter has brought her closer to me once more and given me the courage to try direct address again. What did you do for the five months that you lived in Tegucigalpa before the kidnapping? That's a long time to wait for something to happen. Did you learn that Luis was also in Honduras and hoped to see you and Roberto? Were you disappointed when he did not get permission? Did you know that Guardado had been captured and that the FPL central command was trying to strike a deal for his release? Did your group hear of the arrest in Tegucigalpa on April 24th of another FMLN cell, consisting of five people, or of the shoot-out that killed five men and two women on May 17th?[9] No answer.

Still, I press: were you the woman who accompanied the heavily armed men in the beige car, the woman reportedly wearing a "pañuelo y gafas" (headscarf and sunglasses) who kidnapped the industrialist Casanova on his way to work at 7:45 in the morning on March 10th?[10] No answer. I am left on my own.

I know for sure that she was much more experienced than those two raw recruits, Rosa and Blanca. I have to imagine it was Iris who partici- pated in the kidnapping. But that is a drama I would rather keep at a dis- tance. I prefer to picture her in a domestic scene in the safe house, feed- ing Roberto and then watching him crawl across the tile floor of the kitchen, or giving Rosa a tip on deep breathing for her upcoming child- birth, or rocking Blanca's little girl to sleep. In that context I can even think of her with a Galil machine gun in her hand, taking a turn at sen- try duty, with Casanova safely out of sight below.

I have come to believe—with Mamá Chila and Derek, as well as Mila's children—that she was sure what she was doing was for a just cause and that she hoped by this means to gain a better future for her country and by implication for her offspring. But sometimes I feel crit- ical of her actions. When she took Roberto with her to Honduras she surely knew that she was placing him directly in harm's way. Having seen her other children so rarely, she probably just longed to keep this baby close; what mother would not want that? But she must have com- prehended how dangerous it was. Wasn't the whole idea that the cell would appear to be a normal extended family so that they could under- take kidnappings or other subversive acts?

For that the FPL needed women with children, but women who un- derstood what they were doing, ones who were willing to sacrifice their child if need be.[11] Mila had pledged in no uncertain terms: "I am ready to defend the people with my life or that of someone I cherish." What kind of courage—or foolhardiness—did it take to be willing to risk Ro- berto's life as well as her own in this way? Mila had seen to it that her other two children were safe. Why not this one? Perhaps she simply had no other choice once the order came. What would they have done to her if she had refused to take the child or gotten on a bus for Costa Rica in- stead? I do not know.

Mila's children, of course, concentrate on the idea of their mother's love for them and her bravery—and so they should. But as the other mother in this story, I have pondered whether she might not have felt divided in her loyalties, alone with compas who did not know her, and even afraid at the end. I would have been. I realize I will never really be able to understand her.

And I cannot ignore my own ambivalence. From time to time I have to reflect on the irony that had Mila not been willing to set out on this terrible path, Tom and I would never have had this particular child to love. Like Eva, there have been moments when I find it impossible not to judge Mila pretty harshly for endangering her child, but that emotion always overlaps somewhat with my gratitude that she did, as well as my amazement at all the improbable circumstances that led him to become our child. That he escaped from the shoot-out unharmed and was later entrusted to our care was—at least for us—a miracle.

«   »

No one in the family really wants to think or talk about what comes next in the narrative. I feel bereft. The only photo I have is the one in the newspaper of the dead woman face down in a pool of blood on the tile floor. She was shot dead immediately upon opening the door. She was unarmed. She probably felt no pain. Derek imagined this being the end of the central episode in his piece of writing, and I echo the pretense in my poem: "La policía hondureña te mató. / Tu sangre enrojeció la solería" (The Honduran police killed you. / Your blood reddened the floor). But the family insists: the woman in the photo is not Mila. And I have come to doubt it also.

If I accept their other scenarios instead—that Iris was either already stationed at the second safe house or was out for some reason without Roberto and escaped when she heard the first house was under attack and made the phone call—I have to think through the consequences. So much was written in the Honduran papers about the shoot-out at the first house, but nothing was written about the second house or any related captures. The journalists missed some details; so did the investigators. Or the police weren't sharing them. We know that the first shoot-out was at 10:30 in the morning. By 11:45—in the disinterested language of the newspaper reporter—"the medical examiner [had] finished his work and the three cadavers were taken to the morgue of the General Cemetery of Tegucigalpa."[12]

When did the police go to the second safe house—eleven, noon, one o'clock—and what happened there? Exactly when did Mila make the phone call—that day or another? It hardly matters. The end remains the same. I want to believe they killed her right away, if not in the first house, then the second. But if I am willing to go this far, I also have to imagine the other possibility, that she was captured and tortured first.

Didn't the Hondurans already know everything they needed to know? Why would they have resorted to torture in this case? I have read enough books and articles about the armed conflicts in Latin America and can answer myself. There was always a chance that valuable information could be extracted. My reasoning tells me that if the leadership or a mole had not betrayed the three guerrillas supposedly already killed, then torture would be the only other way the authorities could have found out their pseudonyms: Olga, Néstor, and Alex. My emotions revolt at the thought, for I know too much about the authorities' interrogation methods.

I have read, for instance, about what Battalion 3-16 did to Inés Consuelo Murillo, the twenty-four-year-old Honduran who was seized on March 13, 1983, and held for seventy-eight days. They "tied [. . .] her hands and feet, hung her naked from the ceiling and beat her with their fists. They fondled her. They nearly drowned her. They clipped wires to her breasts and sent electricity surging through her body."[13] I went numb when I first read what Murillo had endured and realized that her last days in captivity overlapped with the time Tom and I were in Honduras.

On the very day we arrived, May 27, 1983, her parents had taken out a full-page ad in *El Tiempo* with the words "Courage, my daughter" above Inés's portrait. Occupied with other things, we had not seen it. She was freed four days later, perhaps only because her parents had international connections. Her mother was a German citizen who worked for the United Nations, where her boss made inquiries and appealed to General Álvarez through diplomatic channels. Ambassador Negroponte reportedly "expressed interest in the Murillo case," and promised to "ask about her."[14] In May 1982, only a year before, there was no one asking about Ana Milagro.

I also recall all too clearly the sketch drawn by Sheila Cassidy concerning her torture: a stick figure, gender-neutral and impersonal, lies spread eagle on the *parrilla*, a metal, bed-like apparatus. Ankles, wrists, and shoulders are tied down, a blindfold placed over the eyes and a wide band around the abdomen and chest. The electric cable that is labeled as such and the transformer box lie harmlessly on the floor, mercifully unconnected. And the chair in which an interrogator should be sitting stands strangely empty beneath a map labeled Santiago (Chile).[15]

I try to imagine Mila in such a room with an actual member of FUSEP's Cobra battalion in the chair and a map of Tegucigalpa on the wall, electrodes fastened to her nipples and vagina. Electroshocks have the advantage of leaving no visible trace on her body. Every time I get to this point, I dissolve. My own crying cannot drown out her cry for help; it still reaches me every time. "Take care of the children!" There is so much we will never know about what happened, but somehow I'm sure those *were* her last words.

I've reached the end of what I'm capable of imagining about Mila. We do not know if or where she was buried, but I do know that she is alive in us, and I take some comfort in the fact that in the process of trying to imagine Mila for myself, I have helped release Eva. She's even more like her mother than she may realize, wanting to keep things tucked away in her heart. In her blog on January 1st, shortly after our long talk, she recalls the turning point:

My last birthday, Margaret asked Roberto and [me] for an interview to talk about my mother. Margaret knows how difficult it is for us, especially for me, to talk about all of these things, to remember and open up, but I knew she really needed to do that, and I agreed. During the interview I tried so hard not to cry. It is always painful to release my Mom from my heart, but there was something Margaret said that made me understand a lot of things that suddenly made sense for me that day: My Mom would never do a thing like this if she wouldn't have been 100% sure it was the right thing to do! Of course, Margaret was right! And then, everything became so clear to me. In an instant, my daughter Dany came to my mind, and I knew why she was doing it and that it was for me, for my brothers, for my family!

Then, I understood that was my Mom's way to do something for other people and that makes me think about how brave she was, since she actually DID something. She didn't wait to see the change, she WAS the change, the force to make it real. She fought for something she really believed in, and I wonder how many of us can do that without hesitation? How many of us can fight for other people just to make a difference? My Mom was a really brave woman. She had determination and in her plans she knew that we (her children, her blood) would have a different opportunity, a chance to be better and improve ourselves, even if that didn't make any sense at that moment. Perhaps she had a vision of the future that not all the people had back then.

I used to think about me as her living memory since I look a lot like her. I like to think that I am her representation today, and let me tell you, that is a huge responsibility because sometimes I am not sure if I am as brave as she was, as strong as she was, as caring and loving as she was, but there is something I am sure about. I am so proud to be the daughter of my mother, a woman one of a kind . . .

Eva's writing touches me so often, especially as I see her finally forgive as she moves beyond the sheer pain of missing Mila. In the video blog with her brother by her side, the one whom she has found to be so much like herself, the one I helped raise, she reaches her own brave conclusion:

> It would be so easy to hate the whole world for not having a mom at the beginning. It would be so easy to hate our country, the people in the war, the people who killed my mother. [. . .] That would be the easy way for us to handle this. [. . .] But we haven't learned how to hate the others. [. . .] Even if it hurts a lot, we're trying to focus on the good things that have come out of our story. Even though we've been through a lot of difficulties, we're trying to do the good. [. . .] What we have written is from the bottom of our hearts, and I hope that it has touched you. [. . .] For so many years I was blaming the people involved. I'm not anymore. [. . .] I think our mother would be so proud of us.

I am proud of them too.

Los monstruos gigantescos,
aterrizan en la aldea pequeña.
La gente grita.
Los niños chillan.
Los militares con caras severas,
y ametralladoras frías,
raptan a los pequeños niños,
y se ponen en las barrigas hambrientas,
de los monstruos,
y entonces vuelan.
La gente llora.

Ésta es la Guerra verdadera.
Éstas son las cosas,
que no lees en un libro,
los sufrimientos,
de la gente olvidada.
Voy a hablar para ellos,
porque el mundo,
no se puede oír,
no se puede oír.
Es necesario contar,
su historia también.

—DEREK WARD DE WITT

The gigantic monsters
land in the small town.
The people yell.
The children scream.
The soldiers with severe faces,
and cold machine guns,
kidnap the small children,
and put them in the hungry bellies,
of the monsters,
and then they fly.
The people cry.

This is the true War.
These are the things,
that you don't read in a book,
the suffering,
of the forgotten people.
I will speak for them,
because the world,
cannot hear,
cannot hear.
It is necessary to tell
their story as well.

SIX

The Disappeared Children
of El Salvador

B y the time Derek wrote this poem for an assignment in his
Spanish class in tenth grade, he understood that no matter
how important his brother was to us, and no matter how riveting Nelson's birth family's narrative, our story and theirs provide only
a few threads in a much broader and bloodier fabric. From our contact
with Pro-búsqueda and Physicians for Human Rights (PHR), and on the
basis of our extensive research into Nelson's background, we had learned
that in addition to the tens of thousands who are known to have perished
in the years leading up to and during the Salvadoran civil war, at least
eight thousand people went missing or were "disappeared," among them
hundreds, perhaps thousands, of children.[1]

We cannot forget the incident in Arcatao that nearly cost Luis Coto
his life, in which a child figured as a human shield for his adversary.
How many times did such unspeakable things occur, but with different
outcomes? We do not know, but it is certain that children were among
the massacred in the village of El Mozote, and others were killed as they
tried to cross the Sumpul or Lempa rivers to escape during government
incursions.[2]

Children could be caught in the crossfire when bullets rang out at
demonstrations or when a safe house was stormed in the cities. They
could get lost in the chaos of a battle, or while on a *guinda* (flight), when
campesinos hastily abandoned their village to avoid an attack and fled
into the surrounding area. How many babies suffocated when a parent
tried to stifle their cries in the night? How many child soldiers or child
guerrillas died, after being recruited at twelve years old by the government and the FMLN? We don't know, but we do know that members of

the Armed Forces, the National Guard, and ORDEN forcibly separated children from their families. These are the ones of whom Derek speaks in his poem and for whom Pro-búsqueda still advocates before Salvadoran courts and international tribunals.[3]

One of the ways that the Fuerzas Armadas instilled fear in the rural population was to disappear people in the midst of firefights. As one report states, "Forced disappearance was part of a military strategy." The plan was to "disperse and destroy populations that were considered the 'social base of the guerrilla' movement."[4] Children were targeted. Sometimes infants and toddlers were literally ripped from their mother's arms and hoisted into a truck or into the "bellies of the monsters," as Derek writes, referring to the helicopters that swooped down on rural villages and terrorized the populace.

On March 29, 2007, the first Salvadoran national day of remembrance for disappeared children was declared.[5] At a ceremony marking the occasion, the gathered families cried out in their desire for reunion and reiterated their demand for a peace with justice: "The search will continue until the last disappeared boy or girl has been found; the relatives will not consider themselves defeated, their hope remains alive, their struggle persists each day more than the last."[6] By contrast, when General Adolfo Blandón, chief of staff of the Salvadoran Armed Forces from 1983 to 1988, was interviewed about the search for disappeared children, he replied, "Is it worth it to reopen wounds when we have been able to throw some forgetting on them?"[7]

I have been advised to take a similar attitude, to move on quickly to our happy ending and not subject readers to yet more details of this bygone conflict. I have also been warned not to appropriate the heartwrenching testimonies of other children or other adoptive families for this chapter. I understand these objections, but I must align myself with Derek's assertion: "It is necessary to tell / Their story as well." I believe that if one only heaps forgetting on such terrible wounds, they will continue to fester, not heal.

At first, Tom and I refused to identify with these other families we were reading about. While we eagerly tried to grasp all the details of our son's intricate story, we hesitated to consider it as part of this larger phenomenon. We tried to keep the word "disappeared" at arm's length. I reacted quite testily as recently as the summer of 2007 when Nelson participated in a news conference organized by Physicians for Humans Rights, for in the press release and the titles provided for the videotaped proceedings, he was identified as one of the children "abducted from their families by El Salvadoran government forces during the El Salvadoran Civil War in the 1980s and given up for adoption to American families."[8]

"Not true," I said to myself. "'Abducted' is not the right word for what happened to him, and they were not Salvadoran forces." I objected to the lack of precision in their reporting, to the way he had been lumped together with others whose experiences had been quite different. After talking with Nelson about it, though, I grasped that for the purposes of introducing the topic of forced disappearances of Salvadoran children to a U.S. press corps, the specifics of his story did not matter as they do to us. Generalization was required. And I had to concede that there was liable to be more sympathy for those introduced as victims of a "kidnapping" or "abduction," uncomplicated by the thought that the mother of a child victim might be a kidnapper herself.

My reaction to this simplification of Nelson's story, though, heightened my already painful awareness that our knowledge of other families is limited to the information provided by secondary sources. Each story is bound to be as multilayered as ours, and the ones included here I have only second or third hand. I also appreciate that the perspectives of individuals may have changed over time, as ours have. Despite these caveats, I can't shake off the sense of urgency represented by Derek in his poem and by the Pro-búsqueda staff who continue to search for missing children. That is why I insist on this chapter—I want to situate our story firmly within a larger context that deserves to be better known.

« »

Between 1994—the year of its founding—and 2007, 787 cases of missing children were registered with Pro-búsqueda. Of these, 323 (41 percent) have been resolved, and nearly two hundred reunions have taken place, ours included. More are pending. The search for 464 other children continues, children who—if they are alive—are in their twenties or thirties by now.[9] Of the 686 cases analyzed in its 2003 report, the highest number of disappearances occurred in the early 1980s, with 132 children in 1981 and 197 in 1982. Thereafter the number began to taper off, dropping to twenty-one in 1985, and in the last two years before peace—1990 and 1991—there was a total of six reported disappearances. It is estimated that as many as fifty to sixty of the registered missing may be living as adoptees in the United States.

Although Nelson certainly counts in the statistic of the resolved cases, he was not a victim of Salvadoran state-sanctioned violence per se, since his forced separation occurred in Honduras, and General Álvarez's FUSEP was responsible for that particular brutality. Moreover, his parents' involvement at the midlevel echelon of the FMLN leadership and Mila's willingness to place her child at risk, as well as the value the FPL may have placed on Facundo Guardado's life above theirs, were all contributing factors.

Moreover, because Luis and Mila were both well educated, and their extended family is urban and largely middle class, their life is not so different from that of our immediate family. That has made it easier for Nelson to reconnect with them. We cannot forget all these complex variables that contributed both to the particular nature of his disappearance and to the way he now interacts with his birth family. My readers know his story in large part. The question remains: what happened to other children?

Some were taken to military installations where they lived for years, serving as veritable mascots for Salvadoran Army or Air Force units. In many instances officers' families took them in.[10] When this fact emerged in the late 1990s, some were confronted with the truth that their birth parents were illiterate peasants who had been fighting against the very people in the oligarchy who had raised them. They were not always grateful to find out from whence they had come within their fractured society.

In a cover article that appeared in the New York Times Magazine in 1999, investigative journalist Tina Rosenberg told of such re-encounters. One mother who had been a guerrillera refused to speak with her daughter once she saw a picture of the president from the right-wing ARENA party on the wall of her room. Reportedly, at another reunion held at Pro-búsqueda's office, "the children shouted at their blood parents: 'Why did you try to find us? Why didn't you just leave us alone!'"[11]

More often, children taken by soldiers were eventually turned over to the Salvadoran Red Cross and brought to orphanages, where they might linger for a decade or more until their families could be repatriated and search for them.[12] Others quickly entered the court system. The so-called Salvadoran Tribunal for the Protection of Children readily declared them "abandoned" and allowed international adoptions. Thus it was possible for well-meaning people in Europe and North America to become the unwitting beneficiaries of a practice that had essentially abused human rights.

In its 2003 report, Pro-búsqueda identified seventy children separated during military operations that were subsequently adopted abroad. Other adoptees had been separated from their families in myriad other ways. The countries with the largest number of adoptions were France, Italy, and the United States. Missing children have also been located in Belgium, England, Holland, Spain, and Switzerland, in addition to Honduras and Guatemala.

During the 1980s, U.S. citizens adopted more than two thousand Salvadoran children.[13] The court readily released "orphans" on the basis of "moral and material abandonment," and the U.S. Consulate issued visas that allowed prospective parents to complete the adoptions in the United States. Our adoption agency made us aware in early 1983 that unscrupulous doctors and corrupt lawyers and judges were being accused of trafficking—this was why it had discontinued adoptions from El Salvador.

The military was also implicated in the scandal, but its role was less clear until specific accusations surfaced in the late 1980s, directed at the U.S.-trained Atlacatl Brigade.[14] Belatedly the U.S. Embassy introduced safeguards into the adoption process in 1989, including an anti-fraud unit with an ombudsman to verify the children's backgrounds. The number of adoptions dropped significantly.

It needs to be emphasized that not all adopted children were victims of forced disappearances. Some just got lost in the chaos of civil war, and there were other kinds of tragedies that could befall them. One adoptive mother discovered after a long search that her daughter's birth mother had died from a fall off a Ferris wheel in the town of San Vicente. Yet the seven-year-old, adopted in 1984, also suffered from earlier traumas associated with the war, as she was the child of landless peasants. The award-winning book *Salvador's Children: A Song for Survival* gives a moving, lyrical account of their journey of rediscovery and healing.[15] From what I know now, I have to believe that most adoptees were touched in some manner by the violence that marked El Salvador in the 1980s, for the country is so small and vulnerable, like the children themselves.

«   »

We were reminded that the search for these missing children goes on to this day when we heard in 2007 about a young woman who had just been reunited with her birth family in El Salvador after twenty-five years.[16] At the time Suzanne Berghaus Norton had been pursuing a master's degree in social work at Salem State College in Massachusetts.

Her professor, Dr. Robert McAndrews, was leading a college-sponsored trip to El Salvador, and Suzanne had explained her personal reason for wanting to go. While the group was in San Salvador, Suzanne met with a staff member of Pro-búsqueda and told what she knew of her background, based on her adoption papers. From age seven, Suzanne had known that she was born December 10, 1980, as María Lorena Sáenz in a village in Morazán, but she had always been reluctant to find out more about her origins. Now that she planned to marry, she was ready to investigate, and not long after her return to Boston, she received word that her birth mother had been located.[17]

The details of Suzanne's disappearance are much more shocking than Nelson's because she was abducted from a family consisting of ten unarmed civilians. Only fourteen months old, baby María was taken in February 1982 when soldiers stormed the place where the family had sought refuge on a flight toward the Honduran border. The troops already had two other children in their custody, and the officer who entered the makeshift shelter noted how cute the baby was, as she swung in a hammock. Her mother recalls the lieutenant saying, "I like this girl. Would you give her to me?" Twice she refused.[18]

One can only imagine that fearing for their own lives and those of the other seven children, her parents must have finally ceded to this man's repeated demand. What is most surprising to me is that these soldiers and other officials did not even try to cover their tracks, so the correct information about the girl's birth name and date was conveyed at the time of her adoption. In August 1983, a year and a half after her abduction, a U.S. family brought Suzanne/María to Wilmington, Massachusetts.

Mario Sánchez of Pro-búsqueda thinks that she was probably caught up in a whole network of profiteers, a "wartime system that had tinges of compassion [but also] of greed" and by means of which the adoptive families also became "victims." Since more than a year is missing from the narrative he has been able to construct, he assumes the little girl was probably first taken to a *casa de engorde* (fattening house), a place where children were treated for parasites or any other maladies and fed well before being passed on to an orphanage.[19]

Suzanne realizes that she "may never know the whole story [. . .] because different people have different versions of what happened."[20] She was reunited with some brothers and sisters in the winter of 2006 after she discovered that four of them had gone to North America. In April 2007 she went back to El Salvador to meet her parents and other members of her birth family: three more siblings, many nieces and nephews, an aunt who had walked six days to be at the reunion, and—as in Nelson's case—countless cousins. She was accompanied to a rural village about four hours' drive from the capital by her professor, representatives of Pro-búsqueda, and a small media entourage. By publicizing such poignant reunion stories in the U.S. and European press, Pro-búsqueda hopes to heighten awareness of its ongoing search efforts, perhaps reaching other adoptees who know little of their origins.

This young woman had the same kind of experience that Nelson did when he saw his birth father for the first time, for the two Marías—mother and daughter—looked so much alike. Moreover, the first thing her birth father did was to ask her forgiveness, just as Luis had in his first letter. She knew little Spanish, but she connected to her birth family immediately through tender hugs, kisses, and tears.

When Nelson read that Suzanne was working in the Boston area, he phoned her. Soon thereafter Professor McAndrews enlisted him, along with Suzanne and several others, to start a group of local Salvadoran-American adoptees, "Advocates for the Disappeared," that could support other young adults anticipating reunions. The young people met and shared their stories with each other, then participated in the 2007 press conference arranged by PHR.[21]

Each of them spoke of the circumstances of their disappearance and about what the reunion with their biological family meant to them. The event also featured two Pro-búsqueda staff members who had come to the United States in order to bring seven more cases to the attention of the Inter-American Commission for Human Rights. Since 1993, when a blanket amnesty was hastily spread over the atrocities committed during the war, the Salvadoran government has consistently denied that the forced disappearance of children was ever used as a military strategy. The peace treaty called for changes in the judicial system, but even after the reform of 1998, the Salvadoran courts have consistently failed to investigate these cases.[22]

« »

So vital to the fate of disappeared children, Pro-búsqueda ironically had its genesis after the kidnapping of the daughter of President Duarte by the FMLN in 1985. In an attempt to save the girl, Father Ellacuría of UCA and Archbishop Rivera Damas traveled to Chalatenango to have the first face-to-face meeting with guerrilla commanders in the field. Their driver that day was Father Jon de Cortina, a professor of engineering at UCA. Born in Bilbao, Spain, he had come to El Salvador in 1955 at the age of twenty-one and eventually became a citizen.

Nothing substantial came of this unusual meeting between the priests and the FMLN commanders, but the trip had repercussions, for by leaving the capital the priests saw "at first hand the 'other' reality of El Salvador," the immense suffering the war had caused the rural populace.[23] Although the war was not yet over, firefights in the northern countryside had subsided, and some refugees had returned from camps in Honduras.

These campesinos wanted to rebuild their villages and—if they could—their families and lives. Entire hamlets had been burned to the ground, and many had seen family members killed or disappeared. De Cortina was moved by their plight and vowed to return to serve them. By 1988 he was traveling regularly each week from the capital to the border towns of Chalatenango in order to work with the so-called repopulated communities—San Antonio Los Ranchos, San José Las Flores, Guarjila, Guancora, and Arcatao, the same town where Luis was wounded in December 1979. It was also in Arcatao that de Cortina first heard mothers tell of children who had been snatched from them during military reprisals.[24]

A photograph of Father Jon—as his parishioners called him—shows the padre-professor much as I remember him—a vigorous man, tall and lean with a shock of gray hair, dressed casually in a red polo shirt and khakis, and smiling broadly, as he is surrounded by a bevy of children. The photo appears on the cover of a book of oral testimonies that reveal just how much these small communities cherished him. Its title, *Con Jon Cortina Dios pasó por Guarjila* (With Jon Cortina, God Passed through Guarjila), echoes an expression that had been coined for Archbishop Romero: "With him God passed through El Salvador."[25]

Father Jon lived austerely and devoted himself to the welfare of the people. He celebrated mass in the open air, for building houses or getting clean water or health care for his parishioners was more important to him than building a church.[26] As an engineer he was able to bring needed expertise for essential projects. He saw to it that a new wooden bridge across the Sumpul River replaced the hanging bridge that had been destroyed.[27] In the last years of the war, he even managed to raise enough money from private donors in the United States and Germany to build a modern clinic with a laboratory. It was inaugurated in 1992, the year the peace treaty was signed, and served not just the Salvadoran villagers, but Honduran peasants as well.[28] De Cortina also believed in the

importance of commemoration; he told the villagers stories of the martyred Father Rutilio Grande and Archbishop Romero, who had been his
teachers and role models.

On November 16, 1989, de Cortina was in the village of Guarjila
when Ellacuría and the other Jesuits, along with their housekeeper and
her daughter, were murdered at the UCA campus where he lived. He
heard a radio report naming him as one of the victims. "I touched myself to make sure I was alive," he recalled in an interview.[29] He was, and
during the sixteen years remaining to him, he continued to make a profound difference in the lives of the people whom he loved, and in the
lives of families he barely knew, like ours.

Once the Truth Commission report had been filed and the associated general amnesty passed in March 1993, there seemed little hope
that the government—dominated by the far-right—would pursue cases
involving the disappeared. Moreover, CODEFAM, the organization devoted to investigating all kinds of human rights abuses, was overwhelmed
with demands on its meager resources. De Cortina realized there was a
need for an organization dedicated just to finding disappeared children.
By enlisting the energy of the affected families, he was able to start Pro-
búsqueda in 1994 with two thousand dollars in donations from Holland.
Ralph Sprenkels, a twenty-five-year-old Dutchman, served as its first
chief investigator.

The two men had already started searching the year before on behalf of some mothers they knew in the repopulated communities, like
María Magdalena Ramos. As a sixteen-year-old, she had been terrified
by a series of incursions that the villagers refer to as *La Guinda de Mayo*,
generally translated as the 1982 May Massacre. She fled with her mother
and six-month-old child, also called Nelson. A group of several hundred
civilians were being herded by soldiers to the top of a hill not far away,
where two helicopters had found a landing site. The soldiers were taking
children, as she recalls:

> The first (helicopter) filled up quickly and so did the second. It was in
> the second they took my baby. I had him in my arms and my mother
> threw herself over him, and we begged them that if they had to kill us
> to please kill us all with the baby. They told us: "No, the young ones
> don't have to suffer because of you."
>
> Then they hit my mother in the face and pushed her to the
> ground. The baby was crying because they were pulling him and I was
> pulling him. They got him loose and I ran to try to find him inside

the helicopter. I was looking and looking for him in the window, but I couldn't see him with all the children. The helicopter was completely full and he was the smallest one.

A soldier grabbed me by the belt and threw me down. I ran to the other side, but I couldn't see him from there, either. Then the helicopter took off and I was left underneath it. It was green, almost black, and when it took off with my baby, a soldier said to me: "Don't cry . . . those children, they're going to serve the government."[30]

For years afterward she had a recurring nightmare about how her Nelson would come back and face her in the uniform of a soldier, a gun in hand.

De Cortina and Sprenkels were fortunate to quickly locate five children in the private SOS Children's Villages orphanage in Santa Tecla. A reunion took place in Guarjila in mid-January 1994. This initial success raised the hopes of other grieving families. By the time we first heard about Pro-búsqueda three years later, the staff had grown to fourteen. Sprenkels was its chief executive and continued as primary investigator. De Cortina acted as honorary director. Five years after its founding, they had already succeeded in finding nearly a hundred children, about half of whom—like our Nelson—had been adopted abroad. Of these, fourteen were located in the United States.[31]

«   »

In January 1999, during my first trip to El Salvador, our whole family met Sprenkels at the Pro-búsqueda office in San Salvador, but de Cortina was out of town. In 2005, however, Dalila and I were able to arrange a meeting. I feel fortunate to have gotten to know this gentle yet forceful man in person. De Cortina was dressed casually that February morning in a white guayabera shirt. He showed us into a tiny office adorned with posters, each documenting the reunions that had taken place during the course of a single year.

De Cortina's light blue eyes under dark bushy brows radiated a warm welcome as he spoke joyously of their most recent discoveries. They had just located a girl in Spain, and a boy would be coming soon from Switzerland to spend two days with his relatives. It was obvious to me that he cared deeply about these hundreds of families, each with its own complicated story of separation and reunion. He could remember that ours was a rather unusual case that they had nevertheless agreed to take on when

contacted by CODEFAM in 1994. On the poster for 1997 we found a photograph of Nelson and Mamá Chila taken by the poinsettia at her house in Heredia on Christmas morning.

I expressed how grateful we were for the work of both Salvadoran organizations, and I indicated how well our son was doing seven years after our reunion. De Cortina spoke of how important it was for the young people involved to figure out where and how they would live in this world. "It is not the idea to force those who were taken abroad to return to El Salvador permanently," he emphasized. And he acknowledged that adoptive parents like Tom and myself had acted "for the most part with good will."

Our conversation turned to *Voces inocentes* (Innocent Voices), a Mexican film that had just been released in El Salvador.[32] Dalila had taken me the previous evening to see this cinematic rendering of the Salvadoran childhood of scenarist Óscar Orlando Torres. I could still feel the emotional force of one harrowing scene in which the army storms a village school near the end of the war in order to forcibly recruit prepubescent boys. Some were already allied with the guerrillas. Hemmed in by violence on all sides, one mother takes the desperate step of getting her eleven-year-old son smuggled out of the country. He may be saved, but she knows she will probably never see him again.

I asked de Cortina whether he had seen the film. "Yes. The film is no exaggeration," he assured me. "Dreadful things like that happened. And people sometimes had to make terrible choices about how best to protect their families." Several weeks later Dalila gave me an article in which de Cortina expressed the same opinion he shared with us that morning. This film, he stated, "has helped to contribute to our history, to remembering and therefore to the reconciliation of the country."[33]

De Cortina clearly believed that each family reunion also has the potential to move El Salvador toward a necessary reconciliation that could not be achieved by either the Truth Commission report or the general amnesty. This elusive goal was the most daunting part of his life's work, however, since he argued that for reconciliation to be complete, the actual searching should be done not by a nonprofit organization, but by the Salvadoran government.

In a tribute at the time of his death later that year, the cultural editor of *La Prensa Gráfica* recalled how de Cortina appeared before the Committee on Family, Mothers, and Children of the Salvadoran Legislative Assembly in October 2002 to press his case. This otherwise mild-mannered man "lost his serenity for a moment," she writes, when he exclaimed, "We should not have to beg for it; it is the obligation of the state to create a national commission to hunt for disappeared children."[34]

Dominated by ARENA at that time, the legislature continued to stall. Finally in October 2004, a commission was created by executive order, but therefore without the force of law that would oblige the defense department to open its files. With the FMLN now in the legislative majority and having also won the presidency in March 2009, the government may become more proactive. The number of new cases being brought to Pro-búsqueda's attention has increased in recent years and its international profile has been heightened because of the organization's repeated appeals before international tribunals.[35]

During our visit in 2005, I asked de Cortina if I could have copies for Eva and Toto of the book published by Pro-búsqueda in 2002, *Historias para tener presente* (Stories So That They May Remain Present). It gathers the stories of five disappeared children who remained in El Salvador throughout the war. De Cortina was close to these four boys and one girl since they were among the first children located and reunited with their families.

After inscribing the books to Nelson's siblings he looked up and remarked, "It may never be possible for some of these young people to reconcile in the way Eva, Ernesto, and Roberto can, who in the long run have led much more fortunate lives. More important is that we preserve the memory of their past experiences, because forgetting it does not provide a path to true reconciliation." I told him about my plan to include this chapter in my book. The poignant testimonies of others provide a window on a whole range of experience and make me realize that I can only generalize up to a point. Tracy Kidder describes the effect perfectly in *Strength in What Remains*: "It lingered in my mind, the secondhand memory of someone else's memories, as strange and unresolved as the memory of a dream."[36]

«   »

Mauricio and Amílcar Guardado's story is one I simply cannot shake off. I think it moves me so profoundly because it involves two little boys, so like my two in the number of years that separate them and in the fact that they remain so close, even though their personalities are quite different. It also offers an eyewitness account of what unfolded at the Sumpul River near the village of Las Aradas on May 14, 1980, a massacre I have read about so often. Each time I am forced to recall that this was the very route Mamá Chila would otherwise have taken that same month with the three children—Eva, Toto, and René—if Mila had not counseled so wisely against it.

The Guardado brothers were growing up in the village of El Portillo in the river valley at the north-central border.[37] It was hardly more than a hamlet with a dozen huts and neither a school nor a chapel. The boys were cared for by an extended family. Part of the time they spent with their mother, Lidia, who shared an adobe hut with a brother who kept a few animals and farmed a nearby "milpa" (a small plot of land to grow corn). When she left each year to pick coffee, the boys moved in with a maternal aunt in another village. From Aunt Goya's house they could see the river. There they fished, caught crabs, and learned to swim. Their mother got involved with a man, but he didn't stick around after their little brother, Antonio, was born.

By the end of 1979, an undeclared war had already begun in these remote areas of Chalatenango. The National Guard of San José Las Flores began to spread terror. People known to believe in agrarian reform might be taken in the night, decapitated, and thrown into a ravine. The guerrillas had also shown up. Children began to pick up the tunes and even the words of their songs. Occasionally the boys saw people carrying weapons. Their uncle left to join the guerrilla force, but they were too young to comprehend what was happening. Mauricio was eight and Amílcar five.

By February 1980 the conflict was escalating; people were beginning to flee. Lidia took her sons first to the border village of Las Aradas, then crossed the hanging bridge into Honduras, but a few months later the authorities made it clear that they wanted no squatters in an area that had been designated as a buffer zone. Honduran troops told the refugees they had twenty-four hours to clear out. Lidia returned with her brood to Las Aradas along with hundreds of others.

As the Salvadoran Army, assisted by the National Guard, ORDEN, and the Air Force, approached on the morning of May 14th, two helicopters fired on this village swollen with refugees. People panicked and headed pell-mell for the bridge. The rainy season had begun; the water was high and the current swift. On the opposite shore, Honduran troops prevented their re-entry. Turned back, people were trapped between the two armies. Some were trampled to death; others drowned as entire families jumped into the swift-moving river to try to save themselves. Most were simply shot by Salvadoran forces as the Hondurans looked on. Estimates range from three hundred to six hundred or more that were killed at the shores of the Sumpul that day.[38]

The two little boys were witnesses. They could see how the river ran red until the current began to sweep some of the bodies downstream. Their mother told them to duck as they hid in a thicket, and when the first barrage subsided, they managed to hide further away. Lidia gave them something to eat and started to nurse the baby. That's where the soldiers found them, Mauricio and Amílcar by her side, and Antonio at her breast. The soldiers shot and killed their mother and brother on the spot. Only minutes later, still holding hands, their shirts splattered with blood, the two were whisked away, up over a terrain littered with the dead and dying.

The helicopter took them back along the path to Las Aradas first. There a soldier urinated on Almícar's head while others made fun of them. After that the boys were swept up once more into the belly of the monster. In little more than an hour they landed at the Ilopango Air Force base near the lake of the same name, just east of the capital. They were taken to the clinic, bathed, and put in a small room where they could sleep in one bed. They lived on base for eleven years.

Colonel Juan Rafael Bustillo, commander of the Air Force, took up a collection to buy the boys shoes and clothes and ordered a member of the medical team, Sergeant Meléndez, to look after them. Interviewed in 1996, Bustillo, by then a retired general, made clear that he considered his actions a humanitarian effort. "I feel very content," he reportedly stated. "Despite being abandoned, someone extended them a hand and they overcame these problems and now they have studied, they have stable jobs and have established a better life for themselves."[39] He appeared totally oblivious to the atrocities committed by his troops.

Besides the clinic staff, Mauricio and Amílcar had contact with mechanics, and some pilots who took them along on noncombat missions. There was little personal warmth in any of these relationships, however. Occasionally Sergeant Meléndez took them home so they would have some other children to play with, but the boys failed to bond with his family.

Once they were told a German family would adopt them. They hoped for months that they would be released from their boring isolation. But no one came. As they got older, they learned to distinguish the different kinds of aircraft, and Mauricio recognized the number twenty-two that identified the Alouette helicopter that had brought them to Ilopango. Mauricio could vividly remember their earlier life, and he seems to have been deeply traumatized. At first he cried piteously whenever he recalled the details of the massacre. Later on he would lapse into a trance as he remembered that day.

The boys did have each other, and their most basic needs were taken care of. Once a year they got new clothes. Twice they were given bicycles that helped them get around the huge installation. When the commander determined that they should go to school, the Air Force took care of the paperwork and bought their schoolbooks. Mauricio and Amílcar were not imprisoned, but they were closely watched. They were not allowed to leave the base on their own. When they started school, an Air Force ambulance would deliver them and pick them up each day.

Occasionally some major event punctuated daily life. In 1982 they experienced the FMLN surprise attack that destroyed six of the fourteen UH-1H helicopters newly delivered by the United States. The following year on March 6th they were on hand for the arrival ceremonies for Pope John Paul II. And in 1986 they witnessed a DC-6 exploding on takeoff. All seventy on board were killed—the crew and many mechanics they knew that were going to Panama for training. There was talk of sabotage, but—ironically—the crash was proven to be due to mechanical failure.

As the civil war wore on, the clinic that had been nearly empty the day of their arrival began to fill up with wounded soldiers. They had a hard time relating to what was going on at the front, but they were frightened by what they saw. The corridor right outside their room became a morgue. They tried to avoid going to the bathroom at night because they would have to walk past the piled-up cadavers in the hallway.

As teenagers the brothers had gotten too big to share the same bed, and the clinic needed their room for the severely wounded, so they were given space in a portable trailer, but they still had to share a bath with the infirmary, and the medical staff expected them to provide some assistance with the sick and injured. When the fighting got much more intense during 1989, the boys were even enlisted to inject formaldehyde into corpses.

Once they had finished the ninth grade, both were offered the opportunity for more advanced study in aviation technology. Mauricio could not abide the military routine in the base boarding school and quit after the first year, preferring an apprenticeship. He learned to fabricate airplane replacement parts and completed his degree at night school. Amílcar stuck it out in the institute's barracks, but without his brother, he felt even more isolated. He was studying to become a mechanic for the U.S.-made Huey helicopters that since 1985 had made up the bulk of the Salvadoran fleet.

The brothers hardly realized that the war was winding down or that General Bustillo had already retired. But gradually things began to change. No one objected when Mauricio moved off base to share a house with some co-workers in 1991. He began to ask questions about what had happened in other parts of the country. During his vacation he accompanied a friend back to Chalatenango to see for himself. By chance, the man's girlfriend provided a connection to the brothers' former life, for her mother had worked with Lidia Guardado on a coffee plantation, and she was originally from the same town as their aunt. They were able to locate their Aunt Goya.

Another breakthrough came when one of Sergeant Meléndez's sons saw a newspaper ad placed by Pro-búsqueda with the names of fifty-four missing children. He had not forgotten the boys who had been brought to his home years before, and he noticed that their names were on the list. He let Mauricio and Amílcar know. They were suspicious of the organization at first, but that changed after Pro-búsqueda arranged a surprise reunion with the uncle who had been looking for them.

Their maternal uncle had been a father figure for them in their infancy, and they eventually found they could talk with him. He was willing to share his experiences of the war. They learned that he had been with the guerrillas on the Guazapa volcano, and that his wife had made it to Honduras. One day he simply decided to leave the FMLN and went to find her at the Mesa Grande camp. They had been among the first to return to the region in 1987.

Eventually they went with him and some cousins to see the hamlet where they had been born. El Portillo was practically deserted in 1994 as only two families had returned, but they were able to locate the hearthstones where their hut once stood. They also wanted to find the place where their mother and Antonio had died. They walked from Las Aradas toward the river along the same path that the Alouette #22 helicopter had traced back to the village that day, but there had been such a change in the vegetation that they could not be sure of the exact spot.

The boys—now young men—could not readily express what they had suffered. Mauricio in particular was given to long silences. On May 14, 1995, the Guardado brothers participated for the first time at the annual commemoration of the Sumpul massacre in Las Aradas, and after mass, Mauricio gave a brief testimony. Even though they found it difficult to talk about it, they wanted their story to be better understood. At a forum on the issue of disappeared children, held at UCA late one November afternoon in 1995, none other than General Adolfo Blandón, the former chief of staff, tried to use them as a prime example of the supposed compassion the armed forces had shown "abandoned" children. Amílcar listened quietly in the darkening auditorium, then rose to speak, wanting to set the record absolutely straight. What the general had said about their education and mechanical training was true, but he objected to the rest of the characterization. He and Mauricio were by no means "abandoned," for their mother had been beside them "until the very last step" when she and their baby brother had been shot in cold blood by the soldiers who later took them away from the scene. The audience, made up largely of searching families, applauded.[40]

Mauricio and Amílcar were beginning to forge independent lives. Pro-búsqueda provided the first step on this path with group therapy. At the time the book of testimonies was published, Mauricio was still working at the base, but Amílcar had left his job with the Air Force in order to study electrical engineering. Then he took a maintenance job with a civilian airline. He had bought a horse that he stabled with his uncle, and both he and Mauricio were thinking of buying a place in the country. In addition, the brothers were helping their cousins get an education, for they knew it could give the next generation of their family a way out of rural poverty.

« »

At the therapy sessions, Amílcar met a special young woman who could really understand him, Andrea Dubón, another disappeared child. De Cortina had spoken to Dalila and me about the "terrible choices" that parents sometimes had to make when it came to protecting their families and surviving. Andrea's story illustrates this in a most excruciating way.[41] Like the Guardado brothers, she came from a hamlet in the municipality of Arcatao in Chalatenango department. But unlike them, she had no memory at all of where she came from or what had happened to her before she was delivered to the orphanage in Santa Tecla by a Red Cross ambulance.

It must have been obvious in 1982 that the girl had suffered both physical and psychological traumas. She had only one arm, and injuries to her spine so severe that she could not walk. And like Mauricio, Andrea was rather easily frightened, especially whenever soldiers passed by in the street in front of the orphanage.

Often she got angry because her physical disabilities frustrated her desire to run around in the yard with the other children. Six of them, including a baby boy called Juan Carlos, had been brought in at the same time. They were singled out by the staff as war orphans, told that their families were guerrillas, that their relatives had died, and that they shouldn't think about them or what had happened.

Andrea had already forgotten. She knew only that she was acquainted with two of the others, Marta and Elsy. Elsy claimed to be her

cousin, and she was the most reliable source of information, even supplying the names of Andrea's older siblings. Elsy recalled that her own
father had been killed, and she provided the bare outline of what must
have happened to all of them: she was taken with other children to a
military camp and then by helicopter to a barracks in the provincial capital, turned over to the Red Cross, and brought by ambulance to Santa
Tecla.

To Andrea it seemed as if life had only begun with the orphanage.
Her only fond memory of the first few years is the March 1983 papal
visit, because she was taken to the Ilopango airport to hand John Paul
II flowers and afterward her picture appeared in all the papers. During
her first year at elementary school, the director of the orphanage summoned Andrea once to tell her that her parents were alive and living in
Honduras; she wrote them a letter but got no response. After this surprising revelation, a silence that she could only construe as rejection proved
even more devastating than the total uncertainty she had lived with up
to then.

Eventually Andrea was taken to an orthopedic surgeon who recommended several operations. The first surgery—a major reconstruction of
her spine—was especially painful and the rehabilitation arduous. She
was placed in a body cast for three months and underwent extensive
physical therapy before she could even move her legs. She missed six
months of school, but the struggle to learn to walk and to keep up with
her class helped her build up reserves of confidence and self-esteem. As
she grew, her legs became different lengths, and another operation was
required three years later.

Over the years her little group had a series of "tías" (aunts) who
shared their rooms and looked after them. Some were cruel, according
to Andrea, others kind. One tía even took the children on occasion to her
home. Those outings gave Andrea an inkling of what a warm family life
might be like, and from time to time, she allowed herself to "fantasize"
about a reunion with her own family. She hadn't forgotten what she'd
been told about them, although it was never mentioned again. This "il-
lusion" sometimes helped her get through the hard times.

After Andrea had been in the orphanage for ten years, it was rumored that someone had showed up asking after her. Andrea was infused with hope at the mere idea that someone was still alive who might
know her. She got the full story much later. A young man was working
at a coffee plantation near San Salvador volcano. As the pickup truck he
was riding in passed through Santa Tecla, he caught a glimpse of a girl

of a certain age with only one arm among a group of kids standing outside the orphanage. He thought she might be his missing cousin. When he had the chance, he followed up, but for some reason the orphanage staff prevented an investigation, and no connection to her family was established at that time.

Then in January 1994, the children were invited to meet with the director, who revealed that a delegation had come from the repopulated villages in Chalatenango and had been searching for disappeared children. The news was overwhelming. Elsy's mother, Francisca Romero, was alive. Also there was a man who was definitely looking for Marta and a younger girl in another dormitory, Angélica; they were sisters! The visitors also knew of a woman named María Magdalena Ramos who might be Juan Carlos's mother.[42] The director then confirmed what he had told Andrea so many years before—her parents were still alive. They had returned from Honduras to one of the repopulated villages. Moreover, in addition to the two whose names she knew, she had many younger siblings.

After so many years of uncertainty and delay, everything occurred in a great rush. The very next day the children were taken in a microbus all the way out to Guarjila, first on the Pan-American highway, then, as they got closer, on a stone-filled and rutted dirt road. Andrea noticed that the mountains were "dry and deforested." When they got off the bus in the center of an unprepossessing village, a crowd had gathered. She looked about uncertainly. Everyone else seemed to be embracing someone. Marta and Angélica's father was there, and the woman thought to be Juan Carlos's mother was hugging him and calling him Nelson. Then Father Jon de Cortina pointed to a large group of people coming down the street: "There is your family." When Andrea finally caught sight of a little boy who looked like her she started to cry. After twelve years of separation, "such emotion—such joy!"[43]

Return visits were organized, and in the following weeks, Andrea's elder brother and sister, Arturo and Carmen, came to see her. They explained that after her disappearance they had joined the guerrillas, whereas their parents had gone to the Mesa Grande camp. Once, a foreign aid worker had helped them find out about her. They discovered that she was alive and would get the medical care she needed. They even received a photograph that Arturo later used to hunt for her. But this tenuous connection was broken as suddenly as it had been established when the foreigner left the refugee camp. That explained why she had never gotten an answer to her letter.

After the reunion, the orphanage staff was at first overprotective and acted as if the families were some kind of "threat." They were suspicious of the fact that some had been guerrillas, and they tried to limit contact to once in three months. The director emphasized that the young people needed to focus on finishing their schooling, but eventually he agreed to some concessions: relatives were allowed to come once a month to see the children, and the children could spend their vacations with their families.

For all of these so-called war orphans, the road to a full restoration of their familial relationships was as rutted as the road to Guarjila. After the initial excitement, each child reacted somewhat differently. Elsy had left the orphanage to get married and had missed the first reunion. When she saw her mother and five siblings later on, the re-encounter proved a mixed blessing, as it also brought back a much sharper memory of the traumatic moment when her father had been shot before her eyes. Afterward, the seven-year-old had been heaved into a helicopter and taken away while her mother watched in terror from behind a thorn bush.[44]

Juan Carlos's situation was especially fraught with uncertainty. When María caught sight of him as the children got off the microbus, she was sure he resembled her dead husband. She embraced the boy, calling him Nelson. He hung his head and wanted to know why she had "abandoned" him. Then he doubted altogether that this woman was his birth mother and remained skeptical until a DNA test proved the link positively, but it took a whole year before they got the result. Interviewed by a journalist several years later, he recalled their reunion and admitted, "I felt nothing. I felt no love for her. It is difficult to think of her as my mother."[45]

For Andrea it also took a long time to build trust. She enjoyed the Holy Week vacations when her family always had a picnic by the Sumpul River. She began to have a sense for the first time in her life of being really "loved and protected." But she did not want to risk asking too many questions, for she sensed that her parents had guilty feelings that of all their children, she alone had gone missing. Her father shared the story reluctantly and only bit by bit. He had difficulty feeling close to a daughter whom he remembered as a badly injured, totally dependent seven-year-old and who was now a self-assured young woman of nineteen with the ambition to go to university.

Andrea's family had been living in a hamlet near the town of Arcatao. In November each year, the parents left to go harvest coffee, but they always returned by Christmas. Andrea was born there on January 2,

1975. As I re-read this, I am reminded that this was also Ana Milagro Escobar's eighteenth birthday. I pause to try to imagine how these two Salvadoran families spent that day. Did Mila and Luis choose it, perhaps, to announce their engagement? Did Andrea's family even have the wherewithal or time for a celebration of her birth? I think her mother probably just got up and went on with her chores, pounding the cornmeal dough on a flat stone to make the tortillas for her growing family as she worried about having another mouth to feed.

By the end of 1979, when Andrea was almost five years old, things began to change. The National Guard of Arcatao was responsible for some assassinations, and the armed opposition was getting stronger. Her parents went to Arcatao to hear Archbishop Romero that year. After that, they decided to leave their village. The place they ended up—a three-hour walk away in the mountains—was an FPL camp. Her father didn't join, because he liked to drink and alcohol consumption was forbidden among the guerrillas. Nevertheless, the family stayed in that place under the protection of the revolutionaries. Here her grandma died.

Helicopters sometimes flew reconnaissance over the area, but they weren't attacked until six months later. When that happened they evacuated during the night. They got caught up in the midst of a terrible battle on this guinda, but made it to another village called Patanera. At first, things seemed calmer. The extended family was staying in houses "abandoned by former residents," but the village was functioning because of the presence of the guerrillas, and Andrea and her older sister Carmen were even able to go to school. Andrea's father still didn't formally join the guerrillas, but he helped with things like sowing, and occasionally he took a rifle and stood guard.

Inevitably the government forces unleashed another attack. The civilians evacuated. The family got separated this time because Carmen wandered off and the rest of them had to hunt for her, while their mother stayed behind somewhere along the way to give birth. She resumed the flight on her own, clutching her newborn daughter, Argelía. About a week after this incursion the family was able to regroup, and they enjoyed a few months' respite. During this interval the guerrillas enlisted their help to build a field hospital.

Finally, her father added the day Andrea lost her arm to the narrative. It had been amputated at this brand new FPL clinic. He was out in the fields and saw the planes coming, but the women and children were surprised. After the first plane passed over, Andrea, who was six then, went outside to play with another child, ignoring the shouts of the adults.

She evidently didn't hear the second plane. The bomb fell nearby, killing the other child instantly. The trunk of a tree protected Andrea from most of the shrapnel. From this point on, as she puts it, "the war opened a wound in my parents' hearts."[46]

Andrea's parents had advanced her story this far, but still could not bring themselves to relate its final chapter. Years went by. The orphanage helped Andrea finance her first year of university study in social work. After she completed her degree, she got a job with the Salvadoran Foundation for Health and Human Services. She even managed to get a visa so she could go to the United States to visit her brother Arturo, who had gone there to work. In addition, Andrea participated in the group therapy arranged by Pro-búsqueda, met Amílcar Guardado, and fell in love.

In those meetings Andrea expressed her belief that each victim of a disappearance must confront that past and fight in his or her own way for psychological recovery, just as she had struggled for physical recovery after her operations. Those experiences gave her the confidence that she could deal with the pain she might yet have to face when the whole truth came out. It was nearly eight years after their first meeting when her father finally told her exactly how she had gotten separated from the rest of them.

Eventually, the family needed to leave for the greater security of the Chichilco volcano. Her father was carrying both Andrea and Carmen, and they were walking at night over rugged terrain, hiding during the day in "tatúes" (shelters consisting of holes in the ground that the guerrillas had constructed so they could not be seen from the air). When soldiers passed close by these hiding places, pieces of wood had to be placed in infants' mouths so they would not cry and reveal the whereabouts of the civilians. Some of them suffocated that way. Andrea adds that her family was lucky because Argelía was such a "tranquil" child.

Toward the end of May 1982—the same month that Ana Milagro lost her life in Tegucigalpa—the family had come to a place near the Sumpul River called Los Amates. There, the Fuerzas Armadas began mounting surprise attacks. Not long after a narrow escape from the first attack, the family found themselves once again surrounded by soldiers in the border area. Helicopters circled overhead shooting at the people corralled below. As they ran, they stumbled over the wounded lying everywhere underfoot. Andrea's father guided the family toward a ravine. They would have to jump over to get to a safer place. It was their only hope. He realized he couldn't make it with one daughter in his arms and another on his back. He could only take one girl across. Kissing Andrea good-bye, he left her under a tree and took the leap with Carmen.

Andrea understood perfectly well that her father had struggled to preserve his family, and that he had been forced to make a "life or death" choice. In the end, the one he made saved them all. Because she was raised in the private SOS Children's Villages orphanage, Andrea had gotten the medical care she needed to be able to walk, as well as the advantage of higher education. Her parents realized this too, but the terrible decision her father had made to abandon her still weighed heavily on them. Although Andrea had been miraculously restored to him, her father was afraid she would not be able to forgive him for leaving her under that tree twenty years earlier. He thought he might lose her again, but Andrea was fully prepared to forgive him "a thousand times."[47]

«   »

For some, the road leading to reunion was much rougher. Armando, a boy from Cabañas in Andrea's dormitory group, is a case in point.[48] He might have been only three or four, but maybe as much as six or seven years old, when he got lost. He could remember his name and that of his mother—Bacha for Bonifacia—but not much more than that. He could conjure up the precise taste and smell of certain tropical fruits he ate as a child, however, and also recall how he got separated from his mother when a bomb dropped in their midst during a guinda. He and another boy hid in a cave. Then they were told they would be taken to their mothers but instead were hustled into a helicopter and flown to an army headquarters in the regional capital. There a stranger claiming to be his aunt cared for them. He was well fed, and for the first time in his life he watched television.

This interlude ended without warning. Armando speculates that his "aunt" might have gotten tired of them, but what he describes sounds to me like a stay in one of those way stations where children were fattened up so that they could be adopted abroad. Another unknown woman in a white jeep, probably from the Women's Auxiliary of the Salvadoran Red Cross, delivered them to the orphanage. Andrea recollects that Women's Auxiliary members visited shortly after her arrival later that year, pushing for the adoption of all the so-called war orphans, but the staff resisted the idea.[49]

As a teenager, Armando was thrown out for misbehavior and sent to a boarding school for difficult children. After he was expelled from this reformatory, he began leading a "nomadic" life, working in the lowest-paying jobs as a coffee picker or a waiter. He didn't have proper papers, and he had trouble keeping any position for long; he would either get bored or get into a fight with a co-worker. He was in a downward spiral, living from hand to mouth and consorting with, as he puts it, "addicts and thieves." He had no family, no home, and, despite his ninth-grade education, no real future.

One part-time job took him to Santa Tecla from time to time. Armando would stop by the orphanage to see his old friends, and when he learned they had been reunited with their families, he thought he might be able to find his too. He contacted Pro-búsqueda. The search was painstaking, and the process filled Armando with mixed emotions.

The investigations coordinator first accompanied Armando to Aguilares, the place so closely associated with the ministry of Father Rutilio Grande and—for us—with the secret field hospital where Luis was taken after he was critically wounded. Many Salvadorans had been internally displaced during the war. In this town Armando was slated to meet a woman who might know something about his mother. By chance it was another refugee who recognized her nickname, Bacha. He told Armando that his mother had been taken prisoner during the attack in which the boy had gotten lost and that she and his baby brother were dead. The teenager reacted to this news much as Nelson had when he learned about Mila; it was like he was losing his mother all over again "at that very moment."

With Pro-búsqueda's help Armando patched together what was left of his family. Later on, his Uncle Vidal pointed out the place where they had been when the bomb dropped, scattering the whole extended family. Armando's relatives also took him to his birthplace, San Felipe, a hamlet near the Copinolapa River that empties into the Lempa. It was totally deserted, but the "sincuya" tree—the one thing he could vividly call to mind from his early childhood—still stood there, bearing its seedy fruit and spreading its sweet aroma over the place. Uncle Vidal talked of moving back to this fruitful spot, and eventually he did.

After Armando attended therapy sessions and got the opportunity to go back to school, he began to feel content instead of restless. As he puts it in his testimonial, he acquired "a personal history" and found with it "a reason for being," including serving on Pro-búsqueda's board of directors. "My life turned around 180 degrees," he exclaims.[50] But he still got angry when he thought of how his mother—not only with a baby in arms, but pregnant—was killed after her capture: "The only thing I ask for is a little respect for her and for all the people who died, for this entire huge void that has remained in our lives."[51]

«   »

In some instances, reunions were less fraught with anxious feelings, even though the complexity of their situation seemed to demand them. One of these provided the lead narrative in Tina Rosenberg's excellent exposé, "Salvador's Disappeared Children: What Did You Do in the War, Mama?" As we know from Nelson's story, not all the disappeared children were the offspring of unarmed civilians.

On January 12, 1981, only days after the FMLN had launched its so-called final offensive, the Fuerzas Armadas retaliated by burning villages to the ground. Every man or woman above the age of twelve was considered a guerrilla, and the soldiers killed any adult they could find. Rosenberg focuses on one of the villages under attack, El Limón, a cluster of fifty mud and stick houses on a steep mountainside in Morazán. None of its inhabitants were combatants, but there was an FMLN encampment within earshot.

At the encampment, as Rosenberg tells it, "Felipa Díaz stood in impotent horror as gunshots crackled and smoke rose from the village."[52] She had left three of her children—Esteban (eleven), Ricardo (eight), and Elsy (seven)—in the village with her mother when she joined the guerrillas a few months earlier, after her father had been murdered in bed. She had taken her baby girl and twelve-year-old son with her. They were safe, but what was happening to the others?

Back in the village, as soon as the mayhem appeared to be over, their grandmother had left their hiding place to find food. By the time she returned the three children were gone. They had been taken by the Armed Forces. After about a week of eating and watching TV at military headquarters, the siblings had been separated. "They gave us out like chickens," Ricardo remarked to the journalist.[53] A soldier took him home to another part of the country, but returned to the front and was killed a short time later. One of this man's aunts then took the boy in and adopted him. She did not try to disguise the fact that Ricardo had been abducted and even promised they would hunt for his brother and sister when he grew up.

Still, her whole family was pro-military, and at age fourteen—lured by the idea of wearing a snappy uniform and defending his country from communism—Ricardo left his adoptive home to become a "child assistant" in the National Guard. Later he served in the regular army. Up close, military life did not appeal to him. He stuck with it for only one six-month tour of duty, but it was long enough to see combat. Although Ricardo moved to San Salvador after his military service, he continued to visit his adoptive mother, of whom he was very fond, until she died in 1989, and he told Rosenberg it never occurred to him that his birth mother might be alive.

Felipa stayed with the FMLN to the bitter end. She, her mother, and the two children she had with her that afternoon had all survived. Once the war was over, she was determined to find the three who had been disappeared. Although in this case mother and son had actually fought on either side of the conflict, they seem to be have been able to quickly get beyond that fact once they were reunited. As one Pro-búsqueda counselor stated, "Each understands why the other fought, and now both play it down."[54]

Felipa, who has a ninth-grade education—unusual for a rural woman—worked after the war as a traveling promoter of women's health. At the time Rosenberg interviewed her she was also raising corn and chickens on a small plot of land in the department of San Miguel. After their reunion, Ricardo moved in with her, but he soon realized he had no aptitude for farming and went to live with his grandmother in the provincial capital of the same name, about an hour away, and got a delivery job. Apparently he was able to integrate himself rather seamlessly into their lives, all without breaking the remaining ties to his other family. When Felipa and Ricardo accompanied Rosenberg to the abandoned site of their former home in El Limón to share their story, Esteban and Elsy—still missing—were "the great void that remained" in their lives. (Esteban was later located in Honduras in 1998.)

« »

Among the stories Tom and I have read in which disappeared Salvadoran children came to the United States through adoption, there are many that begin with brutal abductions or psychologically traumatic separations. One hears of physical injuries, but also of nebulous memories, nightmares, and painful silences—especially among the older children, who remember but cannot find the words to express their anguish—all the voids that adoptive families cannot entirely fill. Despite similarities between the adoptees, one ought not reduce their varied experiences to a generalized plotline, for each story of disappearance, adoption, and re-union has its own drama, its attendant sorrows, and—sometimes quite unexpectedly—its great joys.

Tom and I were unsettled by the first story we heard about. It was highlighted in a series of *Boston Globe* articles that were sent to us by the director of PHR only a few months before we were due to meet Nelson's birth family. At that point we were still in shock over the investigative re-port we had received and nervous about what was in store. Despite some obvious similarities, we were reluctant to place Nelson or his family in the context of the forced disappearances the journalist described. We learned that much had been made of Gina Craig, the first U.S. adoptee to be identified the previous summer as a disappeared child of El Salva-dor, and wished to avoid such publicity.

Gina was seventeen, only a little older than Nelson, we noted. The first report, published in advance of her reunion, made clear she was struggling with identity issues, even before Pro-búsqueda traced her to a suburb of Akron, Ohio, and offered DNA testing. She was excited about the prospect of meeting her birth family, as we knew Nelson was, but her estrangement from her adoptive parents gave us pause.[55]

Gina had grown up with two older brothers "in a two-story colo-nial, with her own bedroom" decorated to her taste, as the reporter de-scribes it.[56] She had evidently enjoyed all the accoutrements of a middle-class American life—a stereo, television, and telephone; participation on sports teams; and family trips to Disney World and Lake Erie. The teen was dreaming of going to college. She was imagining she would make a lot of money in "computers or cosmetology" so she could help her birth family, maybe even bring them to Ohio.[57]

Gina was about to be reunited with her biological parents, six broth-ers and sisters, and other relatives in a village not far from the town of San Vicente. As the reporter points out, the contrast could not have been starker. Her birth father, a subsistence farmer, was leasing a milpa on which he was growing a few beans and some corn he cut with a ma-chete. Her mother cooked "over a wood fire" and made the tortillas for pupusas "on a stone slab in a dirt-floor kitchen by the light of a single bulb." The bathroom was a "concrete outhouse across the street."[58]

A second article described their July 1996 re-encounter. Gina's en-tourage included a television crew from *60 Minutes*, one of her adoptive brothers, and Father Jon de Cortina, who said mass on this occasion. The whole village of four hundred had helped prepare the festivities, and there were more relatives to embrace than Gina (or Imelda, as she had been named at birth) could count. Her father called her rediscovery "a gift from God."[59] Certainly, for her birth family, the reunion was nothing short of a miracle, but when I first read about it, I identified with her adoptive parents, and I was disturbed by the fact that they were not part of this picture.

The Craig family had gone to El Salvador to adopt in the fall of 1984. Just as Tom and I will never forget the moment when we first laid eyes on Nelson, the Craigs could not forget what the little girl looked like when she was first brought to them. Her "clothes were infested with lice. Her right toes pointed down as if she were 'a permanent ballerina,'" as Tom Craig described the six-year-old, and she could only crawl, not walk. "Her head was tucked into her chest."[60] They ignored the quizzical looks of the nurse—one of eight or nine adults taking care of about four hundred kids at the state-run orphanage outside San Salvador. She was evidently amazed that anyone would want a child who was paralyzed from the knees down. The Craigs did.

Stephanie and Tom had two healthy biological sons, but they wanted a daughter, and they had committed to this child from a war-torn country about whom they knew little or nothing—like us, without so much as a photo. The judge—for whom they had brought a ham and a bottle of wine at the suggestion of their adoption agency—assured them Imelda's parents were dead. The Salvadoran court provided a "declaration of moral and material abandonment" and readily issued a provisional guardianship that allowed them to complete the adoption in the United States. The U.S. consular scrutiny was perfunctory. The whole process took them only a few days.[61]

I'm not sure I realized it as clearly in 1997, but as I re-read these articles now I am struck by these particular details. An adoption on the fast track, the presents their agency recommended they bring for the judge, and the little they were told about the child's background should have been red flags. But who am I to pass judgment, given the strangeness we tolerated at the time of our adoption?

Back home, the Craigs made sure their daughter got the medical care she needed. Gina was not expected to walk again, but she was tough. She had an inner resilience and determination. She not only walked, she played basketball and volleyball. Andrea Dubón, wounded in much the same way at roughly the same age, had blocked it all out, but Gina could vaguely remember what had happened to her. She thought she had been shot.

After she met her birth family, they explained what had actually happened. Her parents had been with the FMLN. They had been digging trenches to protect both guerrillas and civilians from aerial bombardment. A bomb wounded both her hip and leg, causing the paralysis, and her eight-year-old sister died instantly when shrapnel from the same bomb hit her directly in the eye. An uncle carried Imelda all the way to a secret field hospital.

The family came several times to see how she was doing. Her father still recalls the exact day of their last visit—June 14, 1984. Imelda's cries tore his heart. She was begging to go back with them, but they could not care for her; they could barely afford to feed her. The next day, the FMLN clinic came under attack. When they returned they found the building destroyed, the body of one nurse, and no trace of their little girl. It was impossible to search for her without revealing their allegiance, but they did not forget her, and, like Mamá Chila, they bided their time until the war was over.

Imelda had been taken by members of the Armed Forces to San Pedro Hospital in Usulután and given a different middle and last name, probably because she could not remember hers. Only a few months passed, and without anyone making any effort to find her family, she entered the court system.[62] A scant three months later she was released to the custody of the Craigs and taken to Ohio.

As a teenager, Gina became prone to angry outbursts directed at her adoptive parents. The main bone of contention had been her repeated insistence that her Salvadoran parents were alive. She certainly knew how to throw it in their faces: "I don't have to listen to you, you're not my real parents. My real parents are alive." Stephanie and Tom had sent her to child psychologists, but that only made matters worse. No one believed her. The experts said that these other parents were a figment of her imagination, a fantasy that was fueling her teen rebellion. After she found her birth family, she made plans to change her name back to Imelda Lainez, telling a journalist, "Gina doesn't exist anymore [. . .]. Gina never existed. She was just something that (my adoptive parents) wanted me to be."[63]

In 1996, Gina/Imelda was a teenager rejecting the idea that she might actually have two identities and two sets of parents who loved her. She was overwhelmed by the "crowd of brothers and sisters, grandmothers, nephews and cousins" who greeted her in Los Cocos, so many who looked like her, who had "familiar faces."[64] This experience of discovering a family resemblance was thrilling for Nelson too, but his relationship with us remained strong.

Gina/Imelda could grudgingly concede that the Craigs had acted in her "best interests," but she still blamed them for taking her away from her family. "They still don't know me, they're not my parents," she insisted adamantly at the time of the second report.[65] The Craigs, however, were hoping that by finding her biological family their daughter might also find a path to reconciliation with them. When I first read these articles, I couldn't help admiring Stephanie Craig, who—despite her own pain at the separation from the daughter she had raised—could empathize with Gina's birth mother, who for twelve years had not even known whether her daughter was dead or alive.

« »

By the time we first read Tina Rosenberg's article "Salvador's Disappeared Children," our reunion was more than a year behind us, and we felt less threatened and also more receptive to the idea that Nelson's story actually fit into this larger picture. In fact, Rosenberg had contacted us in November 1998, hoping to include our family in the piece. This was about a month before we were due to leave on our second trip to Central America, where Hurricane Mitch's torrential rains had just wreaked havoc.

I was trying to comprehend how the Rio Choluteca, which I remembered as a harmless, dry riverbed in which boys could play soccer, could rip through the middle of Tegucigalpa, washing adobe houses, roads, and people away. Anticipating our visit to El Salvador, Ralph Sprenkels had written to us about the landslides that had demolished entire villages there, when hovels made of little more than mud and sticks, perched precariously on deforested hillsides, crashed into ravines. No one knew yet how many casualties there were in either country.

After talking with Rosenberg on the phone, we declined to be interviewed, since we were still grappling with our own understanding of Nelson's disappearance and Luis and Mila's involvement in the civil war. It all seemed too complicated for a journalistic treatment. When the cover article came out three months later, we noted approvingly that Rosenberg had not settled for any simplistic idea of the war or its aftermath, as she did offer individual stories of disappeared children within a complex framework—Ricardo, for one, mentioned above, the son of an FMLN combatant.

The journalist also told the story of Peter Cassidy, the sixteen-year-old son of a single adoptive mother in New Jersey. His birth mother, Eulalia Sibrián, had been part of the extended rear guard that had supported the FMLN, working as a cook for the guerrillas. Once again, I found myself identifying most closely with the adoptive mother, for Kathleen Cassidy was about my age and Peter was about Nelson's. And while the story was different in its particulars, their situation in some ways closely resembled our own.

Kathleen explained her motivation for adopting this boy to Rosenberg straightforwardly: "My feeling was that he was almost three, and had been in the orphanage for a period of time. What were the chances that he was going to end up with a family? Either I adopt him, or he is in an orphanage."[66] I also admired the way she had dealt with the news that his birth family was hunting for him, although her first reaction to Robert Kirschner's call had not been much different from Tom's—panic.

In 1985, the year of Peter's adoption, the records had indicated that his name was Ernesto Sibrián. Thirteen years later, Dr. Kirschner told Kathleen that Pro-búsqueda was hunting for a boy with an injured arm on behalf of the Sibrián family. Peter still carried bullet slivers in his right arm, of which he had only partial use. There was no need for DNA testing. It was certain that the Ernesto they were looking for was her son, a ninth-grader at Princeton High School at the time. She only needed some basic reassurance that he would not be taken away before she acted decisively. The two of them shared a sense of urgency and decided to meet Peter's birth family during his upcoming spring break, only a month later.

When I first read about this mother and son, it occurred to me that they had been much better prepared for the news than we had. Kathleen had always thought Peter might have some family in El Salvador, and they had traveled there twice, first when Peter was eleven years old, and again the year before he was reunited with his birth family. While Peter couldn't speak Spanish, he knew a lot about his birth country's recent history, an understanding Nelson totally lacked since we didn't even know he was Salvadoran. Against those pluses, I weighed some differences that had eased things for us.

First, we had had the advantage of five months in which to exchange letters and photos with Nelson's birth family before we met them. Kathleen had more difficulty at the time of their reunion figuring out where she fit into it all. "I couldn't imagine how they could meet Peter and accept me," she frankly admitted to Rosenberg. And Peter also had a much harder time at first, since his birth family—like most of the victims' families—were rural peasants and very poor. They lived without electricity and their "plumbing consist[ed] of an outhouse and a hose a five-minute walk away."[67] Peter admitted he wasn't ready yet at sixteen to give up his American lifestyle in order to stay with them for a longer period.

By contrast, nearly all Nelson's relatives live in urban areas, and Luis's house and workshop in Panama, or his Uncle Reinaldo's home in San Salvador, would be considered opulent by these standards. Even the poorest of Nelson's relatives have electricity. They enjoy the convenience of basic appliances, and they have running water, warm showers, and flush toilets, although the water and electricity can be shut off without notice. Nelson seemed at ease with them from the start, although he—like Peter—communicated more by roughhousing and shared activity, than with words. Given the vast social differences Kathleen and her son had to confront, though, in addition to the language barrier, I couldn't help admiring her pluck, her preparedness, her whole attitude.

Eulalia Sibrián had been part of an FMLN encampment in the village of El Tamarindo. On August 28, 1984, the Atlacatl Brigade attacked with air support. The noncombatants—mostly women and children—wasted no time vacating the village. As they fled toward the Gualsinga River, at least fifty of them were surrounded and slaughtered. The bullet that wounded Peter/Ernesto was probably the same one that killed his mother. Ernesto, not yet two, was too young to remember, but he suffered from terrible nightmares until the age of five, according to Kathleen.

As in so many of these stories, the children were taken away from the bloody scene in one of the U.S.-supplied helicopters that were, by then, a mainstay for this elite rapid reaction force. When they got back to an army base, his six-year-old sister Lilian tried to hang on to her little brother, but Ernesto got separated.

We could understand that despite Peter Cassidy's initial reactions to his birth family's poverty, he clearly wanted to engage with them, and his adoptive mother supported him. Just as we decided to have Nelson's brother visit us only a few months after the reunion and to let Nelson return to Costa Rica and Panama for a visit the following summer, Kathleen allowed Peter to return to Guarjila for a week on his own that first summer and arranging for Lilian to come to Princeton in December.

Although Peter admitted he didn't "feel connected" to his sister at first, by the time this article was published, the teen had signed on with a New York priest to work on an aid project in Guarjila the following summer. Ties were being firmly forged. And Kathleen looked toward the future optimistically: "I felt this is a journey we were supposed to take. [. . .] He looks like them, smiles like them, has an energy level like them. I understand him better because of it."[68] I could relate to this sentiment because it was true of Nelson and me too.

Now a young adult, Peter Ernesto Cassidy has written a moving testimonial that is featured on the Pro-búsqueda website in both English and Spanish. He speaks of his gratitude toward his adoptive mother for giving him the opportunity to meet his birth family, and of the close ties he has developed to them and to his native land since. He writes eloquently of his grandmother's unconditional love and generous spirit, and of his admiration for Jon de Cortina and the social activist John Guiliano.[69]

« »

Any unexpected familial reunion of this kind across time and cultures is bound to be a life-changing event. For most of the disappeared Salvadoran children, the mystery about their origins has been a source of questioning and sometimes terrible suffering. When their uncertainty suddenly disappears, and they meet their blood relatives for the first time, it can be an epiphany, as it certainly was for Nelson. For some, however, the initial joy of being reunited can be eclipsed by a realigned future that feels more like a cross to bear.[70]

Suzanne Berghaus Norton, a founding member of the Boston support group, has had to contend with ambivalent feelings as she hears the various versions of her disappearance told over and over again by her birth family, and as she painstakingly uncovers more details. Like Andrea Dubón, Suzanne knows with certainty, "I have to face that past."[71] Like us, she also realizes that some pieces of her story are irretrievably lost. But at the time of her reunion, she expressed optimism as she began to balance her identities: "I'm becoming more of a person. I'm expanding who I am. I'm this whole new person now."[72] In the same way, for more than ten years, Nelson has been incorporating a missing part of his past into his sense of who he is as an individual. At the same time, his birth family and Tom, Derek, and I have been expanding our idea of who we are as a family.

My perfect world
I would live with both families
There would be sunny weather every day
It would be warm
We would live in a place like Costa Rica
There would be no violence
No unnatural death
No bad temptations
It would be the best life ever!
However without this imperfect world
I wouldn't be writing this poem about
My perfect world

—NELSON WARD DE WITT

One Story

*Just being a family is not enough. There has to be agreement, not
a narrowing but a widening, not bitterness and misunderstanding
but sensibility and justice.*

—MARJORY STONEMAN DOUGLAS, *VOICE OF THE RIVER*

Around the time we first read the articles about Suzanne
Berghaus Norton in 2007, we were thinking a great deal
about the fact that on May 19th it had been exactly twenty-
five years since Ana Milagro's death at the hands of the Cobra battalion of the Honduran police force and the disappearance of one-year-
old Roberto from his birth family. Just a little over a year later, as I write
this epilogue, I have been reflecting on the twenty-five years that have
passed since Tom and I got that unexpected phone call from our social
worker and set out for Tegucigalpa with little more than a hope and a
prayer—and the assurances of the U.S. ambassador's wife—to adopt that
two-year-old as our son.

Another anniversary falling exactly between these two also holds
special significance, because it marks the first meeting of "both families"—as Nelson referred to us in his poem for a school assignment in
May 1998, the spring after the reunion. In Chapter 3, I described the way
Tom and I experienced December 20, 1997, and the days that followed.
On February 20, 2007, Eva recalled that turning point on the siblings'
blog in a post titled "The Meaning of Family":

> It was late at night. It seemed that every Christmas flight was delayed
> on this day. It was the longest waiting I've ever had. We didn't talk

too much; we were just there waiting. Time passed, and we just looked at each other trying to guess what was going through each other's mind.

Suddenly a bunch of people came to the exit door and there he comes . . . Oh my God! That's him, that's Roberto! We don't need any DNA test in our hands to know it's him; he is an exact copy of my father standing there! We didn't know what to do but go over to him and hug him. All of us wanted to hug him and touch him, maybe to see if it was truly happening . . . I remember my grandma's face, she wanted to cry but she was trying so hard not to.

After all the hugs and kisses, I looked back, and they were there. It was his family. It was his father, his mother and little brother. They were like the definition of family. They were there right behind him, supporting him, but so stumped. I don't know what they were thinking at that moment. I can't imagine the overwhelming feeling they could have been experiencing then, but they were so brave. They just were standing there and letting him reunite with his family and I mean— they are his family . . . I believe maybe they were thinking: "we are going to lose him!"

What a difficult decision to make: keep him with them by not saying a word about his family, or let him get together with his family with the risk to lose him. Myself I don't know what I would do, being in their place.

She also wrote in the same post about how our relationships have developed since then, how we have become one family:

Today I wonder: How is it that you can become family to people you've never met? How is that you can also love these people since the very beginning? How is that you get to know them just by looking into their eyes? Would it be because all of this was meant to be? What a perfect plan!

Everything fit since the beginning even if it didn't look like it. [. . .] God gave [Roberto] three amazing people that really loved him, cared about him and raised him as the wonderful guy he is. We love them just knowing they took care of him as their own, but then we got to know what wonderful people they are! [. . .]

Today I am glad I have them, as well [as Roberto]. I've never felt so supported and never felt someone who is not my own blood takes care of me so much like they all do. They give me support, they give me confidence, they give me advice, and they give me love—all of this on top of material things. Love is what I truly appreciate and keep in my heart.

In his first contribution to the blog dated July 20, 2007, Derek also had something to add about being a family:

> Obviously I knew from early on that Nelson was "different" and my parents explained to him and me as best they could about who he was and what they knew, which wasn't much. At that age, it doesn't really matter. Family is family. Nelson was and is my brother in every meaning of the word. He has always looked out for me and I knew that he cared. We were very close, even though he was four years older than me. [. . .]
>
> Pretty soon, it will have been ten years since that night [we first heard about Nelson's birth family], and instead of losing a brother, I've gained an entire second family. I can understand the apprehension that somebody might feel in this situation. I experienced a lot of new things, and it wasn't always easy, but I'm glad now that it happened. Everyone has been so welcoming, from the very first letters that our parents read to us that night through all of the visits and the other correspondence. I have never once felt like an outsider, but always like a member of the family.

As I reflect on the whole astonishing development of the past ten and a half years, I am in awe of the way Nelson negotiated this passage with so much emotional intelligence from the age of sixteen. He could have been crushed by having to juggle two identities; instead he managed to meld them and emerge as a mature and integrated adult: "Roberto and Nelson at one and the same time," as Eva puts it in one of their video interviews.

I've learned only because of their blog that after meeting his birth family for the first time, Nelson did think a great deal about what it would have been like to grow up with them rather than us, and he grieved for the losses he had sustained by being separated from them at such an early age. But in his own way he gradually came to terms with the situation.

It wasn't too many days after we came back home at the end of December 1997 that Nelson asked us whether he could change his name. We said that he could but pointed out that it might be quite complicated.

So many things he relied upon were tied to his legal name and contrived date of birth: his medical, dental, and school records, his birth certificate and naturalization papers, his driver's license, and his passport. We indicated he would probably need a lawyer, money and patience with bureaucracies here and abroad. He thought it over and settled for having the initials R.A.C.E. (Roberto Alfredo Coto Escobar) embroidered on his school backpack. Now he uses both names interchangeably and has left the legal record as is. We switched to celebrating his birthday in the month of May, along with Derek's, our wedding anniversary, and his adoption.

In one of his posts, Nelson quotes from James Baldwin's *The Fire Next Time*: "Know whence you came. If you know whence you came, there is really no limit to where you can go."[1] Being sure now where he comes from, Nelson/Roberto looks to the future with the confidence suggested by Baldwin's words. On December 23, 2007, he posted from Panama:

> It's hard to believe that it has been ten years since we first met. Sometimes people say, "It feels like just yesterday." For me it feels like a lifetime. It seems like so long ago that I walked out of the airport into the arms of my father and sister. I don't think that's a bad thing either. I have so many good memories since then that I can hardly believe it was only ten years ago.
>
> People sometimes ask, "Where do you see yourself in ten years?" Well I can tell you that ten years ago I would have never guessed this. I would have never guessed I would be sitting in Panama in front of the Christmas tree. I never would have guessed I would be working for my dad and brother here and [designing software] with my cousin [from El Salvador]. I never would have guessed I would have such wonderful brothers and sisters to spend the holidays with. I never would have guessed that my [adoptive] mother would be writing about my story or that people would want to hear me talk about it.
>
> [. . .] I really wanted to write something about how incredible these past years have been and how they have affected my life. I also wanted to talk about what a great family I have, both here and in America. Maybe it's just too hard to sum up ten years of memories in a couple of paragraphs. I'm at a loss for words. Perhaps I shouldn't even try and just enjoy being here with my family.
>
> All I can say for sure is that I am so lucky to have found these incredible people and to be a part of their lives. I know they feel the

same way. I love all of you and you all mean so much to me. Happy ten years!

Considering Eva's remembrance and loving appreciation, Derek's matter-of-fact "family is family," and Nelson's sunny tenth-anniversary greeting, it would be easy to act as if this process of becoming one family had been effortless. Frankly, for me, it was not—at least not at first. Even though the reunion had gone smoothly and the signals from Nelson's biological family were reassuring, I sensed just how seductive this huge other family must be for him, and I was afraid that we three might be the losers. I believed in 1997 that a contest could ensue, if not overtly, then in Nelson's heart and mind. Initially, it just wasn't possible for me to see that the loss I feared would instead become a gain.

«   »

This book is dedicated to the memory of Lucila Angulo, who passed away in August 2008 while I was drafting the epilogue, although I made sure that she knew of my intention to honor her in this way. Mamá Chila was the person most entitled to be bitter about so many losses over the years, but instead of indulging her pain over the death of her youngest daughter—after having previously lost her only son to a firearm accident and her father either to random or politically motivated violence—she took care of the grandchildren entrusted to her and remained determined to find the one who had disappeared.

And when Roberto had been so improbably found, she truly rejoiced that he was safe and well cared for, making it clear from the start that she would not try to wrest him away from us. With a sensibility to everyone's needs, she showed us that it was not a time for recriminations or "what ifs," and that the only way to arrive at any justice and peace was not to narrow, but rather to widen, our idea of family. I'll never forget the way she managed to embrace us all in that first letter after the reunion with her salutation to twelve-year-old Derek: "My dear grandson." She set the tone and pointed the way. But it took time and emotional effort for relationships to evolve that truly bind.

Tom's generous nature also had a lot to do with the way this all played out. From the very moment we found out about Nelson's family, he was the one promoting contacts—booking our flights to Costa Rica even before the DNA results were in. Of the two of us, it was Tom who more readily overlooked the threat implied by the whole situation and who best understood that we would need to make the bonding process a financial as well as an emotional priority. We had the resources to let Nelson travel to Central America, and for members of his birth family to come to visit us. During our visit with relatives in El Salvador in January 1999, we discovered how little it would take for us to help some of his cousins get a university education. That figured into our thinking. Mireya has recently completed her degree in computer engineering, the latest fruit of that educational support.

Tom started planning for Ernesto to visit during the reunion in 1997. As soon as he found out that Toto had several months' break between his high school graduation and the start of university studies, he suggested that he come to Boston. By enrolling Toto in an English language school, we made sure that he could get a visa. We also knew that it was important for Nelson's siblings to improve their English language skills, just as we encouraged him to learn Spanish.

Toto's first visit to our home overlapped with our boys' two-week spring break. After that, the three commuted together on the subway, with Nelson and Derek hopping off to go to school, and Toto—accustomed by then to Boston's public transit—heading on to the institute near Harvard Square for his language classes. During these two months the brothers had a chance to discover they had much more in common than the manner in which they sauntered. They are both interested in technology and have a knack with computers. They also engaged in silly contests with each other, as if they were much younger kids, making up for their lost childhood. Only a few years later, they were collaborating on one of Nelson's business projects, with Toto spending the summer with us doing programming for the administrative system Nelson was designing for a bank's loan office. Another summer Nelson arranged for Toto to be a volunteer counselor at the camp our boys had attended growing up.

Having Toto in our home for eight weeks so soon after the reunion jump-started these relationships. We also let Nelson fly to Costa Rica by himself the following summer. He stayed with his grandmother and sister for a few days, then Mamá Chila accompanied him to Panama to see his father, stepmother, brother, and half-sister. It didn't take long for this trek to become routine—a plane ride from Boston via Atlanta, Miami, or Houston takes him as far as San José, then he has another eight hours by bus. He thinks nothing of going unaccompanied now, since he's been making this trip at least twice a year for more than a decade.

Even though Nelson was soon able to solidify his relationship with

Toto and loved fooling around with his fun-loving half-sister, Éstefany, who was going to a bilingual elementary school, he really wanted to spend more time with Eva, whose sensibilities seemed so much like his own. In the meantime she had married and had a baby girl, Daniela Sophia, born in July 1998. We had seen her and the baby only briefly the following December when our family of four flew first to Panama City, where we were met by Luis, Miriam, and Éstefany and drove with them the eight hours north to David for Christmas. After that we took Toto with us to Costa Rica and on to El Salvador—his first visit to his homeland since he had left at ten months old, but Eva could not come with us.

«   »

It must have been sometime in 1999 when Nelson was undergoing a battery of tests, required to certify that he was entitled to have extra time to take the SAT exams, that he wrote about his deep longing to know his sister. The testing psychologist wanted him to write a sample paragraph or two, so the assignment was to choose any person in the world with whom he would like to spend a day. The examiner was so surprised by the response Nelson gave—so different from most of the kids she tested who dreamed of spending time with a movie or sports star—that she made a copy for her files and handed me the original:

> If I could spend a day with one person, it would be my sister. I don't know her at all, and I really want to know her. Everyone else in my family I have spent a lot of time with except my sister. She lives very far away so it is hard to see her but if I had a day with her, it would be something like this.
>
> We would probably be staying at the same house so we would eat breakfast together. I would help her with the baby. Later we could go sightseeing or just go out. I would really want to know her and speaking different languages would make this hard. We would do a lot of stuff and come home later during the day. I think we would have a lot of fun and we would get to know each other.

In these first few years after our reunion, Nelson's longings to draw closer to his birth family were as strong as my fear of losing him. Despite the positive way things seemed to be developing with visits back and forth, I still harbored a deep-seated anxiety that Nelson would favor his "other family" and perhaps even suddenly disappear from our lives entirely. He was a teenager after all, and school remained such a challenge for him.

We were insisting that he complete his college education in the United States, where he had many more opportunities, but there were days when we wondered whether he would get through high school. I remember clearly how during a church service one Sunday morning I suddenly began to cry. I don't know what set me off—music perhaps—but I had this sudden premonition that Nelson would not return from Central America. I can't remember whether he had already left or was just preparing to go, or whether it was Christmas or summer. But the strength of the emotion that welled up in me I still recall viscerally, for I experienced it as physical pain.

Preoccupied by my worries about the risks we were taking each time we let him go to visit his birth family, and given that he still didn't talk with me about his feelings, I couldn't appreciate how much he was really struggling with identity issues, nor fully understand how he had experienced the anxiety of feeling different from the time he was aware of difference at all. Nevertheless, my fears began to recede, for he always did come back. In addition, there were some early signs that the two families would draw closer. When Nelson kept referring to his father as Luis, Tom admonished him to call him "Dad" or "Papá." The breakthrough on that score came one Christmas holiday when Nelson called us from David, remarking to Tom quite unconsciously, "Wait a minute, Dad, my dad wants to say hello."

In December 2000 we even let Derek go to Central America with his brother. Nelson—by then a college student—began to divide his time more evenly between his family in Panama and his sister in Costa Rica; he drew closer to Eva, and so did we. As her marriage foundered and disintegrated, she had to deal with being on her own and raising her daughter. Eva turned to us for advice, and we tried to give her the kind of support she needed to cope with her new situation as a divorcée and single mother. Tom and I encouraged her, among other things, to finish her university degree. Almost before we knew it, she and Dany had become an integral part of our circle of care.

«   »

Nevertheless, I still did not fathom the extent to which Nelson dreamed of his birth mother, nor could I appreciate the depth of his sadness over the fact that while the rest of his family had been miraculously restored to him, she was lost to him forever. Eva became the person he could most easily talk to about their shared feeling of missing Mila. It took a long time for him to work it out, but eventually he was able to be at peace with everything that had happened—to truly accept "whence he came" and "who he was," both Luis and Mila's son and ours, at the same time.

Nelson wrote about this transformation shortly after he got back from a six-week stay in Central America. Because of the tenth anniversary of the reunion he had been writing a lot about his birth family, and he told me later that he thought I might be feeling a little sad and missing him. I was. One morning, I noticed that there was a new post entitled "The Moment It All Changed" on the blog, dated February 4, 2008:

Through most of my life I struggled with the fact that the family that I lived with was not my biological family. I am sure this is something that many adopted persons go through at sometime in their lives. I think much of that came from the fact that when I was younger I knew so little about where I came from and who I was. Your birthday and background are such an important part of your identity and for the first fifteen years of my life this was surrounded in mystery.

I think this also stemmed from the fact that I could see my little brother as the child of my parents. He was like them in so many ways, and I was so different. Not having people in my life who were like me and who understood me was hard. Then I found my family, and I found a piece of my self. However, part of me would not let go of those childhood dreams of seeing my mother again. How are you just supposed to let go of the one thing you wanted all your life?

In the last [video] interview my sister asked at what point did it all start to make sense? When did everything change for me? I can re-member the day. The day where I was finally able to let go of my birth mother and accept who I was.

It was May 2003 and I was in Central America visiting Eva. I was talking with her about our biological mother, because May 19th is the day that she was taken from us, and a day that I always think about her. It used to be a very difficult day for me, for in my mind this is the day that my world was ripped apart.

I was talking with Eva about this. I was so sad and trying desper-ately to understand why this happened to us. Then Eva said something that I will never forget. She said that I had a great mother in Margaret and behind her, looking down on us, was our mother.

A few days later I was back in Boston. I think I was still feeling a little down. When I got home Margaret had something for me. It was a letter she had sent me while I was in school. The letter was part of something the school was doing and was supposed to be posted somewhere in school for us to find. For whatever reason they received the letter too late and ended up sending it back home.

I opened it up and started to read. The letter said how proud she was of me, and what a joy it was to raise both Derek and myself. On the back she wrote "You are my sunshine, my only sunshine. Do you remember I used to sing that to you when you were little?"

I broke down. I remembered very clearly when she used to sing that song. I remembered all the difficult times we had had. But most of all I remembered how she loved and cared for me over the years. How both my adoptive mother and father gave me so much when I was little. How they stood by me when I struggled to understand who I was and what had happened to me. How they always believed in me. How they taught me right from wrong and so many other valuable life lessons.

It was exactly what I needed to hear. My sister was right. Behind my mother was . . . my mother. I couldn't believe it. This letter I was supposed to receive during school got sent back but arrived when I was away. So I ended up reading it just when I needed it the most. I guess you might call it fate, but from that moment on, things got easier. I felt a peace about the situation that I had not felt before.

Looking back years later I can appreciate so much more what my adoptive family was able to give me. Perhaps my longings for growing up with my birth family came from my youthful ignorance. Or maybe it was easier for me to dream of my perfect family than face the difficulties that every family deals with. Whatever it was, I know now how fortunate I was to have them. After getting to know my biological family more, I see how they struggle with the love and understanding that were given to me unconditionally, how they have a hard time looking past each others' shortcomings and just loving each other for who they are. What I realize now is that the perfect family I longed for in my youth, I had all along.

I recalled the letter that I had written and sent to Nelson's school, only to have it returned to me unopened. I also remember giving it to him when he returned from Central America, but I really had no idea of the impact it had on him at the time. When I re-read what he has written about it I am moved to both tears and a smile, for he is "my sunshine" now more than ever.

Nelson has summed things up better than I possibly could in the conclusion of an electronic book he has put together containing a selection of his and his sibling's posts to their blog:

> In the end I wonder how much finding your birth parents really matters. Yes, finding them did answer a lot of my questions and it did take away the awful feeling of uncertainty, but I don't think that's what mattered most. I think what mattered the most was the family that we have become. I hardly think of my "adopted" family and my "birth" family anymore.
>
> When people say, "Oh, you found your real parents," I say, "No, I found my birth parents." I don't even like to make the distinction between them. I just like to think I have two sets of parents and one BIG family. Family is more than just being related because sometimes even our own blood relatives don't treat us as they should. Family is about caring for people and loving them unconditionally. Family is what we found in them and what they found in us.

When I read words like these by Nelson or Eva's above, when I listen to the candor of their video interviews that demonstrate how close they have become, I am deeply touched by their love for each other and for us. When I imagine the idealistic young Mila, I am inspired. When I remember the indefatigable and wise Mamá Chila, I am humbled. Above all, I am grateful for the way their stories and ours have become one.

Abbreviations and Acronyms

ANDES   Asociación Nacional de Educadores Salvadoreños (National Association of Salvadoran Educators). Teachers' union that joined with the FPL to create the BPR; one of its leaders, Dr. Mélida Anaya Montes (Ana María), became second in command of the FPL.

ARENA   Alianza Republicana Nacionalista (Nationalist Republican Alliance). Political party on the right founded in 1981 by former major Roberto d'Aubuisson; has dominated the presidency and legislature in the post–civil war period.

BPR   Bloque Popular Revolucionario (Popular Revolutionary Block). The largest of five mass organizations on the Salvadoran left, it included both workers and peasants; by 1979 it could turn out eighty thousand to one hundred thousand at demonstrations.

CODEFAM   Comité de Familiares de Víctimas de las Violaciones de los Derechos Humanos de El Salvador "Marianella Garcia Villas" (Committee of Relatives of the Victims of Human Rights Violations in El Salvador, "Marianella Garcia Villas"). Nongovernmental organization founded in 1981 that investigates human rights abuses; one of four organizations involved in the search for Roberto.

COFADEH   Comité de Familiares de Detenidos Desaparecidos en Honduras (Committee of the Families of Disappeared Detainees in Honduras; www.cofadeh.org). Nongovernmental organization founded in 1992 that investigates human rights abuses; one of four organizations involved in the search for Roberto.

CO-MADRES   Comité de Madres y Familiares de Presos y Desaparecidos Politicos de El Salvador (Committee of Mothers and Relatives of Political Prisoners and the Disappeared of El Salvador); since 1992 changed to COMADRES (Comité de Madres Monsignor

Romero). Founded in 1977 to give support to families of prisoners and the disappeared, it continues to search for around four thousand individuals.

ERP   Ejército Revolucionario del Pueblo (Revolutionary Army of the People). Clandestine armed group that split from the Christian Democratic Party in 1970, joined by some PCS members; one of five groups in the FMLN.

FAL   Fuerzas Armadas de Liberación (Armed Forces of Liberation). See PCS.

FARN   Fuerzas Armadas de la Resistencia Nacional (Armed Forces of National Resistance). Clandestine armed group that split off from the ERP after the execution of the poet Roque Dalton in 1975; one of five groups in the FMLN.

FDR   Frente Democrático Revolucionario (Revolutionary Democratic Front). Created in April 1980 as a united front of parties, mass organizations, labor unions, and federations. Five of its original leaders were assassinated in November 1980. It became the political face of the FMLN and is sometimes referred to as the FMLN-FDR.

FMLN   Frente Farabundo Martí para la Liberación Nacional (Farabundo Martí National Liberation Front). Formed in November 1980 as an umbrella organization on the far left, bringing together all five clandestine armed groups (ERP, FARN, FPL-FM, PCS [FAL], and PRTC-ES).

FPL-FM   Fuerzas Populares de Liberación—Farabundo Martí (Popular Liberation Forces—Farabundo Martí); also called the FPL. Clandestine armed group under the leadership of Salvador Cayetano Carpio (Marcial) that split off from PCS in 1969; the organization to which Luis (José) and Mila (Iris) belonged.

FSLN   Frente Sandinista de Liberación Nacional (Sandinista National Liberation Front). Revolutionary party under Daniel Ortega in Nicaragua that came to power in 1979; it allowed FPL leaders to live and train combatants in Nicaragua.

FUSEP   Fuerza de Seguridad Pública de Honduras (Force for Public Security of Honduras). Security police headed by General Gustavo Álvarez Martínez; its Cobra battalion was responsible for the shoot-out in Tegucigalpa on May 19, 1982.

ORDEN   Organización Democrática Nacionalista (Nationalist Democratic Organization). Organized in the 1960s and trained by the CIA as the rural arm of the Salvadoran National Guard; after 1971 became a paramilitary force.

PCS   Partido Comunista Salvadoreño (Salvadoran Communist Party); also called the PCES (Partido Comunista de El Salva-

	dor; Communist Party of El Salvador). Political party outlawed in the 1930s. After 1979 it moved from an electoral strategy to one of armed struggle and developed its own clandestine armed wing, FAL, one of five groups in the FMLN.
PHR	Physicians for Human Rights (physiciansforhumanrights.org). A nongovernmental organization based in Cambridge, Massachusetts, that supported Pro-búsqueda's investigations with DNA testing and other services; one of four organizations involved in the search for Roberto.
Pro-búsqueda	Asociación Pro-búsqueda de Niñas y Niños Desaparecidos (Association Searching for Disappeared Girls and Boys; pro-busqueda.org.sv). A nongovernmental organization founded by Father Jon de Cortina in 1994 that searches for disappeared children of the Salvadoran conflict; one of four organizations involved in the search for Roberto.
PRTC-ES	Partico Revolucionario de Trabajadores Centroamericanos–El Salvador (Revolutionary Workers' Party of Central America–El Salvador). A group of dissenters from FARN and the PCS, together with exiles then in Costa Rica, who formed a regional organization with Trotskyite leanings in February 1977. The Salvadoran branch became more mainstream Marxist-Leninist and joined the FMLN in December 1980.
UCA	Universidad Centroamericana "José Simeón Cañas" (University of Central America, "José Simeón Cañas"). Private university located in San Salvador, and in November 1989, site of the massacre of six Jesuit priests, their housekeeper, and her daughter.
UGB	Unión Guerrera Blanca (Union of White Warriors). Death squad specifically charged with attacking Jesuits; it was founded by Major Roberto d'Aubuisson.

Family Names

Those mentioned more frequently in the text are in **bold**.

The Ward–de Witt Family (partial list)
(Granny) Margaret S. Ward (d. 2004) m. Nelson Ward (d. 1968)
    Margaret E. Ward m. **Thomas (Tom) E. J. de Witt**
    Nelson Ward de Witt
    Derek Ward de Witt

The Escobar Family (partial list)
Salvador Ramón Angulo (d. 1975)
    Oscar
    Lucila Angulo (**Mamá Chila**, d. 2008) m. Héctor Escobar (d. 1990)
    Vilma
        Cony
            Lucy (Cony's daughter)
        Evelyn
        Martha Haydée (d. 1972)
        Nena
    Dalila
        Juan Carlos
        Fernando
    René (d. 1963)
    Haydeé
        René
        Jorge
        Eugenia
        César
    Tina
        Betty

Tita
   Mireya
   Claudia
   Diana
Inés
Ana Milagro (Mila, d. 1982) m. **Luis Noé Coto**
   Eva Nátaly
      Daniela (Dany, Eva's daughter)
   Ernesto Arnoldo (Toto)
   Roberto Alfredo (Nelson)

The Coto Family (partial list)
Adrián Coto m. Estebana Amaya
   Reinaldo m. **Ana-Doris**
      Reinaldo Jr.
   Noémi
   Mariano m. **Reina**
      Sergio (d. 2004)
   Luis Noé m. **Ana Milagro** (d. 1982)
      Eva Nátaly
      Ernesto Arnoldo (Toto)
      Roberto Alfredo (Nelson)
   Luis Noé m. **Miriam**
      Jennifer Éstefany

Notes

PROLOGUE

1. A political map of Central America and a map of El Salvador showing the departments, as well as major cities and towns, will help to orient the reader. Excellent ones can be found on the website of the University of Texas, Perry-Casteñeda Library Map Collection, Central America and the Caribbean, at http://www.lib.utexas .edu/maps/americas/america_caribbean_pol_97.jpg and http://www.lib.utexas.edu/ maps/americas/elsalvador.jpg.

2. Brockett suggests the lower figure is more accurate (130 n. 1). For a detailed study of the complex political, economic, ethnic, and class factors that led to the insurrection and affected the way it is remembered, see Gould and Lauria-Santiago.

3. Montgomery 37. For a fuller consideration of the relationship of these counterrevolutionary military massacres to racism, see the nuanced analysis in "The Question of Genocide" in Gould and Lauria-Santiago 217–221.

4. For the issue of remembrance see Lindo-Fuentes, Ching, and Lara-Martínez.

5. Allende 179

CHAPTER ONE

1. Ann Colamosca, "International Adoption: Considering *All* Families," *Ms. Magazine,* January 1983: 96–98. According to this article I kept in my adoption files, of one hundred thousand children being adopted every year, about five thousand came from abroad. An increase in international adoption was anticipated, especially among older couples and single mothers. U.S. Office of Immigration statistics show a steady increase from 1995 to 2007. By 2007 the figure of 19,471 intercountry adoptees was quadruple what it had been in the 1980s. Five thousand came from

Guatemala alone that year. U.S. Department of Homeland Security, "Immigration Statistics, Table 12, Immigrant Orphans Adopted by U.S. Citizens by Gender, Age, and Region and Country of Birth: Fiscal Year 2007," accessed May 19, 2008, http://www.dhs.gov/ximgtn/statistics/publications/LPR07.shtm.

2. "The Convention on Protection of Children and Co-operation in Respect of Inter-country Adoption" was approved by sixty-six nations on May 29, 1993. It covers adoptions among countries that become parties to it and is intended to protect children, birth parents, and adoptive parents. It was signed by the United States in 1994, ratified by the U.S. Congress in 2000, and went into effect on April 1, 2008, after many federal regulations were enacted to support its guidelines.

3. In 2005 thousands of abandoned children languished in Romanian orphanages after a new law suddenly prohibited further international adoptions. Elisabeth Rosenthal, "Law Backfires, Stranding Orphans in Romania," *New York Times*, June 23, 2005: A1+. In 2007 and 2008 procurement practices in Guatemala and Vietnam made news, as international adoptions in progress were disrupted and further placements suspended, pending investigation. Laura Smith-Spark, "Guatemala Adoptions: A Baby Trade?" *BBC News*, December 17, 2007, accessed May 6, 2008, http://news.bbc.co.uk/go/pr/fr/-/2/hi/americas/7125697.stm; "Guatemala Halts Foreign Adoptions," *BBC News*, May 6, 2008, accessed May 6, 2008, http://news.bbc.co.uk/go/pr/fr/-/2/hi/americas/7385122.stm; see also Embassy of the United States, Hanoi, Vietnam, "April 2008 Warning Concerning Adoptions in Vietnam," Adoption News Archive, accessed November 4, 2010, http://vietnam.usembassy.gov/adoption_warning0408.html.

4. International adoption continues to be controversial, especially in light of some high-profile celebrity adoptions. In 2010 attention was drawn once again to the issue after the January 12th earthquake in Haiti, when an Idaho-based church group tried to remove children to the Dominican Republic without proper papers, and when Russia briefly halted adoptions after a seven-year-old boy was put on a plane unaccompanied and "returned" by his U.S. adoptive mother. For a historical overview of international adoption in the United States, as well as a moving personal story, see John Seabrook, "The Last Babylift: Adopting a Child in Haiti," *New Yorker*, May 10, 2010: 44–53.

5. Congress passed the "Multiethnic Placement Act" in 1994, but issues around transracial adoption remain controversial. See Dorow; Trenka, Oparah, and Shin; and Heather M. Dalmage, "Interracial Couples, Multiracial People, and the Color Line in Adoption," in Wegar 210–224. See also Ron Nixon, "De-emphasis on Race in Adoption Is Criticized," *New York Times*, May 27, 2008, accessed May 27, 2008, http://www.nytimes.com/2008/05/27/us/27adopt.html.

6. U.S. Office of Immigration statistics for 1995–2007 show these continuing biases. Of 19,471 international adoptions in 2007, 7,625 were males and 11,846 females; 7,789 were under one year old, 8,462 were between ages one and four, and 3,220 were five years or older. U.S. Department of Homeland Security, "Immigration Statistics, Table 12."

7. Less than a year later, in 1984, junior officers deposed Álvarez. After five years in exile, he returned to Tegucigalpa where he was assassinated. For more on Battalion 3-16, see the first in a series of investigative reports by Gary Cohn and Ginger Thompson, "When a Wave of Torture and Murder Staggered a Small U.S. Ally, Truth Was a Casualty," *Baltimore Sun*, June 11, 1995, accessed May 18, 2008, http://www.baltimoresun.com/bal-negroponte1a,0,1769421,print.story. The remainder of the series appeared on June 13th and June 15th. Negroponte responded at the end of the year: Cohn and Thompson, "Former Envoy to Honduras Says He Did What He Could," *Baltimore Sun*, December 15, 1995, accessed May 17, 2008, http://www.baltimoresun.com/bal-negroponte5,0,4501192,print.story.

8. Colamosca, "International Adoption" 96.

9. "The Negroponte File," *National Security Archive Electronic Briefing Book* 151, parts 1 and 2, ed. Peter Kornbluh, April 12, 2005, accessed May 19, 2008, http://www.gwu.edu/~nsarchiv/NSAEBB/NSAEBB151/index.htm. Declassified by Negroponte in 1998, the file highlights the close working relationship between General Álvarez and the U.S. ambassador from 1981 to 1984. During hearings for his confirmation as ambassador to the United Nations in 2001, Negroponte reportedly said, "Some of the abuses during the 1980s might have been committed by police units commanded by Gen. Gustavo Álvarez, who later oversaw Battalion 316." Jay Hancock, "Senate Panel Confirms U.N. Ambassador: Negroponte Is Approved Despite Questions about Honduran Rights Abuses," *Baltimore Sun*, September 14, 2001: A27.

10. Ellipsis in square brackets [. . .] indicates material deleted from a quoted text. Ellipsis without brackets indicates that the punctuation was part of the original text.

11. The first SOS Children's Village orphanage in Honduras, part of SOS-Kinderdorf International, opened in 1970. Because the building was considered substandard, it was replaced by an entirely new facility in 1995. See SOS Children's Villages International, "SOS Children's Village Tegucigalpa," accessed November 4, 2010, http://www.sos-childrensvillages.org/where-we-help/americas/honduras/tegucigalpa/pages/default.aspx.

12. Cohn and Thompson, "When a Wave of Torture."

13. Robert E. White, ambassador to El Salvador under Carter, alleged as early as the summer of 1982, "Honduras today is alive with United States military uniforms: Green Berets advising on counterinsurgency at the Salvadoran border; Air Force officials flying obscure missions in United States helicopters on loan to Honduras." See White, "Central America: The Problem That Won't Go Away," *New York Times Magazine*, July 18, 1982: 28. Ambassador Negroponte issued a denial: "There are no United States Air Force officers flying helicopter missions." John D. Negroponte, "Honduras Perspective," *New York Times Magazine*, September 12, 1982: 158.

14. Painfully aware now of our ignorance of these massacres at the time, it is small comfort to have confirmed that "the major U.S. news media ignored the

Sumpul river killings, and so did the State Department's country reports on human rights for 1980"; Lamperti 186.

15. White, "Central America" 28, 43.

16. John Brecher with John Walcott, David Martin, and Beth Nissen, "A Secret War for Nicaragua," *Newsweek*, November 8, 1982: 42+. See also Robert S. McFadden, "U.S. Is Said to Plot against Sandinists: *Newsweek* Says Ambassador Is 'Overseeing' Rebel Effort on Honduran Border," *New York Times*, November 1, 1982: A6.

17. The *New York Times* ran a front-page exposé on the subject of this connection only a month before our call from Mary Duggan. Raymond Bonner, "U.S. Said to Plan a Military Base in Honduras to Train Salvadorans," *New York Times*, April 10, 1983: A1+. The day after our return home, it carried an article by Barbara Crossette, "Base Plan Raises Honduran Tension: Accord with the U.S. to Train Salvador Troops in Nearby Nation Causes Concern," *New York Times*, June 26, 1983: A14.

18. Statistics on international adoption show that Honduras has never been a major source. The number peaked with 249 children in 1992 and fell to 179 in 1993. By 1995 only twenty-eight children were adopted out of country, and in 2001 and 2002 only five and six, respectively. Holt International, "International Adoption Statistics, Significant Source Countries of Immigrant Orphans, 2002–1992," accessed May 23, 2008, http://www.holtintl.org/insstats.shtml. Government statistics show that in 2009 ten children were adopted to the United States from Honduras. U.S. Department of Homeland Security, "2009 Yearbook of Immigration Statistics," accessed June 10, 2010, http://www.dhs.gov/files/statistics/immigration.shtm.

19. Photograph courtesy of my colleague Thomas S. Hansen.

CHAPTER TWO

1. "En inteligente operativo liberan joven secuestrada," *La Prensa*, October 11, 1982: 1–4.

2. The girl was the granddaughter of Jorge J. Larach, the owner and director of two of the largest newspapers in the country, *La Prensa* and *El Heraldo*, both based in San Pedro Sula.

3. Dr. Kirschner has since passed away, and PHR works with other forensic labs. We sometimes saw his name in the news in conjunction with investigations having to do with human rights abuses and remembered his role in our story. See the International Forensic Program page on PHR's website, accessed June 18, 2010, http://physiciansforhumanrights.org/forensic/.

4. Betancur, Planchart, and Buergenthal.

5. Copies of the correspondence between COFADEH and CODEFAM, as well as Pro-búsqueda's case file, provided to us later on by members of the family, reveal that Lucila Angulo began her search in 1992 by making a direct inquiry to an

FMLN legislator. She got no help from him. Only after August 1994, when she gave testimony to CODEFAM and was put in touch with Pro-búsqueda, was there any progress. From that point, her search took three more years.

6. Steve Fainaru, "El Salvador: Searching for a Stolen Past," *Boston Globe*, part 1, "A Country Awakes to the Reality of Its 'Disappeared' Children," July 14, 1996: A1+; part 2, "'Imelda (Gina)' Struggles for Identity," July 15, 1996: A1+; part 3, "Lost Children Find Reunions Bittersweet," July 16, 1996: A1+. See also Steve Fainaru, "In the Language of Love, a Salvadoran Reunion," *Boston Globe*, July 19, 1996: A1.

7. COFADEH describes the Cobra battalion as a unit of the police force organized after 1980 and especially trained for antisubversion. Within FUSEP it played the same role that Battalion 3-16 did in the army proper. "Historia," COFADEH website, accessed May 27, 2008, http://www.cofadeh.org/html/historia/index.htm.

8. Two articles about the shoot-out sent to us with the investigative report were "ABATIDOS PLAGIARIOS DE JACQUES CASANOVA: Tres facciosos murieron en el espectacular rescate del empresario," *El Tiempo*, May 20, 1982: 12–13; and "MORTAL GOLPE A SECUESTRADORES: Abatidos tres terroristas en su propria 'cárcel del pueblo,'" *La Tribuna*, May 20, 1982: 1+. In May 2009 we discovered these were incomplete and that there were many other articles not included.

9. By early 1982 the biggest problem for the FMLN was not lack of combatants but lack of arms and munitions. The main source of money for buying arms was the ransoming of hostages. See Montgomery 117–118. For more on kidnapping by insurgents that ended violently, see Lamperti 141–142.

10. Daniel Balí Castillo is described by COFADEH as follows: "Infantry Colonel, Ex-Commander of FUSEP. Balí Castillo was indicted for the illegal detention and disappearance of Amado Espinoza Paz and Adán Avilez Fúnez in 1995. The Colonel remained a fugitive from justice for six years." "Violadores de derechos humanos en la década de los 80's," COFADEH website, accessed August 4, 2009, http://www.cofadeh.org/html/violadores%20ddhh/index.htm.

11. "ATIENDE LA POLICIA A NIÑOS QUE VIVIAN CON PLAGIARIOS," *La Tribuna*, May 31, 1982: 2.

12. "SIN IDENTIFICAR 3 NIÑOS UTILIZADOS POR SUBVERSIVOS," *El Tiempo*, September 4, 1982: 16.

13. PHR, *Record* 8, no. 2 (August 1995): 1.

14. The kind of test used at that time did not use the cell's nucleus, which includes chromosomes from both father and mother, but analyzed only the mitochondrial DNA inherited from the mother alone.

CHAPTER FOUR

1. Lisa J. Adams, "Negroponte Draws Criticism South of Border," *Associated Press*, February 18, 2005, accessed May 28, 2008, http://www.commondreams.org/headlines05/0218-10.htm.

2. Peter Kornbluh, a senior analyst at the National Security Archives in Washington, quoted in ibid. See also "The Negroponte File," *National Security Archive Electronic Briefing Book* 151, parts 1 and 2, ed. Peter Kornbluh, April 12, 2005, accessed May 19, 2008, http://www.gwu.edu/~nsarchiv/NSAEBB/NSAEBB151/index .htm.

3. Leo Valladeres, quoted in Adams, "Negroponte Draws Criticism."

4. "John Negroponte, nuevo director inteligencia EUA," *La Prensa Gráfica*, February 18, 2005: 72. "¡Qué barbaridad! EUA hasta inventó un cargo para premiar a un nefasto personaje de la historia Centroamericana."

5. "Lo sabrá todo, todo," *La Prensa Gráfica*, February 20, 2005: 16. "Impulsor de la doctrina de seguridad nacional que Estados Unidos aplicó en los ochenta, Negroponte ha sido vinculado con generales golpistas, violadores de derechos humanos y escuadrones de la muerte en varios países centroamericanos, incluido El Salvador."

6. Duncan Campbell, "Veteran of Dirty Wars Wins Lead US Spy Role," *Guardian*, February 18, 2005, accessed May 28, 2008, http://www.guardian.co.uk/ world/2005/feb/18/usa.duncancampbell.

7. For more on these programs, see the newsletter of Save the Children: El Salvador, *¡Celebremos!* (Spring 2006): 1–4.

8. For the Soccer War, or "Hundred Hours War," with Honduras, see Lamperti 100–103.

9. The Roman Catholic bishops met at Medellín, Colombia, in 1968, marking the beginning of a shift by some to "liberation theology," but this also had immediate political repercussions. A radicalized youth branch split off from the Christian Democratic Party in El Salvador. By 1971 this group, joined by some former PCS members, developed into the ERP (Ejército Revolucionario del Pueblo), one of five armed groups later part of the FMLN. For more on liberation theology and the role of the Catholic Church, see Montgomery 82–99 and Whitfield 36–40.

10. On Salvador Cayetano Carpio's background, see Brockett 80–81 and Alegría, *They Won't Take Me Alive* 42–44. On Carpio's theories, see Armstrong and Shenk 66; McClintock 254–256; and Lungo Uclés 139.

11. Lungo Uclés 49–50. He emphasizes that 1974–1980 saw the development of an "extended rearguard." Like Luis and Mila, these middle managers of the various militant organizations tended to be urban and somewhat better educated, as was the top leadership, with the exception of Carpio, who came from the working class. For more on the leadership ranks of the FMLN, see Lungo Uclés 131ff. and McClintock 252ff.

12. Three of Carpio's first followers were members of the university's medical faculty where Luis's cousin studied. It seems likely that the cousin was recruited early on by one of these professors. According to Carpio's own testimony, "The original seven FPL members were each charged with developing fifteen collaborators who could carry out the necessary organizing among the masses"; Brockett 89.

13. For the FPL's role in labor organizing in rural areas, see Brockett 143.

14. Reprinted in Hermanos 28. I thank Dalila Escobar for giving me her only copy of this document collection.

15. For more on the elimination of Dalton, see Alegría, "Roque Dalton: Poet and Revolutionary"; and Lindo-Fuentes, Ching, and Lara-Martínez.

16. The armed wing of the RN, called FARN (Fuerzas Armadas de la Resistencia Nacional), was one of five groups later part of the FMLN, along with the FPL and the ERP.

17. "Asalto," *La Prensa Gráfica*, February 9, 1975: 1, 3.

18. Brockett (77 nn. 18–19) cites several different estimates of dead and wounded in these incidents.

19. Brockett 95. The BPR "presented itself as an autonomous movement" but had complex origins and covert ties to the FPL. By 1979 it could mobilize 80,000 to 100,000 people for demonstrations"; Brockett 89.

20. For more on Ana María, see Alegría, *They Won't Take Me Alive* 90–96; McClintock 256–257; and Brockett 8, 73, 76, 79. She covertly joined the FPL leadership by 1974 before becoming a central figure in the establishment of the BPR. Facundo Guardado became the BPR's secretary-general; he too was a covert FPL leader. Brockett 89–90.

21. This is also the version given by Dalila Escobar, but published anonymously, in "La esperanza de una madre núnca muere," *En Búsqueda: Identidad—Justicia—Memoria* 1, no. 3 (October 1997): 6–7.

22. The information added in brackets about their compa Eva is derived from Alegría, *They Won't Take Me Alive* 69, not from Luis's testimonial. His account about the members of the cell writing their FPL slogan in blood before committing suicide rings true. See a similar story as told by Ana María in ibid. 92.

23. Accurate data does not exist before 1978, and even after that there are many difficulties associated with getting reliable estimates for each violent incident. See Brockett 233, 261–262.

24. For the assassination of Rutilio Grande, see Whitfield 99, 103–105. For Archbishop Romero, see Whitfield 99–100, 102–107. A film in which both priests figure became popular in the United States: *Romero*, DVD, dir. John Duigan (Lions Gate, 1989; re-released 2000).

25. Montgomery 73.

26. For more on the death squads and their connection to the military at this time, see *El Salvador: Background to the Crisis* 81–86; and Gettleman et al. 136–139, 146–148.

27. On kidnapping for ransom, see Armstrong and Shenk 104–105; Byrne 37–38, 99; and Montgomery 116–117.

28. One captured member of ORDEN describes the kind of perks he was offered as "special preference for agricultural loan credits and the promise of year-round employment"; Clements, *Witness to War* 241. For more on ORDEN, see Alegría 61–63; Brockett 144–147; and *El Salvador: Background to the Crisis* 87–90.

29. Gorkin, Pineda, and Leal 105. On the difficulty of being married and hav-

ing children while being a guerrillera, see Alegría, *They Won't Take Me Alive* 79–80; and Vázquez, Ibáñez, and Murguialday.

30. Facundo Guardado (Esteban) was a founder of the UTC peasants' union and subsequently became involved in both the BPR and the FPL. Brockett describes him as the "only top FMLN leader from a peasant background" (146).

31. Sundaram and Gelber 43.

32. McClintock 108 and Brockett 235. In his foreword to Lamperti's biography of Alvarez Córdova, Clements places the statistic for 1980 in a comparative context. In proportion to the size of their populations, one thousand civilian deaths a month in El Salvador would be fifty thousand U.S. deaths a month, "nearly the total of American casualties in a decade of warfare in Southeast Asia" (2).

33. For the first four months of 1980, for example, the Office of Legal Aid for the Archdiocese of El Salvador attributed 88 percent of such killings to the Squadron of Death. The FMLN-FDR's estimates for the same time period assign 54 percent to this group alone. *El Salvador: Background to the Crisis* 83–84.

34. Clements gives an account of what medical care was like in the Guazapa zone under guerrilla control in 1982, including a photo of a "'Salvadoran ambulance,' a hammock slung between two bamboo poles and hefted down the dark trail by some sturdy compañeros"; *Witness to War* 53. This may be how Luis was transported to Aguilares. In another source, a guerrillera describes a secret field hospital in the Aguilares area where she gave birth: "It was just a room with some beds made out of planks of wood. Good doctors, though. Some international people, I think they were French. Good equipment too"; Gorkin, Pineda, and Leal 106.

35. According to Miguel Castellanos (also known as Napoleón Romero García), Fidel Castro was personally responsible for forcing the unification of the armed factions into the FMLN. After that the "Cubans became the managers, and Nicaragua the warehouse and the bridge to transfer solidarity to the FMLN"; quoted in Prisk 25.

36. Armstrong and Shenk 131–132.

37. Byrne 41.

38. See Whitfield, "The UCA in a Time of War," in *Paying the Price* 231–258. Also McClintock 314 and Montgomery 92.

39. According to one detailed account of this "reform" there were instances where security forces shot and killed the newly appointed directors of agricultural self-management groups in order to quickly eliminate peasant leaders. See Lamperti 187–190.

40. Quoted in Whitfield 138.

41. Some popularized versions mistakenly place Romero's assassination in the main cathedral immediately after his homily on March 23rd. But he was killed the following day in the chapel of the Hospital Divina Providencia.

42. Hermanos 24. For more photos of Archbishop Romero's funeral, the stampede, and its aftermath, see Mattison, Meiselas, and Rubenstein 33–38.

43. Benítez 1.

44. Several literary works use this historical moment for its symbolic power. See works by Bencastro and by Limón.

45. Clements, *Witness to War* 201.

46. McClintock 77. For more on the various reasons women joined the guerrilla groups, see McClintock 270 and Vázquez, Ibáñez, and Murguialday 99ff.

47. To put Luis's participation into context, in 1979 the U.S. Embassy estimated that there were still only about two thousand militant revolutionaries in the five different groups, with the FPL the largest, accounting for about eight hundred; Brockett 84.

48. For more on the massacre, see Betancur, Planchart, and Buergenthal, "Massacres of Peasants by Armed Forces, Sumpul River (1980)," in *From Madness to Hope*, section IV.C.2: 121–124.

49. Quoted in Gettleman et al. 148.

50. Byrne 62.

51. [Dalila Escobar], "La esperanza de una madre núnca muere," *En Búsqueda: Identidad—Justicia—Memoria* 1, no. 3 (October 1997): 7.

52. The armed groups that united under the FMLN umbrella were the FPL, ERP, FARN, FAL (Fuerzas Armadas de Liberación, a remnant of the PCS), and the last to form, the PRTC-ES (Partido Revolucionario de los Trabajadores Centroamericanos-El Salvador).

53. For the political parties and mass organizations grouped in the FDR and for a discussion of its platform, including a nonaligned foreign policy, see *El Salvador: Background to the Crisis* 123–124.

54. Byrne 63.

55. Sundaram and Gelber 59; Brockett 235.

56. For more on the death of the churchwomen, see Gettleman et al. 139–146; Hermanos 29–30; and Betancur, Planchart, and Buergenthal, "Extrajudicial Executions," in *From Madness to Hope*, section IV.B.2c: 62–66. See also the photograph labeled "Unearthing of three assassinated American nuns and layworker from unmarked grave, Santiago Nonualco, December 4, 1980," in Mattison, Meiselas, and Rubenstein 63.

57. Sundaram and Gelber 60. See also photographs in Mattison, Meiselas, and Rubenstein 48–49.

58. Concerning the arrest and later freeing of those responsible, see *El Salvador: Background to the Crisis* 120–122.

59. Quoted in Gettleman et al. 119–120. For more on Radio Venceremos, see Consalvi.

60. For U.S. military aid in this early phase, see *El Salvador: Background to the Crisis* 109–112. For the rationale for commitment to the junta, see Gettleman et al. 206–228.

61. For the role of Honduras, see *El Salvador: Background to the Crisis* 91–94 and Byrne 125.

62. A photograph in *La Prensa Gráfica* shows four of the five former mem-

bers of the National Guard, all young men in their twenties or thirties, hanging their heads and averting their eyes at the time they were sentenced for the crime in May 1984. See Hermanos 30. Three years later these men were released in a general amnesty.

63. See the photograph labeled "Families looking for 'disappeared' relatives in the 'Book of the Missing,' Human Rights Commission Office, San Salvador," in Mattison, Meiselas, and Rubenstein 48.

64. See the photograph labeled "La Virtud Refugee Camp, Honduras," in Mattison, Meiselas, and Rubenstein 52.

65. The Quakers actively helped Salvadoran refugees. Today the AFSC (American Friends Service Committee) continues to support the CISPES (Committee in Solidarity with the People of El Salvador). For example, the AFSC was a signatory to the letter sent to the U.S. Justice Department in May 2008 on CISPES's behalf. See the letter on CISPES's website, accessed May 6, 2009, http://www.cispes.org/index.php?option=com_content&task=view&id=406&Itemid=29.

66. *El Salvador: Background to the Crisis* 84. This link was later proved. See Betancur, Planchart, and Buergenthal, "Death Squad Assassinations," in *From Madness to Hope*, section IV.D: 127–131.

67. See Gill for more on the history of the School of the Americas, renamed WHINSEC (Western Hemisphere Institute for Security Cooperation) in 2001. For current attempts being made to shut down the training facility located at Fort Benning, Georgia, see SOA Watch, accessed May 6, 2009, http://www.soaw.org.

68. *El Salvador: Background to the Crisis* 122. A delegation of the FDR met with State Department representatives and some members of Congress on a visit to Washington, D.C., in 1980. Senator Kennedy was one of the few who "had a better perspective," according to one member of the delegation, quoted in Lamperti 221.

69. Betancur, Planchart, and Buergenthal, "Chronology of Violence, 1981," in *From Madness to Hope*, section III: 29–30.

70. *El día más esperado* 182–186. The ages of the children in the two safe houses as reported in the Honduran press—while inconsistent—seems to jibe roughly with this. The baby of two weeks could indeed be Rosa's child, born in early May, and the other girl, estimated at five months, could be Blanca's. But it is also conceivable that there had been a change of personnel between December and May.

71. The ERP reportedly forbade pregnancies and would secure an abortion for a guerrillera. The FPL, as Facundo Guardado makes clear in a 1995 interview, did not forbid it, but having a child was not encouraged, especially in clandestine environments. "If a woman got pregnant," he explained, it was considered a "lack of seriousness in the work"; quoted in Vázquez, Ibáñez, and Murguialday 191. This skepticism about family ties may help explain his refusal of José's request.

72. Motives for kidnappings varied. Early on, they included "the demand for publication of political manifestos in the newspapers around the world"; Byrne 99. FARN kidnapped Salvadoran businessmen and politicians for ransom, netting $40 million to buy arms by 1979. Late in the conflict, there were some high-pro-

file kidnappings, and the FAL group around Schafik Handal kidnapped President Duarte's daughter in 1985. See Lamperti 141–142.

73. A rumor about a liaison between leaders is not without precedent. After the murder of Ana María, a rumor circulated about a love triangle between her, Marcial, and another woman comandante. See Prisk 51.

74. Beth Nissen, "Our Man in Tegucigalpa," *Newsweek*, November 8, 1982: 46.

75. Miguel Castellanos, another FPL comandante, speaks at length in his memoir of personal rivalries and the jockeying for power between the groups in the FMLN and within each group. He also describes the ideological and strategic conflict and personal animosity that existed between Ana María and Marcial at this time. See Prisk 45–59.

76. Ch. 3, "Casas de seguridad," in *El día más esperado*, gives accounts of women and children in safe houses; Ana Milagro is mentioned on pages 177–186.

77. In 2009 we learned more about the Casanova kidnapping and the shootout on May 19, 1982. Additional newspaper reports further complicate the matter. Before Casanova, two other businessmen had been held in similar circumstances using sophisticated electrical and ventilation systems for breathing in a confined space, in hideaways that would have taken several months to construct. The other two incidents had ended in release of the businessmen with ransom paid, and it is reported that ten million lempiras was being sought for Casanova. In some reports the authorities allege they had already eliminated all the "terrorists." But several assert that after the shoot-out at the first house, three people were still being sought (one report says three men, another two men and a woman). Several articles speak of a six-member cell consisting of four men and two women. Luis told us there were three cells of four adults each in this operation. One report identifies the victims as Salvadoran FMLNistas, possibly working with Nicaraguans. Another says Hondurans were aiding and abetting the action. One article cites two male pseudonyms not mentioned elsewhere. There are many inconsistencies in the reporting, but each article repeats the unfounded claim that the children were kidnapped in El Salvador and used as a cover. No Honduran authority seems to have considered that they might be the offspring of some of the adults killed. One article features a very precise drawing of the safe house. It became clear to me how the police could come through the garage and still be said to be at the front door. The placement of the bodies in the diagram shows that the woman was killed behind the first man, and he—not she—must have been the first person shot. The illustration also shows the room where the two children were found on the left, slightly away from where the three adults were killed. This may explain why the children were unharmed. Perhaps it was all over in a few minutes and there was no crossfire. The unnatural positioning of the guns in the hands of the two men looks as if they might have been placed after the fact. It is noteworthy that pseudonyms of compas Luis knew appear in several of these reports. Of course, we are still left with many questions. Was there a mole within the group? Were the names provided by the woman

domestic mentioned, or were they extracted by torture when some guerrillas were captured? Was Ana María really responsible for the betrayal of the whole group in order to free Esteban? Luis firmly believes this to be true, but his testimony remains uncorroborated. The articles in order by date include "Secuestran empresario!" *El Tiempo*, March 11, 1982: 1–3; "ABATIDOS PLAGIARIOS DE JACQUES CASANOVA," *El Tiempo*, May 20, 1982: 1, 12–15; "CASANOVA LIBERADO!" *El Heraldo*, May 20, 1982: 1–3, 52; "Liberado Casanova," *La Prensa*, May 20, 1982: 1–4; "MORTAL GOLPE A SECUESTRADORES," *La Tribuna*, May 20, 1982: 1, 46–49; "Policia libera Dr. Gomez Zinmermann [*sic*] en el operativo mueren 7 terroristas," *La Prensa*, May 21, 1982: 56; "Como en su casa se encuentran niños rescatados a plagiarios," *La Prensa*, May 21, 1982: 3; "Muestran 'cárcel del pueblo' donde permanecío Herman Eyl," *El Tiempo*, May 22, 1982: 1, 5; "DIEZ MILLONES DE LEMPIRAS PEDIAN PLAGIARIOS DE CASANOVA," *La Prensa*, May 25, 1982: 1, 56.

78. *La paz en construcción* 23. It turns out that the "unnamed" source is an article that was included with our investigative report, but the page on which these three names are given was not included. COFADEH evidently found it more convenient to lead us to believe, without doubt, that the woman shown in the photo was Roberto's mother.

79. [Dalila Escobar], "La esperanza de una madre núnca muere," *En Búsqueda: Identidad—Justicia—Memoria* 1, no. 3 (October 1997): 7.

80. Quoted in Armstrong and Shenk 95.

81. Miguel Castellanos, a FPL comandante who later defected, gives a far different view in his memoir, claiming that only "external support," not that of the rural populace, allowed the guerrillas relative military success at this point. See Prisk 35.

82. McClintock 257 and Brockett 73. Miguel Castellanos, who was brought in to investigate, gives details about the aftermath in his memoir, but the editor mistakenly places the murder in February, not April. See Prisk 45–58.

83. Miranda and Ratliff 144–145 and José Antonio Morales Carbonell, "El suicidio de Marcial: Un asunto concluido?" *Estudios Centroamericanos* 549: 653–688.

84. Montgomery 169. Brockett accepts the theory that Carpio ordered the killing. He argues that Marcial's rigidity had prevented unified action by the FMLN (84). Miranda and Ratliff's history of the Sandinistas describes the international background of the incident in more detail, but their analysis is similar to Brockett's.

85. Morales Carbonell offers a spirited and detailed defense. He explains that Marcelo testified at trial through his defense attorney that Marcial did not know of their plan to kill Ana María and would have tried to prevent it had he known of the plot. The accusation of Marcial's complicity did not surface until December. Futhermore, one of the two letters the comandante left behind was suppressed. I have Luis to thank for giving me a copy of this article.

86. Morales Carbonell 653. For a secondhand account, see Prisk 52.

87. One of Ana María's loyalists, Leonel González (also known as Salvador

Sánchez Céren), a former teacher who also had come to the FPL through ANDES, became the new FPL comandante jefe.

88. Byrne 115.

89. Byrne 176.

90. Betancur, Planchart, and Buergenthal, "Violence against Opponents by Agents of the State, Illustrative Case, The Murders of the Jesuit Priests (1989)," in *From Madness to Hope*, section IV.B.1: 45–53. On November 13, 2008, the Center for Justice and Accountability (CJA) "filed a criminal case in Madrid against former Salvadoran President and Commander in Chief of the Armed Forces, Alfredo Cristiani Burkard, and 14 former officers and soldiers of the Salvadoran Army" for their role in the "Jesuits Massacre Case." See the page for "The Jesuits Massacre Case" on the CJA's website, accessed June 16, 2010, http://www.cja.org/article .php?list=type&type=84.

91. Congressman Joe Moakley of Massachusetts headed an independent investigation that showed that the Armed Forces chief of staff and his top generals had ordered the killings, and the Atlacatl Brigade had carried them out.

92. Byrne 205. Only with the March 2009 elections did the FMLN party gain both a majority in the legislature and the presidency. With President Mauricio Funes, a former TV journalist, it appears to have moved to the center-left, although the vice president, Salvador Sanchéz Céren (alias Leonel González), is a comandante of the civil war era.

93. Cited in Vázquez, Ibáñez, and Murguialday 21.

CHAPTER FIVE

1. See Garrard-Burnett; Golden; González and Kampwirth; Gorkin, Pineda, and Leal; Kampwirth; Moreno; Radcliffe and Westwood; Randall; Shayne; and Vázquez, Ibáñez, and Murguialday. See also *A Dream Compels Us*, and the film *Testimony: The Maria Guardado Story*, videocassette, dir. Randy Vasquez (High Valley Productions, 2001).

2. This part is based on an interview Vilma gave to her granddaughter Lucy for an assignment during her university studies in social work. My thanks go to both for their willingness to share this account with me.

3. Luis has told us something of the wedding at arms. To lend the imagined scene more authenticity, I have taken the FPL oath used by Eugenia as remembered by a compa and quoted in Alegría, *They Won't Take Me Alive* 74. All words appearing in quotation marks are taken verbatim from this source.

4. Ibid. 75.

5. Ibid.

6. Gorkin, Pineda, and Leal 100.

7. Towell 52–53. For more on CO-MADRES, see Shayne 28–30.

8. "Detenida," *La Prensa Gráfica*, May 22, 1981: 1+.

9. "Capturan izquierdistas en zona de Tegucigalpa," *La Prensa Gráfica*, April 25, 1981: 7. See also "Policia libera Dr. Gomez Zinmermann [*sic*] en el operativo mueren 7 terroristas," *La Prensa* (San Pedro Sula), May 21, 1982: 56.

10. "LA PESADILLA SE INICIO A LAS 7:45 A.M. DEL 10 DE MARZO . . . ," *La Tribuna*, May 20, 1982: 46.

11. Ch. 3, "Casas de seguridad," in *El día más esperado*, gives several other examples of women with children who served the revolutionary movement in this way.

12. "LOGRA POLICIA EN RESCATE DE EMPRESARIO," *La Tribuna*, May 20, 1982: 47.

13. Cary Cohn and Ginger Thompson, "A Survivor Tells Her Story: Treatment for a Leftist: Kicks, Freezing Water and Electric Shocks; In Between, a Visitor from the CIA," *Baltimore Sun*, June 15, 1995, accessed May 17, 2008, http://www.baltimoresun.com/bal-negroponte3a,0,2686927,print.story.

14. Ibid.

15. Cassidy 174.

CHAPTER SIX

1. See "The Problem of Disappeared Children in El Salvador," *Executive Document*, Pro-búsqueda (January 2007): 1, circulated by PHR at a July 27, 2007, press conference held in Cambridge, Massachusetts. It cites eight thousand disappeared of all ages that have been documented.

2. See Danner for a full account of the El Mozote massacre. Dr. Kirschner was part of the forensic team that investigated. In the laboratory, the skeletal remains of 143 bodies were identified, including 131 children under the age of twelve, 5 adolescents, and 7 adults. They determined that "the average age of the children was approximately 6 years." One of the adults was a pregnant woman. See Betancur, Planchart, and Buergenthal, "Massacres of Peasants by Armed Forces, Illustrative Case: El Mozote (1981)," in *From Madness to Hope*, section IV.C.1: 114–120.

3. See *La paz en construcción* 26. This 2003 Pro-búsqueda report analyzed 686 reported cases of disappeared children. Of these, 51 were attributed to the FMLN and 351 to the Armed Forces. An additional 276 were due to circumstances of the conflict in general. Nelson's disappearance is one of seven in Honduras; there is only one involving Guatemalan security forces.

4. "The Problem of Disappeared Children in El Salvador," 1.

5. El Salvador legislated a day of remembrance after it was cited for violations of human rights in the case of the Serrano Cruz sisters, a case argued by Pro-búsqueda before the Inter-American Commission for Human Rights in 2003. See "The Problem of Disappeared Children in El Salvador," 6.

6. "29 de Marzo: Día de las niñas y niños desaparecidos durante el conflicto armado," *En Búsqueda: Identidad—Justicia—Memoria* 3, no. 17 (May 2007): 4.

7. Quoted in Tina Rosenberg, "Salvador's Disappeared Children: What Did You Do in the War, Mama?" *New York Times Magazine*, February 7, 1999: 59.

8. PHR, "Press Advisory—Photo/Broadcast Opportunity," press release, July 25, 2007. See also Ryan Haggerty, "Reestablishing Family Ties: Cambridge Group Aid Salvadorans' Quest to Find Kin," *Boston Globe*, July 28, 2007: B1+; and Robert K. McAndrews, "El Salvador's Civil War and the Pursuit of Justice," *Salem Statement* (Fall 2007): 10–11.

9. "The Problem of Disappeared Children in El Salvador," 3. Of the 323 cases resolved by 2007, 283 individuals were found; 43 were deceased.

10. Rosenberg, "Salvador's Disappeared Children" 56.

11. Quoted in Rosenberg, "Salvador's Disappeared Children" 59.

12. For more on the role of the Salvadoran Red Cross as a "courier" service, see Steve Fainaru, "A Country Awakes to the Reality of Its 'Disappeared' Children," *Boston Globe*, July 14, 1996: A14. See also *La paz en construcción* 37–39.

13. Fainaru repeatedly uses a figure of 2,354 children adopted in the United States from El Salvador during the 1980s. Pro-búsqueda, citing Fainaru, uses the figure 2,357; *La paz en construcción* 33. In its literature, PHR often rounds this number to 2,300. Careless reporting sometimes leaves the impression that all these adoptees must have been victims of forced disappearances.

14. Steve Fainaru, "At US Embassy, Critics Say, a Failure to Safeguard Adoptions," *Boston Globe*, July 14, 1996: A15; and Fainaru, "'Imelda (Gina)' Struggles for Identity," *Boston Globe*, July 15, 1996: A6; also Larry Rohter, "El Salvador's Stolen Children Face a War's Darkest Secret," *New York Times*, August 5, 1996: A6.

15. See Marenn; and Fehervary.

16. Joseph P. Kahn, "War Child Who 'Disappeared' Finds Her Way Back," *Boston Globe*, April 5, 2007: A1+; and Marc Lacey, "A Daughter Stolen in Wartime Returns to El Salvador," *New York Times*, April 5, 2007: A4. See also Chris Cassidy, "Professor Helps Reunite Students with Relatives in El Salvador," *Salem News*, July 28, 2007: A1–2; Margo W. R. Steiner, "Suzanne's Story: A 'Lost Child' of El Salvador Returns Home," *Salem Statement* (Fall 2007): 6–9.

17. The DNA testing initiated by PHR at the request of Pro-búsqueda in 1994 was turned over to them in 2006. See the International Forensic Program page on PHR's website, accessed June 19, 2010, http://physiciansforhumanrights.org/forensic/. The forensic program is much more sophisticated now than when it was made available to us, consisting of a database containing over eight hundred genetic profiles. In addition, information gathered from searching families by means of a questionnaire has been used to create a computerized database that allows for much more rapid kinship analysis.

18. Quoted in Lacey, "A Daughter Stolen in Wartime Returns to El Salvador."

19. Ibid. Sanchez's use of the word "victims," however, appears in Kahn, "War Child Who 'Disappeared' Finds Her Way Back." For more on the "fattening houses," see Fainaru, "A Country Awakes."

20. Quoted in Kahn, "War Child Who 'Disappeared' Finds Her Way Back."

21. The nucleus of this support group, including Nelson and Suzanne, are pictured in Robert K. McAndrews, "El Salvador's Civil War and the Pursuit of Justice," *Salem Statement* (Fall 2007): 11. See also Ryan Haggerty, "Reestablishing Family Ties: Cambridge Group Aid Salvadorans' Quest to Find Kin," *Boston Globe*, July 28, 2007.

22. "The Problem of Disappeared Children in El Salvador," 4.

23. Whitfield 300.

24. *Con Jon Cortina Dios pasó por Guarjila* 129.

25. Ibid. iii.

26. Ibid. 95.

27. Ibid. 87–88.

28. Ibid. 90–94.

29. Quoted in Rosenberg, "Salvador's Disappeared Children" 56. See also Whitfield 334.

30. Quoted in Fainaru, "A Country Awakes," A14.

31. Rosenberg, "Salvador's Disappeared Children" 54–56.

32. *Voces Inocentes* (Innocent Voices), videocassette, dir. Luis Mandoki, story by Óscar Orlando Torres (Altavista Films, 2005).

33. Quoted in Carmina Castro, "Menores desaparecidos: Possible próximo guión de Óscar Torres," *La Prensa Gráfica*, March 5, 2005: 98.

34. Quoted in Elena Salamanca, "Un hombre sereno," Enfoques (editorial), *La Prensa Gráfica*, December 18, 2005: 10.

35. For more on cases brought by Pro-búsqueda to the Inter-American Commission on Human Rights and the reaction of the Salvadoran government to its findings, see "The Problem of Disappeared Children in El Salvador," 6–7.

36. Kidder 150.

37. In what follows, I retell the brothers' story in *Historias para tener presente* 95–138, in my own words. Whenever I use a Spanish word or closely translate a term or phrase from the Spanish, I so indicate by using quotation marks. Whenever I have taken more than a single word or short phrase directly from the text or used another source, I give a page reference in a separate endnote.

38. The Truth Commission report is based on complaints brought in 1992. It uses the figure 323. Later accounts suggest there may have been twice as many victims. Betancur, Planchart, and Buergenthal, "Massacres of Peasants by Armed Forces, Sumpul River (1980)," in *From Madness to Hope*, section IV.C.2: 120–124.

39. Fainaru interviewed General Juan Rafael Bustillo (ret.) for "Lost Children Find Reunions Bittersweet," *Boston Globe*, July 16, 1996: A1+. He is one of the military men identified as responsible for ordering the November 1989 murders of the Jesuits. See Whitfield 375–377.

40. *Historias para tener presente* 134. Here Amílcar is the one who speaks up on this occasion. In Rosenberg's account, it is Mauricio ("Salvador's Disappeared Children" 56).

41. In what follows I retell Andrea's story from *Historias para tener presente* 15–57, in my own words. See note 37.

42. Fainaru, "A Country Awakes."

43. *Historias para tener presente* 39.

44. For these details of Elsy Dubón Romero's story, see Fainaru, "A Country Awakes." See also *La paz en construcción* 52–53.

45. Quoted in Fainaru, "A Country Awakes," A15.

46. *Historias para tener presente* 52.

47. Ibid. 57.

48. In what follows I retell part of Armando's story in *Historias para tener presente* 59–93, in my own words. See note 37.

49. *Historias para tener presente* 19. The Aldeas SOS (Kinderdorf or Children's Villages SOS), a worldwide network of orphanages headquartered in Austria, supposedly has a no-adoption policy. That makes our adoption of Nelson from its orphanage in Tegucigalpa even more curious. See Fainaru, "A Country Awakes," A15.

50. *Historias para tener presente* 91.

51. Ibid. 92.

52. Rosenberg, "Salvador's Disappeared Children" 52.

53. Ibid. 54.

54. Ibid. 85.

55. Steve Fainaru, "'Imelda (Gina)' Struggles for Identity"; and *La paz en construcción* 30–31.

56. Steve Fainaru, "In the Language of Love," A13.

57. Fainaru, "'Imelda (Gina)' Struggles for Identity," A6.

58. Ibid.

59. Fainaru, "In the Language of Love," A13.

60. Ibid.

61. Ibid.

62. Sometimes attempts were made to locate the families of children who had turned up in hospitals or orphanages. Their photos or a description were placed in the paper. In Nelson's case, the Honduran authorities made at least one such appeal that we know of.

63. Fainaru, "'Imelda (Gina)' Struggles for Identity," A6.

64. Fainaru, "In the Language of Love," A13.

65. Fainaru, "'Imelda (Gina)' Struggles for Identity," A6.

66. Rosenberg, "Salvador's Disappeared Children" 56, 58.

67. Rosenberg, "Salvador's Disappeared Children" 58.

68. Ibid.

69. See Peter Cassidy's testimonial on Pro-búsqueda's website, accessed June 16,

2010, http://www.probusqueda.org.sv/index.php?option=com_content&view=article &id=135&Itemid=88.

70. For examples of such stories, see Yvonne Abraham, "Orphaned by Murder, Two Sisters Meet Their Past," *Boston Sunday Globe*, August 28, 2005: A1+; and "A Lost Daughter Finds Her Way Home," *Glamour*, December 9, 2008: 206–208, 282–283.

71. Abraham, "Orphaned by Murder" A23.

72. Lacey, "A Daughter Stolen in Wartime Returns to El Salvador."

EPILOGUE

1. Baldwin 8.

References and Suggested Reading

Alegría, Claribel. *Flores del volcán / Flowers from the Volcano*. Trans. Carolyn For-
ché. Pitt Poetry Series. Pittsburgh, PA: Pittsburgh University Press, 1982.
———. "Roque Dalton: Poet and Revolutionary." Introduction to *Small Hours of
the Night: Selected Poems of Roque Dalton*. Ed. Hardie St. Martin. Trans. Jona-
than Cohen. Willimantic, CT: Curbstone Press, 1996.
———. *They Won't Take Me Alive: Salvadorean Women in Struggle for National
Liberation*. Trans. Amanda Hopkinson. London: Women's Press, 1987.
Allende, Isabel. *My Invented Country: A Nostalgic Journey through Chile*. New York:
HarperCollins, 2003.
Alvarez, Julia. *In the Time of the Butterflies*. New York: Penguin / Plume, 1995.
Armstrong, Robert, and Janet Shenk. *El Salvador: The Face of Revolution*. 2nd ed.
Boston: South End Press, 1982.
Baldwin, James. *The Fire Next Time*. New York: Vintage, 1993.
Belli, Gioconda. *The Inhabited Woman*. Trans. Kathleen March. Madison: Univer-
sity of Wisconsin Press, 2004.
Bencastro, Mario. *A Shot in the Cathedral*. Trans. Susan Giersbach Rascón. Hous-
ton, TX: Arte Público Press, 1996.
Benítez, Sandra. *The Weight of All Things*. New York: Hyperion, 2000.
Betancur, Belisario, Reinaldo Figueredo Planchart, and Thomas Buergenthal.
From Madness to Hope: The Twelve-Year War in El Salvador. Report of the Com-
mission on the Truth for El Salvador. New York: United Nations, 1993. Accessed
June 13, 2010, at http://www.derechos.org/nizkor/salvador/informes/truth.html.
Brockett, Charles D. *Political Movements and Violence in Central America*. Cam-
bridge: Cambridge University Press, 2005.
Byrne, Hugh. *El Salvador's Civil War: A Study of Revolution*. Boulder, CO: Lynne
Rienner, 1996.
Cassidy, Sheila. *Audacity to Believe*. London: Collins, 1977.
Clements, Charles. Foreword to *Enrique Alvarez Córdova: Life of a Salvadoran Rev-*

olutionary and Gentleman, by John Lamperti, 1–3. Jefferson, NC: McFarland, 2006.

———. *Witness to War: An American Doctor in El Salvador.* Toronto: Bantam Books, 1984.

Con Jon Cortina Dios pasó por Guarjila. Ed. Milto Aparicio. San Salvador: Asociación Pro-búsqueda de Niñas y Niños Desaparecidos, 2006.

Consalvi, Carlos Henriquez. *Broadcasting the Civil War in El Salvador: A Memoir of Guerrilla Radio.* Trans. Charles Leo Nagle with A. L. (Bill) Prince. Intro. Erik Ching. Austin: University of Texas Press, 2010.

Danner, Mark. *The Massacre at El Mozote: A Parable of the Cold War.* New York: Vintage, 1994.

El día más esperado: Buscando a los niños desaparecidos de El Salvador. Ed. Ralph Sprenkels. Asociación Pro-búsqueda de Niñas y Niños Desaparecidos. San Salvador: UCA Editores, 2001.

Didion, Joan. *Salvador.* New York: Simon and Schuster, 1983.

Dorow, Sara K. *Transnational Adoption: A Cultural Economy of Race, Gender, and Kinship.* New York: New York University Press, 2006.

Douglas, Marjory Stoneman, with John Rothchild. *Voice of the River: An Autobiography.* Sarasota, FL: Pineapple Press, 1987.

A Dream Compels Us: Voices of Salvadoran Women. Ed. New Americas Press. Boston: South End Press, 1989.

Duarte, José Napoléon, with Diana Page. *Duarte: My Story.* New York: Putnam, 1986.

Dunkerley, James. *The Long War: Dictatorship and Revolution in El Salvador.* London: Junction Books, 1982. (Rpt. 1983.)

El Salvador: Background to the Crisis. Cambridge, MA: CAMINO (Central America Information Office), 1982.

El Salvador's Decade of Terror: Human Rights since the Assassination of Archbishop Romero. Americas Watch. New Haven: Yale University Press, 1991.

Fehervary, Helen. "Tales of Migration from Central America and Central Europe." In *Aftermaths: Exile, Migration, and Diaspora Reconsidered*, ed. Marcus Bullock and Peter Y. Paik, 15–32. New Brunswick, NJ: Rutgers University Press, 2009.

Garrard-Burnett, Virginia. "El Salvador and Guatemala: Refugee Camp and Repatriation Experiences." *Women and Civil War: Impact, Organization, and Action.* Ed. Krishna Kumer. Boulder, CO: Lynne Rienner, 2001.

Gettleman, Marvin E., Patrick Lacefield, Louis Menashe, David Mermelstein, and Ronald Radosh, eds. *El Salvador: Central America in the New Cold War.* New York: Grove Press, 1982.

Gilbert, Dennis. *Sandinistas: The Party and the Revolution.* New York: Basil Blackwell, 1988.

Gill, Lesley. *The School of the Americas: Military Training and Political Violence in the Americas.* Durham, NC: Duke University Press, 2004.

Golden, Renny. *The Hour of the Poor, the Hour of Women: Salvadoran Women Speak.* New York: Crossroad Press, 1991.

González, Victoria, and Karen Kampwirth, eds. *Radical Women in Latin America: Left and Right.* University Park, PA: Pennsylvania State University Press, 2001.

Gorkin, Michael, Marta Pineda, and Gloria Leal, eds. *From Grandmother to Grand-daughter: Salvadoran Women's Stories.* Berkeley: University of California Press, 2000.

Gould, Jeffrey L., and Aldo A. Lauria-Santiago. *To Rise in Darkness: Revolution, Repression, and Memory in El Salvador, 1920–1932.* Durham, NC: Duke University Press, 2008.

Hayden, Bridget A. *Salvadorans in Costa Rica: Displaced Lives.* Tucson: University of Arizona Press, 2003.

Hermanos, Dutriz, ed. *El conflicto en El Salvador: Documento de La Prensa Gráfica.* 2nd ed. San Salvador: n.p., 1992.

Historias para tener presente. Ed. Ralph Sprenkels. Asociación Pro-búsqueda de Niñas y Niños Desaparecidos. San Salvador: UCA Editores, 2002.

Kampwirth, Karen. *Women and Guerrilla Movements: Nicaragua, El Salvador, Chiapas, Cuba.* University Park, PA: Pennsylvania State University Press, 2004.

Kidder, Tracy. *Strength in What Remains: A Journey of Remembrance and Forgiveness.* New York: Random House, 2009.

Lamperti, John. *Enrique Alvarez Córdova: Life of a Salvadoran Revolutionary and Gentleman.* Jefferson, NC: McFarland, 2006.

Lauria-Santiago, Aldo, and Leigh Binford, eds. *Landscapes of Struggle: Politics, Society, and Community in El Salvador.* Pittsburgh, PA: University of Pittsburgh Press, 2004.

Limón, Graciela. *In Search of Bernabé.* Houston, TX: Arte Público Press, 1993.

Lindo-Fuentes, Héctor, Erik Ching, and Rafael A. Lara-Martínez. *Remembering a Massacre in El Salvador: The Insurrection of 1932, Roque Dalton, and the Politics of Historical Memory.* Albuquerque: University of New Mexico Press, 2007.

Lungo Uclés, Mario. *El Salvador in the Eighties: Counterinsurgency and Revolution.* Trans. Amelia F. Shogan. Ed. Arthur Schmidt. Philadelphia: Temple University Press, 1996.

Marenn, Lea. *Salvador's Children: A Song for Survival.* Columbus, OH: Ohio State University Press, 1993.

Mattison, Harry, Susan Meiselas, and Fae Rubenstein, eds. *El Salvador: Work of Thirty Photographers.* Text by Carolyn Forché. Chronology by Cynthia Arnson. New York: Writers and Readers Publishing Cooperative, 1983.

McClintock, Cynthia. *Revolutionary Movements in Latin America: El Salvador's FMLN and Peru's Shining Path.* Washington, D.C.: U.S. Institute of Peace Press, 1998.

Miranda, Roger, and William Ratliff. *The Civil War in Nicaragua: Inside the Sandinistas.* New Brunswick, NJ: Rutgers University Press, 1993.

Montgomery, Tommie Sue. *Revolution in El Salvador: From Civil Strife to Civil Peace*. 2nd ed. Boulder, CO: Westview Press, 1995.

Moreno, Elsa. *Mujeres y política en El Salvador*. San José, Costa Rica: FLASCO, 1997.

Murray, Kevin. *El Salvador: Peace on Trial*. Oxford: Oxfam, 1997.

Paige, Jeffery M. *Coffee and Power: Revolution and the Rise of Democracy in Central America*. Cambrige, MA: Harvard University Press, 1997.

La paz en construcción: Un estudio sobre la problemática de la niñez desaparecida por el conflicto armado en El Salvador. San Salvador: Asociación Pro-búsqueda de Niñas y Niños Desaparecidos / Save the Children, 2003.

Prisk, Courtney E., ed. *The Comandante Speaks: Memoirs of an El Salvadoran Guerrilla Leader*. Boulder, CO: Westview Press, 1991.

Radcliffe, Sarah A., and Sallie Westwood, eds. *"ViVa": Women and Popular Protest in Latin America*. New York: Routledge, 1993.

Randall, Margaret. *Our Voices / Our Lives: Stories of Women from Central America and the Caribbean*. Monroe, ME: Common Courage Press, 1995.

———. *When I Look into the Mirror and See You: Women, Terror, and Resistance*. New Brunswick, NJ: Rutgers University Press, 2003.

Shayne, Julie D. *The Revolution Question: Feminisms in El Salvador, Chile, and Cuba*. New Brunswick, NJ: Rutgers University Press, 2004.

Sundaram, Anjali, and George Gelber, eds. *A Decade of War: El Salvador Confronts the Future*. New York: Monthly Review Press, 1991.

Towell, Larry. *El Salvador*. Intro. Mark Danner. Center for Documentary Studies. New York: W. W. Norton, 1997.

Trenka, Jane Jeong, Julia Chinyere Oparah, and Sun Yung Shin, eds. *Outsiders Within: Writing on Transracial Adoption*. Boston: South End Press, 2006.

Tula, Maria Teresa. *Hear My Testimony: The Story of María Teresa Tula, Human Rights Activist of El Salvador*. Trans. and ed. Lynn Stephen. Boston: South End Press, 1994.

Vázquez, Norma, Cristina Ibáñez, and Clara Murguialday. *Mujeres-Montaña: Vivencias de guerrilleras y colaboradores del FMLN*. Madrid: Horas y Horas, 1996.

Wegar, Katarina, ed. *Adoptive Families in a Diverse Society*. New Brunswick, NJ: Rutgers University Press, 2006.

White, Christopher M. *The History of El Salvador*. Greenwood Histories of Modern Nations. Westport, CT: Greenwood Press, 2008.

Whitfield, Teresa. *Paying the Price: Ignacio Ellacuría and the Murdered Jesuits of El Salvador*. Philadelphia: Temple University Press, 1995.

Wood, Elisabeth Jean. "The Emotional Benefits of Insurgency in El Salvador." In *Passionate Politics: Emotions and Social Movements*, ed. Jeff Goodwin, James M. Jasper, and Francesca Polletta, 267–281. Chicago: University of Chicago Press, 2001.

———. *Insurgent Collective Action and Civil War in El Salvador*. Cambridge: Cambridge University Press, 2003.

Index